A Treatise on the Law and the Gospel

John Colquhoun

introduction by Joel R. Beeke
and Paul M. Smalley

Reformation Heritage Books
Grand Rapids, Michigan

Reformation Heritage Books
3070 29th St. SE
Grand Rapids, MI 49512
616–977–0889
orders@heritagebooks.org
www.heritagebooks.org

Scripture taken from the King James Version. In the public domain.

Printed in the United States of America
23 24 25 26 27 28/10 9 8 7 6 5 4 3 2 1

Library of Congress Cataloging-in-Publication Data

Names: Colquhoun, John, 1748-1827, author.
Title: A treatise on the Law and the Gospel / John Colquhoun ; introduction by Joel R. Beeke and Paul M. Smalley.
Description: Grand Rapids, MI : Reformation Heritage Books, [2023] | Includes bibliographical references and index.
Identifiers: LCCN 2023009800 (print) | LCCN 2023009801 (ebook) | ISBN 9798886860146 (hardcover) | ISBN 9798886860313 (epub)
Subjects: LCSH: Law and gospel.
Classification: LCC BX9175 .C6 2023 (print) | LCC BX9175 (ebook) | DDC 241/.2—dc23/eng/20230701
LC record available at https://lccn.loc.gov/2023009800
LC ebook record available at https://lccn.loc.gov/2023009801

For additional Reformed literature, request a free book list from Reformation Heritage Books at the above regular or email address.

Contents

Publisher's Introduction

John Colquhoun (pronounced *ka-hoon*) was born on January 1, 1748.[1] His father was a farmer on the estate of Sir James Colquhoun in Luss, Dumbartonshire, of the Scottish Lowlands. John's mother was notable for her Christian piety and is said to have greatly influenced him. Initially, it appeared that John's vocation would be a shepherd and a weaver.

As a young man, Colquhoun attended a school sponsored by the Society in Scotland for the Propagation of Christian Knowledge, a Presbyterian missionary educational organization.[2] The schoolmaster was instrumental in his conversion by teaching him the Westminster Shorter Catechism's question and answer "What is effectual calling? Effectual calling is the work of God's Spirit, whereby, convincing us of our sin and misery, enlightening our minds in the knowledge of Christ, and renewing our wills, he doth persuade and enable us to

---

1. For Colquhoun's biography, see "Memoir of Dr. John Colquhoun," in John Colquhoun, *Sermons, Chiefly on Doctrinal Subjects* (Edinburgh: J. & D. Collie, 1836), v–xxiv. A summary may be found in John J. Murray, "Biographical Introduction," in John Colquhoun, *Repentance* (London: Banner of Truth, 1965), 5–7. Short notices appear in *Oxford Dictionary of National Biography*, ed. H. C. G. Matthew (Oxford: Oxford University Press, 2004), 12:787; and *The Dictionary of Scottish Church History and Theology*, ed. Nigel M. de S. Cameron (Edinburgh: T&T Clark, 1993), 196.

2. The Society in Scotland for the Propagation of Christian Knowledge (SSPCK), established in 1709 by Scottish Presbyterians, should be distinguished from the Society for the Propagation of Christian Knowledge (SPCK), which originated in England in 1698 and was Anglican in theology. It was the former organization, the SSPCK, that supported David Brainerd (1718–1747) in his mission to the Native Americans.

embrace Jesus Christ, freely offered to us in the gospel."[3] Colquhoun so hungered and thirsted after the knowledge of God that, at his teacher's recommendation, he walked about twenty-five miles to Glasgow to obtain a copy of Thomas Boston's *Human Nature in Its Fourfold State*. Colquhoun acquired other books by Boston and studied them fervently.

Sensing a call to ministry and encouraged by a devout farmer who lived nearby, Colquhoun obtained a basic knowledge of Latin and then matriculated at the University of Glasgow around 1768. There he continued his Latin studies and developed proficiency in Greek and Hebrew. After completing his studies at Glasgow and studying briefly at the University of Edinburgh, he was licensed in early August 1780 by the presbytery at Glasgow to preach the gospel. He was called to pastoral ministry at the New Church (St. John's) in South Leith (pronounced *leeth*), and was ordained on March 22, 1781. He ministered there until his health failed him in his older years. He married twice, being bereaved of his first wife just a few years after their wedding and then marrying Euphemia,[4] a woman who was his godly helper to his dying day. He had no children.

Colquhoun was known as a man of mature spiritual experience, thorough knowledge of both doctrine and ethics, and skill in speaking to the particular cases and questions of individuals. He firmly believed in the presbyterian ecclesiological principles by which the Church of Scotland was organized. He deeply grieved over the church's decline in doctrine and discipline. He was profoundly concerned about the rise of Roman Catholic influence in Britain and opposed the government opening doors to that influence by the Catholic Relief Act, which was made law in 1829, a couple years after his death.

Colquhoun's preaching was systematic, evangelical, biblical,

---

3. James T. Dennison Jr., comp., *Reformed Confessions of the 16th and 17th Centuries in English Translation: 1523–1693* (Grand Rapids: Reformation Heritage Books, 2008–2014), 4:357.

4. Euphemia was the name of a Christian woman martyred in Chalcedon in AD 303.

Reformed, experiential, and practical. He preached twice each Lord's Day and gave a lecture every Thursday evening during the summers. Over the course of four decades of lecturing, he gave an exposition of the entire New Testament, the Psalms, and some parts of the Old Testament. He was devoted to the ministry and delighted in private prayer and study of the Word.

A faithful shepherd, Colquhoun regularly visited the members of his congregation in their homes. He publicly catechized them in the doctrines of the Holy Scriptures according to the Westminster Catechisms. He held monthly meetings with the young people to lead them to Christ for salvation and to prepare them to be qualified to partake of the Lord's Supper. Every Friday evening, he welcomed all who would come to talk about the Christian life—meetings frequently attended by ministerial students, among others.

Colquhoun remained a follower of Boston's theology throughout his life,[5] though his sympathy with the Marrow Men put him at odds with his own denomination.[6] When students of theology asked what books he would recommend for their reading, he would acknowledge that the Church of Scotland condemned the *Marrow of Modern Divinity* but said that it never condemned Thomas Boston's notes on the *Marrow*.[7]

---

5. Colquhoun named Boston as a writer to whom his treatment of the covenant of grace is greatly indebted: "I freely acknowledge, that, so far as he has proceeded, I have followed him so closely, as often to adopt, for the most part his method, and even his illustrations and proofs. Indeed, the substance of the greater part of his book on the covenant of grace, is extracted, and will be found in the following pages; though the sentiments are expressed in a different manner." John Colquhoun, *A Treatise on the Covenant of Grace* (Edinburgh: Ogle, Allardice and Thomson; Glasgow: M. Ogle; London: Ogles, Duncan and Cochran; Dublin: Johnson and Deas, 1818), v.

6. The Church of Scotland's assembly condemned the *Marrow of Modern Divinity* in 1722 and forbade its ministers from recommending it. After other developments, a number of ministers, including supporters of the *Marrow*, seceded in 1733 from the church to form the Associate Presbytery. Thomas Boston had already died in 1732.

7. John Macleod, *Scottish Theology in Relation to Church History since the Reformation* (1946; repr., Edinburgh: Knox Press and Banner of Truth, 1974), 219.

Colquhoun published his first book, *A Treatise on Spiritual Comfort*, in 1813, when he was about sixty-five years old. When Archibald Bonar (1753–1816), minister at Cramond, received a copy, he wrote to Colquhoun, "I am more and more convinced that according to the degree of our spiritual consolation, and the measure of our rejoicing in glorious Immanuel as our all, so will be our steadfastness and progress in all the other graces of the divine life…. I rejoice to think that…generations yet unborn will read your work with tears of gratitude, and will magnify the God of Zion."[8] Colquhoun's first book was followed by *A Treatise on the Law and the Gospel* (1815), *A Treatise on the Covenant of Grace* (1818), *A Catechism for the Instruction and Direction of Young Communicants* (1821), *A Treatise on the Covenant of Works* (1821), *A View of Saving Faith from the Sacred Records* (1824), *A Collection of the Promises of the Gospel* (1825), and *A View of Evangelical Repentance from the Sacred Records* (1825).

When John Colquhoun preached on the morning of November 18, 1826, his delivery of the sermon was hindered by much weakness of body. It proved to be the last time he preached. On November 27, 1827, just over a year later, he passed from this world into glory. The inscription on his cemetery tablet reads, "Having studied deeply the doctrines of grace, and experienced their saving and sanctifying power in his own soul, he laboured earnestly and affectionately to communicate the knowledge of them to his fellow-sinners."[9] Colquhoun's *Sermons, Chiefly on Doctrinal Subjects*, was published posthumously in 1836.

Robert Burns (1789–1869), then minister at Paisley (later to join the Free Church of Scotland and to serve as minister and professor in Toronto, Canada), wrote to Colquhoun's widow, "I have always looked upon Dr. Colquhoun as one of our most valuable scriptural divines, while his life and labours afforded a bright pattern of the

---

8. As quoted in "Memoir," in Colquhoun, *Sermons*, xiii–xiv.

9. As quoted in "Memoir," in Colquhoun, *Sermons*, xxiv.

sanctifying tendency of the doctrines he taught, and which are truly doctrines according to godliness."[10]

To whet your appetite for *Law and Gospel*, we give a summary of it below and then provide some practical applications that you can glean from it.

Chapter 1: The Moral Law

The opening chapter of *Law and Gospel* provides a three-part theological overview of the moral law. The first section shows that the law was "inscribed on the heart of man in his creation." Colquhoun says that that law is sometimes called "the law of creation" because it is the will of the sovereign Creator revealed to man as His creature and made in His image, owing "all possible subjection and obedience to God, considered as his benign Creator" (p. 13).

Sometimes this is called "the law of nature" because it was founded in the holy and righteous nature of God, its author, and was woven into the nature of man, who is justly subject to that law. Sometimes it is called "the moral law" because it reveals the will of God as man's moral governor. God uses this moral law, summarized by the Ten Commandments, as the standard and rule of man's moral qualities and actions. Both God and man are bound to this law by their very nature and relationship, a relationship between "God the Creator, proprietor, preserver, benefactor, and governor of man; and man the creature, the property, and the subject of God" (p. 14).

In the second section, Colquhoun explains how the law was given to Adam under the form of the covenant of works. That covenant includes a precept, a promise, and a penalty. Colquhoun says of the precept that it requires "perfect, personal, and perpetual obedience as the condition of eternal life" (p. 17). The gracious promise is "of the continuance of spiritual and temporal life and, in due time, of eternal

---

10. As quoted in "Memoir," in Colquhoun, *Sermons*, xiv.

life" (p. 20). The penal sanction is "an express threatening of death: spiritual, temporal, and eternal" (p. 24).

In the final section, Colquhoun teaches how the law functions in the Mediator's hands as a rule of life to believers. After establishing that the law in Christ's hands is not a new preceptive law but the old law issued to believers under a new form, Colquhoun explains that this law must be given to believers in and through the Mediator. Otherwise, the law could only terrify and destroy. Colquhoun writes, "It was requisite, then, that a mediator should interpose both between the offended Lawgiver and the sinner and also between the violated law and the sinner, who, by satisfying the justice of the one and by answering the demands of the other, might obtain free access for the guilty criminal to both" (pp. 31–32).

God did not give the law through Christ to His people for their justification, for that is complete in Christ alone, but for their sanctification, that the law may "direct and oblige them to walk worthy of their union with Christ, of their justification in Him, of their legal title to and begun possession of life eternal, and of God Himself as their God in Him" (p. 34). In words reminiscent of Luther, who described the law as a stick that God first uses to beat a sinner to Christ, which the believer, saved at the cross, then uses as a cane to help him walk the Christian life, Colquhoun writes, "The precept of the law as a covenant is 'Do and live,' but the command of the law as a rule is 'Live and do'; the law of works says, 'Do or you shall be condemned to die,' but the law in the hand of Christ says, 'You are delivered from condemnation; therefore do'" (p. 34).

The law initially metes out the rewards and punishments of judgment, but in the hands of Christ, it offers the rewards and paternal chastisements of grace. To keep believers from disobedience and sin, the Lord, as their Father, warns that "although He will not cast them into hell for their sins, yet He will permit hell, as it were, to enter their consciences" (p. 38) in the form of afflictions, the greatest being the withdrawing of His favorable and sensible presence in the soul.

Colquhoun concludes that to distinguish "clearly between the law as a covenant and the law as a rule is, as Luther expressed it, 'the key that opens the hidden treasure of the gospel'" (p. 40).

Chapter 2: The Covenant and the Law

In this chapter, Colquhoun explains how the Ten Commandments were published from Sinai in the form of a covenant, then how the Sinaic transaction contained aspects of both the covenant of grace and the covenant of works.

The covenant of grace was promulgated from Mount Sinai. That is evident from the following:

- The Ten Commandments are rooted in the gracious preface "I am the LORD thy God, which have brought thee out of the land of Egypt, out of the house of bondage" (Ex. 20:2).

- The people with whom the Lord covenanted at Sinai were "the people of God," on whom He was to have mercy.

- God commanded that the two tables of the covenant on which He had written the Ten Commandments were to be placed in the ark of the covenant and covered by the mercy seat.

- After Moses read the book of the covenant, he sprinkled the people with the blood of the sacrifices and said, "Behold the blood of the covenant, which the LORD hath made with you concerning all these words" (Ex. 24:8).

- The ceremonial law, which referred exclusively to the covenant of grace, was an important part of the transaction at Sinai.

- Circumcision and the Passover, the two sacraments of the covenant of grace made with the patriarchs, were added to the transaction at Sinai (John 7:22–23; Deut. 16:1–8, respectively; pp. 47–53).

The Ten Commandments were also displayed to the Israelites at Sinai in the form of a covenant of works, Colquhoun says. God did not do this to renew that broken covenant with His people. Rather, in subjection to the covenant of grace, He displayed the covenant of works before His people so that they would see "how impossible it was for them as condemned sinners to perform that perfect obedience" (p. 53) which the law by its very nature requires.

The covenant of works at Sinai is evident in the following:

- The thunderings and lightnings, the noise of the trumpet, the smoking mountain, the thick darkness, and the awful voice of the living God are all symbols of divine justice and wrath.

- Paul's reference to the Ten Commandments given to Moses on Sinai as "the ministration of death, written and engraven in stones" (2 Cor. 3:7) implies a covenant of works, for only this type of covenant includes the penalty of death.

- Christ's command to the rich young ruler to keep the Ten Commandments if he would earn eternal life (Matt. 19:17–19) implies a covenant of works.

- The New Testament presentation of law and grace in contrast to each other (e.g., "The law was given by Moses, but grace and truth came by Jesus Christ," John 1:17) implies a covenant of works, for if the law included only the covenant of grace, there would be no such contrast.

The Israelites at Sinai could not have been placed under the covenants of works and grace at the same time. As Colquhoun explains, "The believers…were internally and really under the covenant of grace and only externally under that terrible display of the covenant of works as it was subservient to that of grace (Gal. 3:24); whereas the unbelievers were externally, and by profession only, under that dispensation of the covenant of grace (Rom. 9:4), but were internally and really under the covenant of works (Rom. 4:14)" (p. 60).

Furthermore, Colquhoun teaches that a national covenant between God and the Israelites was added to the covenant of grace. This is evident because the moral law was given in the context of ceremonial and judicial laws that related to the blessed entrance of Israel into Canaan. This national covenant with Israel, which is embedded in the moral law, is a secondary and subservient dimension to the primary emphasis of Scripture, however, which is that the moral law underscores the covenant of grace.

Chapters 3–4: Properties and Principles of the Moral Law

In chapter 3, Colquhoun offers a traditional Reformed understanding of the properties of the moral law, saying that the moral law is universal, perfect, spiritual, holy, just, good, and perpetual. In chapter 4, he offers several principles for rightly understanding the Ten Commandments. Some of these principles, such as the following, are standard Reformed fare:

- That which is forbidden requires the opposite duty, and a required duty forbids the opposite sin.

- A required duty implies that every duty of the same kind is required; a forbidden sin means that every sin of the same kind is prohibited.

- No sin may be committed to prevent a greater sin.

- Obedience should aim for God's great goals: His own glory and our holiness.

- Love is the beginning, summary, and end of all the commandments.

Some of Colquhoun's principles are quite innovative, however, such as the following:

- That which is forbidden is always forbidden; that which is required is to be done only when the Lord affords opportunity.

- We are obliged to persuade others around us to be, do, or forebear whatever the law commands us to be, do, or forebear.

- The commandments of the second table of the law must yield to those of the first when they cannot both be observed (pp. 79–85).

Chapters 5–6: The Uses of Gospel and Law

In chapter 5, Colquhoun introduces the concept of the gospel as good news, or glad tidings of salvation, to lost sinners of mankind through that Saviour, Christ the Lord (Luke 2:10–11). The gospel includes all the promises of grace as well as God's gracious offers and invitations of His Son to sinners (pp. 91–100). Colquhoun concludes this chapter by stressing that if a reader wants to know if he is truly experiencing the grace of the gospel, he should ask himself such questions as these:

1. Do I know spiritually and believe cordially the doctrines of this glorious gospel?

2. Do I heartily comply with the invitations and accept the offers of the gospel?

3. Do I frequently endeavor to embrace and trust the promises of it, and do I place the confidence of my heart in the Lord Jesus for all the salvation that is offered and promised in it?

4. Do I so love the gospel that I delight in reading, hearing, and meditating on it?

5. Do I find that under the transforming and consoling influence of the gospel that I, in some measure, "delight in the law of God after the inward man" (Rom. 7:22) and run in the way of all His commandments (Ps. 119:32)? (pp. 104–5).

In chapter 6, Colquhoun says that the primary purposes of the gospel are to reveal the following:

• how the believer is reconciled with God in Christ;

• the covenant of grace and how that gives sinners a right, or warrant, to trust in Christ for complete salvation; and

• the grace of Christ to elect sinners by the Spirit, using the gospel as a means to effect a supernatural change of their nature and state. This is the instrument by which the Holy Spirit plants saving faith in the soul and continues to apply Christ to believers for their sanctification and comfort so that they may glorify God before men and angels (pp. 107–12).

The moral law is subservient to the gospel. It reveals to sinners the holy nature and will of God, informs them of their duty to God and neighbor, restrains sin and promotes virtue, convinces sinners of their sinfulness and misery and utter inability to recover themselves from this tragic state, and especially shows sinners their dire need of Christ and His righteousness. It drives them to Him and serves believers as a rule of life (pp. 112–20).

A preacher cannot preach the gospel faithfully unless he preaches the law in subservience to the gospel, Colquhoun concludes. He must press the demands of the law on the consciences of his hearers, particularly on secure sinners and self-righteous formalists. He must "tear away every pillow of carnal security on which they repose themselves" (p. 121) and show "how great is the misery, and how intolerable will the punishment be, especially of those under the gospel who obstinately continue in their unbelief and impenitence" (p. 125).

Colquhoun asks his readers to consider sinners who reject the gracious offer of Christ "a thousand times; they are a thousand times greater sinners than they were when He began to be offered to them, and according to the greatness of their sin will their punishment be" (p. 125).

Chapter 7: The Difference between the Law and the Gospel

Those who do not know the difference between the law and the gospel are prone to mix bondage with freedom of spirit, fear with hope, and sorrow with joy, Colquhoun says. They are prone to misunderstand both justification and sanctification, thus diminishing Christ in the soul and promoting self-righteousness. Some souls will be discouraged from coming to Christ for salvation but will instead look in vain for something to bring with them to recommend themselves to Christ (pp. 127–31).

The major differences between the law and the gospel are these:

- The law proceeds by necessity from the very nature of God; the gospel, from the free gift of His love, grace, and mercy, or from His goodwill to men.

- The law is known partly by the light of nature, but the gospel is known only by divine revelation.

- The law regards us as creatures who are capable of yielding perfect obedience; the gospel regards us as sinners who have no strength to perform perfect obedience.

- The law shows us what we ought to be but not how to become holy, whereas the gospel shows us that we may be made holy through communion with Christ and by the sanctification of His Spirit.

- The law says, "Do and you shall live." The gospel says, "Live, for all is already done; believe, and you shall be saved."

- The law promises eternal life for man's perfect obedience; the gospel promises eternal life for Christ's perfect obedience.

- The law condemns but cannot justify a sinner; the gospel justifies but cannot condemn a sinner who believes in Jesus Christ for salvation.

- The law, by the Spirit, convicts of sin and of unrighteousness; the gospel presents the perfect righteousness of Christ to justify a sinner before God.

- The law irritates the depravity of the sinner and hardens his heart; the gospel melts the sinful heart and subdues depravity.

- The law, when obeyed, prompts boasting; the gospel discourages all boasting because of the law of faith (Rom. 3:27; pp. 131–39).

Chapter 8: The Agreement between the Law and the Gospel

In this chapter, Colquhoun teaches how law and gospel are harmonious. First, the commanding and condemning power of the law harmonizes with the gospel, for both law and gospel seek to lead the sinner to Christ. The law does so indirectly; the gospel, directly. As

Colquhoun explains, while the law is our schoolmaster that teaches us our absolute need of Christ, the gospel presents Christ as the end of the law for righteousness to everyone who believes (p. 146).

The gospel is the law immersed in the blood of Jesus Christ. The good news of the gospel is that for lawbreakers, Christ took on Himself their nature and bore the law's curse and paid the law's penalty for them as their Mediator and substitute. Christ did not merely satisfy the moral and punitive claims of the law, however; on the basis of His finished work on the cross, He transforms lawbreakers into law keepers. And thus the good news of the gospel is that Jesus Christ has been made to us justification (having satisfied the claims of the law) and sanctification, guaranteeing our restoration as image-bearers of God and as keepers of His law.

Second, the law and gospel harmonize in being a rule of life for believers. What the law requires as duty is offered as a privilege by the promise of the gospel. "The commands of the law reprove believers for going wrong, and the promises of the gospel, as far as they are embraced, secure their walking in the right way," Colquhoun says. "The former show them the extreme folly of backsliding; the latter are means of healing their backslidings and restoring their souls" (p. 148).

The law requires true holiness of heart and of life, and the gospel promises and conveys this holiness. Thus, as Colquhoun says, "The gospel, or word of Christ, dwells richly in none but in such as have the law of Christ put into their minds and written on their hearts. The law cannot be inscribed on the heart without the gospel nor the gospel without the law" (pp. 148–49). Finally, the law and the gospel have the same friends and enemies. It is impossible to be a friend of the gospel and an enemy of the law, for both the law and the gospel are transcripts of the moral perfections of God, and those perfections are loved by true believers. Law and gospel, therefore, are not to be seen in opposition to each other (pp. 150–51).

Chapters 9–12: The Believer's Response to the Law

In chapter 9, Colquhoun stresses how the gospel establishes the law. As Paul says, "Do we then make void the law through faith? God forbid: yea, we establish the law" (Rom. 3:31). Believers, by the doctrine of faith, establish the law especially as a rule of life, Colquhoun says. This helps prevent licentiousness, promotes holiness, condemns legalism, and exposes sin in its heinousness (pp. 155–71).

In chapter 10, Colquhoun shows (in a detailed manner reminiscent of Ralph Erskine) how the believer becomes dead to the law as a covenant of works. Dying to this covenant of works includes being delivered from anxiety about being justified by works, he says. Justification by faith alone sets believers free from the commanding, condemning, and irritating power of the covenant of works. Redeemed sinners are divorced from the law, their first master, enabling them to be married "to him who is raised from the dead." The goal of this remarriage, as the apostle says, is that believers "should bring forth fruit unto God" by living unto Him (Rom. 7:4). Living unto God is a holy, humble, and heavenly life, Colquhoun says. It involves living in close communion with the triune God and the inestimable blessings of salvation.

In chapter 11, Colquhoun focuses on why believers must yield obedience to the law as a rule of life. This obligation is grounded in God's nature as the sovereign and supremely excellent Jehovah: in being our Creator and provider and we as His dependent creatures; in being our redeeming, covenantal God; in His holy, revealed will, which commands obedience; and in the great blessings that come to us when we pursue holiness.

Obedience to God is honorable, delightful, and pleasant. Believers, therefore, should make spiritual and moral vows of gratitude to God, voluntarily covenanting and dedicating themselves and all that they are, have, and do to the Lord.

In chapter 12, Colquhoun addresses the nature, necessity, and desert of good works. "Good works are such actions or deeds as are commanded in the law of God as a rule of life," he writes (p. 245).

Such works must be performed in obedience to God's holy will as expressed in His law. They must be motivated by evangelical principles and obedience and based on sound doctrine, especially the glorious doctrine of justification by faith in Christ alone. They must be done out of evangelical graces such as faith, hope, and love, which flow out of the heart. And they must have evangelical goals, which are to glorify God in Christ, to conform heart and life to our great Redeemer, and to prepare for the full enjoyment of God in glory as our infinite portion.

Such good works are necessary as just acknowledgments of God's sovereign authority over believers, as acts of obedience to His righteous commands, as inevitable fruits of God's election of believers, and as the great design of the gospel and of all God's providential leadings of His people. They are also essential expressions of gratitude to God for His great salvation. They are the ordained way that leads to heaven, as confirming and assuring evidences of the faith of the saints, as sources of comfort that help maintain the Spirit's peace and joy in believers, as adornments of the doctrine of God our Savior that promote God's glory before a watching world, as requisites to close the mouths of unbelievers and to prevent offense, and as sources of edification and comfort for fellow believers.

The good works of believers cannot procure the smallest favor at the hand of God, much less eternal life, Colquhoun teaches. They have no merit in themselves. This teaches us several important lessons:

- that we are dependent for all the good works we do as believers in Christ alone;

- that no unregenerate person outside of Jesus Christ can ever perform even the slightest good work;

- that millions today in the visible church are deceiving themselves for eternity when they base their salvation in any measure on their own works;

- that our good works, instead of contributing to our salvation, are evidences of our salvation; and

• that believers receive rewards of grace, not rewards of debt, for good works, and even then, these rewards are all for Christ's sake.

Colquhoun's *Law and Gospel* helps us understand the precise relationship between law and gospel. He excels in showing how important the law is as a believer's rule of life without doing injury to the freeness and fullness of the gospel. By implication, he enables us to draw four practical conclusions:

1. *The law shows us how to live.* Colquhoun shows how both the Old and New Testament teem with expositions of the law that are directed at believers to help them in the ongoing pursuit of sanctification. The Psalms repeatedly affirm that the believer relishes the law of God in the inner man and honors it in his outward life (see especially Psalm 119). One of the psalmist's greatest concerns is to understand the good and perfect will of God, then to run in the way of His commandments.

Likewise, the Sermon on the Mount and portions of Paul's epistles in the New Testament are prime examples of the law being used as a rule of life. The directions contained in these portions of Scripture are intended primarily for those who are already redeemed to encourage them to combine a theology of grace with an ethics of gratitude. In this ethics of gratitude, the believer finds his life in Christ and follows in the footsteps of his Savior, who was Himself the servant of the Lord and law fulfiller, daily walking in all His Father's commandments throughout His earthly sojourn.

2. *The law combats faulty understanding.* The law as a rule of life combats both antinomianism and legalism. *Antinomianism*, meaning "anti-law," teaches that Christians have no obligation toward the moral law because Jesus has fulfilled it and freed them from it. Paul strongly rejected this heresy in Romans 3:8, as did Luther in his battles against Johann Agricola, and New England Puritans in their opposition to Anne Hutchinson.

Likewise, Colquhoun teaches that antinominians misunderstand the nature of justification by faith, which, though granted apart from works of the law, does not preclude the necessity of sanctification. One of sanctification's most important elements is grateful obedience to the law. As Colquhoun writes, "When the law as a covenant presses a man forward, or shuts him up to the faith of the gospel; the gospel urges and draws him back to the law as a rule" (p. 148).

Antinomians charge that those who maintain the necessity of the law as a rule of life for the believer fall prey to legalism. It is possible, of course, as Colquhoun warns us, that abuse of the law can result in legalism. When an elaborate code of conduct is developed for believers to follow, little freedom is left for them to make personal decisions based on the principles of Scripture. In such a context, man-made laws smother the divine gospel, and legalistic sanctification swallows up gracious justification. The Christian is then reduced to bondage like that of the medieval monks of Roman Catholicism.

The law offers us a comprehensive ethic but not an exhaustive application. Scripture provides us with broad principles and illustrations, not the particulars that can be applied to every circumstance. The Christian must bring the law's broad teaching to his particular situation daily, carefully weighing all matters according "to the law and to the testimony" (Isa. 8:20), praying all the while for a growing measure of Christian prudence.

Legalism and thankful obedience to God's law are totally different, Colquhoun says. They differ as much from each other as compulsory, begrudging slavery differs from willing, joyous service. Sadly, too many people confuse law with legalism. They do not realize that Christ did not reject the law when He rejected legalism. Legalism is indeed a tyrant, but law is our helpful and necessary friend. Legalism is a futile attempt to attain merit with God. Legalism is the error of the Pharisees; it cultivates outward conformity to the law without regard for the inward attitude of the heart.

The law as a rule of life steers a middle course between antinomianism and legalism. Neither antinomianism nor legalism are true to the law or the gospel. Antinomianism stresses freedom from the law's condemnation at the expense of the believer's pursuit of holiness. It accents justification at the expense of sanctification. As Colquhoun points out, antinomianism fails to see that abrogation of the law's condemning power does not abrogate the law's commanding power.

By contrast, legalism so stresses the believer's pursuit of holiness that obedience to the law becomes something other than the fruit of faith. Obedience becomes a constitutive element of justification. The commanding power of the law for sanctification suffocates the condemning power of the law for justification.

Legalism denies in practice, if not in theory, the Reformed concept of justification. It stresses sanctification at the expense of justification. The Reformed concept of the law as a rule of life helps the believer safeguard, both in doctrine and in practice, a healthy balance between justification and sanctification. Justification leads to and finds its proper fruit in sanctification. Salvation is by grace alone and cannot help but produce works of grateful obedience.

3. *The law shows us how to love.* As 1 John 5:3 says, "For this is the love of God, that we keep his commandments: and his commandments are not grievous."

God's law is evidence of His tender love for His children (Ps. 147:19–20). It is not a cruel taskmaster for those who are in Christ. Rather, in giving His law to His own, God is like a farmer who builds fences to protect His cattle and horses from wandering into roads and highways.

This became clear to me (Joel Beeke) when I witnessed a horse belonging to a farmer break through a fence and wander across a highway. The horse was struck by a car. Both the horse and the seventeen-year-old driver were killed immediately. The farmer and his family wept all night. As broken fences can cause irreparable damage, so can broken commandments. But God's law, obeyed out of Spirit-worked love, will promote joy and rejoicing, Colquhoun says. Let us thank God for His law, which fences us in so we may enjoy His word.

In Scripture, law and love are friends rather than enemies. Indeed, the essence of the law is love. As Scripture teaches, "Thou shalt love the Lord thy God with all thy heart, and…thou shalt love thy neighbour as thyself. On these two commandments hang all the law and the prophets" (Matt. 22:37, 39–40; see also Rom. 13:8–10). As a loving subject obeys his king, a loving son obeys his father, and a loving wife submits to her husband, so a loving believer yearns to obey the law of God.

4. *The law promotes true freedom.* Today there is widespread abuse of the idea of Christian liberty, which is only an excuse for freedom to serve the flesh. But true Christian freedom is both defined and protected by the law of God. When God's law limits our freedom, it is only for our greater good, and when God's law imposes no such limits, the Christian enjoys freedom of conscience from the doctrines and commandments of men. In matters of daily life, true Christian freedom consists of willing, thankful, and joyful obedience to God and Christ. As John Calvin wrote, true Christians "observe the law, not as if constrained by the necessity of the law, but that freed from the law's yoke they willingly obey God's will."[11]

God's word binds us to Him as believers. He alone is Lord of our consciences. We are truly free in keeping His commandments, for freedom flows out of grateful service. We were created to love and serve God above all and our neighbor as ourselves in accord with God's will and word. Only when we realize this purpose do we find true freedom. True freedom is a free servitude and a serving freedom. True freedom is obedience. Only those who serve God are free. Such liberty is used promptly and readily to obey God.

This, then, is the only way to live and to die.

—Joel R. Beeke and Paul M. Smalley

---

11. John Calvin, *Institutes of the Christian Religion*, ed. John T. McNeill, trans. Ford Lewis Battles (Philadelphia: Westminster Press, 1960), 3.19.4.

A

TREATISE

ON THE

LAW AND THE GOSPEL

BY

JOHN COLQUHOUN

MINISTER OF THE GOSPEL, LEITH

For the law was given by Moses, but grace and truth came by Jesus Christ.
—John 1:17

Do we then make void the law through faith? God forbid: yea, we establish the law.
—Romans 3:31

1816

Advertisement

The immediate design of the following treatise is to promote conviction of sin and misery in the consciences of sinners and true holiness in the hearts and lives of saints.

There can be no evangelical holiness, either of heart or of life, except it proceed from faith working by love, and no true faith either of the law or of the gospel unless the leading distinctions between the one and the other are spiritually discerned. Though in the external dispensation of the covenant of grace the law and the gospel are set before us as one undivided system, yet an immutable line of distinction is drawn between them so that the works of the law cannot pass over to the gospel as a proper condition of the blessings promised in it, nor can the grace of the gospel pass over to the law as a recompense for the works of men therein prescribed. To blend or confound them has been a fatal source of error in the Christian church and has embarrassed many believers not a little in their exercise of faith and practice of holiness. Troubled consciences cannot ordinarily be quieted except the doctrine of the gospel is rightly distinguished from that of the law.

Though to some readers there may appear in several passages of the following work a redundance of words and too frequent a recurrence of the leading sentiments and even of the same modes of expression, yet the author cannot but hope that to others these will, in some degree, serve to render his meaning more obvious and determinate.

As it has been his constant endeavor to render his subject easy and intelligible to candid and devout readers even of the lowest capacity, so it is his unfeigned desire that this feeble attempt to promote the faith and holiness of believers may obtain the gracious approbation of the divine Redeemer and, by His blessing, be made subservient to the glorious cause of evangelical truth and of vital godliness.

Leith
September 11, 1815

Introduction

The subject of this treatise is, in the highest degree, important and interesting to both saints and sinners. To know it experimentally is to be "wise unto salvation" (2 Tim. 3:15), and to live habitually under the influence of it is to be at once holy and happy. To have spiritual and distinct views of it is the way to be kept from verging toward self-righteousness, on the one hand, and licentiousness, on the other; it is to be enabled to assert the absolute freeness of sovereign grace and, at the same time, the sacred interests of true holiness. Without an experimental knowledge of and an unfeigned faith in the law and the gospel, a man can neither venerate the authority of the one nor esteem the grace of the other.

The law and the gospel are the principal parts of divine revelation, or rather they are the center, sum, and substance of all the other parts of it. Every passage of sacred Scripture is either law or gospel or is capable of being referred either to the one or to the other. Even the histories of the Old and New Testaments, as far as the agency of man is introduced, are but narratives of facts done in conformity or in opposition to the moral law and done in the belief or disbelief of the gospel. The ordinances of the ceremonial law, given to the ancient Israelites, were, for the most part, grafted on the second and fourth commandments of the moral law; and in their typical reference they were an obscure revelation of the gospel. The precepts of the judicial law are all reducible to commandments of the moral law, and especially to those of the second table. All threatenings, whether in the

Old or New Testament, are threatenings either of the law or the gospel; and every promise is a promise either of the one or the other. Every prophecy of Scripture is a declaration of things obscure or future connected either with the law or the gospel or with both. And there is not in the Sacred Volume one admonition, reproof, or exhortation but what refers either to the law or the gospel or both. If then a man cannot distinguish aright between the law and the gospel, he cannot rightly understand as much as a single article of divine truth. If he does not have spiritual and just apprehensions of the holy law, he cannot have spiritual and transforming discoveries of the glorious gospel; and on the other hand, if his view of the gospel is erroneous or wrong, his notions of the law cannot be right.

Besides, if the speculative knowledge that true believers themselves have of the law and the gospel is superficial and indistinct, they will often be in danger of mingling the one with the other. And this, as Luther in his commentary on Galatians well observes, "doth more mischief than man's reason can conceive."[1] If they blend the law with the gospel or, which is the same thing, works with faith, especially in the affair of justification, they will thereby obscure the glory of redeeming grace and prevent themselves from attaining "joy and peace in believing" (Rom. 15:13). They will, in a greater degree than can be conceived, retard their progress in holiness as well as in peace and comfort.

But on the contrary, if they can distinguish well between the law and the gospel, they will thereby, under the illuminating influences of the Holy Spirit, be able to discern the glory of the whole scheme of redemption, to reconcile all passages of Scripture that appear contrary to each other, to try doctrines whether they are of God, to calm their own consciences in seasons of mental trouble, and to advance

---

1. Colquhoun's source for this quote was Martin Luther, *A Commentary on St. Paul's Epistle to the Galatians* (Wigan: William Bancks, 1791), on Gal. 1:7 (26). For a modern edition, see Martin Luther, *Galatians*, Crossway Classic Commentaries (Wheaton, Ill.: Crossway, 1998), on Gal. 1:7 (52).—Ed.

resolutely in evangelical holiness and spiritual consolation. In order, then, to assist the humble and devout reader in studying the law and the gospel, and in learning to distinguish so between them as to attain those inexpressibly important objects, I shall, in humble dependence on the Spirit of truth, consider the following:

First, the law of God in general.

Second, the law of God as promulgated to the Israelites from Mount Sinai.

In the third place, the properties of the moral law.

Fourth, the rules for understanding rightly the Ten Commandments.

In the next place, I shall endeavor to explain the gospel.

Then, I shall point out the uses of the gospel and also of the law in its subservience to the gospel.

Afterward, it will be proper to consider the difference between the law and the gospel.

Next, the agreement between them.

Then, the establishment of the law by the gospel, or the subservience of the gospel to the authority and honor of the law.

In the next place, the believer's privilege of being dead to the law as a covenant of works, with a necessary consequence of it.

After which, I shall consider the great obligations under which every believer lies, to perform even perfect obedience to the law as a rule of life.

And last, the nature, necessity, and desert of good works.

CHAPTER 1

The Law of God in General

The term *law* in Scripture is to be understood in either an extended or a restricted sense.

In its extended or large acceptation, it is used sometimes to signify the five books of Moses (Luke 24:44); at other times all the books of the Old Testament (John 10:34); sometimes the whole word of God in the scriptures of the Old and the New Testaments (Ps. 19:7); in some places the Old Testament dispensation as distinguished from the New (John 1:17); in others the Old Testament dispensation, as including prophecies, promises, and types of Messiah (Luke 16:16; Heb. 10:1), and in several the doctrine of the gospel (Isa. 2:3; 42:4).

In its restricted or limited sense, it is employed to express the rule that God has prescribed to His rational creatures in order to direct and oblige them to the right performance of all their duties to Him. Or in other words, it is used to signify the declared will of God, directing and obliging mankind to do that which pleases Him and to abstain from that which displeases Him.

This, in the strict and proper sense of the word, is the law of God; and it is divided into the natural law and the positive law. The natural law of God, or the law of nature, is that necessary and unchangeable rule of duty which is founded in the infinitely holy and righteous nature of God, to obey which all men, as the reasonable creatures of God, are and cannot but be indispensably bound. The positive law of God comprises those institutions that depend merely on His sovereign will and which He might never have prescribed, and yet

His nature has always continued the same, such as the command not to eat of the forbidden fruit; the command during the period of the Old Testament dispensation to keep holy, as the Sabbath of Jehovah, the seventh day of the week, which under the New Testament is altered to the first day; the ceremonial law given to the Israelites that prescribed the rites of God's worship, together with many of the precepts of their judicial law; and the positive precepts concerning the worship of God under the gospel.

The dictates of God's natural law are delivered with authority because they are just and reasonable in their own nature previous to any divine precept concerning them inasmuch as they are all founded in the infinite holiness, righteousness, and wisdom of His nature (Ps. 111:7–8). On the contrary, the dictates of His positive law become just and reasonable because they are delivered with authority. The former are "holy, and just, and good," and therefore they are commanded; the latter are commanded, and therefore they are "holy, and just, and good" (Rom. 7:12). Those commandments of God founded in the holiness and righteousness of His nature are unalterable and perpetually the same, whereas these founded on the sovereignty of His will are in themselves alterable, and He may, by His own express appointment, alter them whenever He pleases. But till He Himself alters them, they continue to be of immutable obligation (Matt. 5:18).

Although the positive precepts of God are capable of being changed by Him, yet our obedience to them is built on a moral foundation. It is a moral duty, a duty of perpetual obligation, to obey in all things the revealed will of God. It was on a moral ground that Christ as Mediator proceeded when He changed the seals of the covenant of grace, altered the Sabbath from the seventh to the first day of the week, and instituted new ordinances of worship and government for His church. And it is on the same ground that we are bound to obey the positive commands of Christ respecting those ordinances.

The law of God strictly taken in the aspects that it bears on mankind is to be considered in a threefold point of view: first, as written on the heart of man in his creation; second, as given under the form of a covenant of works to him; and third, as a rule of life in the hand of Christ the Mediator to all true believers.

✦ SECTION 1 ✦
The Law as Inscribed on the Heart of Man in His Creation

God, in creating the first man, made him after His own moral image (Gen. 1:27). This image, as the apostle Paul informs us, consists of knowledge, righteousness, and true holiness (Col. 3:10; Eph. 4:24, respectively). God, then, created man in His own moral image by inscribing His law, the transcript of His own righteousness and holiness, on man's mind and heart. The law of God is to be taken either materially, as merely directing and obliging the rational creature to perfect obedience, or formally, as having received the form of a covenant of works. Now it is the law not formally, but materially considered, that was inscribed on the heart of man in his creation. Man, therefore, as the creature of God, would have been obliged to perform perfect obedience to the law in this view of it, though a covenant of works had never been made with him. This law and sufficient power to obey it were included in the image of God, according to which He created man (Eccl. 7:29). Although the law, in this view of it, contained no positive precepts, yet it required man to believe everything that God should reveal and to do everything that He should command (Deut. 12:32).

Since the first man, on whose heart his Creator had inscribed this law, was not confirmed in rectitude of nature and life and so was fallible, it implied a sanction of eternal punishment to him as the just recompense of his disobedience if he should at any time transgress it (Rom. 1:32; 6:23). I say it implied this sanction, for as it was never designed by God to be in that simple form either a rule of duty to man or of judgment to himself, and as Adam was not permitted to transgress till after the covenant of works was made with him, there does not seem to have been any express threatening of eternal punishment annexed to it. But though it implied a penal sanction, and though disobedience to it would deserve even eternal death, yet there is no ground from the Scripture to conclude that a penal sanction or a threatening of eternal wrath is inseparable from it.

For glorified saints and confirmed angels in heaven are all naturally, necessarily, and eternally bound to perform perfect obedience to it as the law of creation; but to affirm that they have a threatening of eternal punishment annexed to it would be rash and unscriptural. The truth is, there is no place for a penal sanction where there cannot be a possibility of sinning. Besides, if a threatening of eternal punishment was inseparable from the law of creation, true believers, who are and always must be under this law, should inevitably remain under that threatening. Although their justification for the righteousness of Jesus Christ, received by faith and imputed by God, is perfect and irrevocable, yet if even in that state they committed but a single sin, it would lay them afresh under condemnation to eternal wrath. And that would be contrary to these consoling passages of Scripture: "He that heareth my word, and believeth on him that sent me, hath everlasting life, and shall not come into condemnation" (John 5:24). "There is therefore now no condemnation to them which are in Christ Jesus, who walk not after the flesh, but after the Spirit" (Rom. 8:1).

Indeed, if a penal sanction were inseparable from the law of creation, believers should at once be both justified and condemned. For as all men, considered as creatures of God, are subject to the law of creation (Rom. 2:15), so this law cannot but forbid the smallest degree of sin and cannot but require perfection of obedience from all believers as well as all unbelievers. It may be proper here to remark that no mere man, even by perfect obedience to the law in that simple form, could ever have merited from God eternal life. It therefore implied no promise of eternal life, even no promise that mankind should ever be confirmed under it as a rule of life. It was only when it received the form of the covenant of works that a promise of life eternal and, consequently, of confirmation in holiness and happiness was annexed to it.

The law as written on the heart of the first man is often styled the law of creation because it was the will of the sovereign Creator revealed to the reasonable creature by impressing or engraving it on his mind and heart. To this law, so inlaid in the mind and heart in creation as to the natural instinct and moral rectitude of the rational creature, every person, as a reasonable creature, is indispensably bound. It obliges to perfect and perpetual obedience in all possible states of the creature, whether he be on earth, in heaven, or even in hell. Since man is the creature of God and since, in his creation, he was made in the image of God, he owes all possible subjection and obedience to God, considered as his benign Creator.

The same law is also denominated the law of nature because it was founded in the holy and righteous nature of God and was interwoven with the nature of the first man because it corresponds to both the nature of God, who is the author of it, and to that of man, who is subjected to it; because to act according to this law is the same as to act naturally and reasonably; because writing it on the heart of Adam was so distinct and the impression of it on his nature was so deep that they were equal to an express revelation of it; because the dictates of this law are the very same that the dictates of natural conscience in the first man were; and because the obligation to perform perfect obedience to it proceeds from the nature of God and lies on the nature of man. The knowledge that man in innocence had of this law was concreated with his nature.

It is sometimes called the moral law, and is so called because it was a revelation of the will of God as His moral governor to the first man and was the standard and rule of all the man's moral qualities and actions because, while it was manifested to his reason, it represented to him the moral fitness of all his holy inclinations, thoughts, words, and actions; because while it regulates the manners or morals of all men, it is of perpetual obligation; and because it is summarily comprehended in the Ten Commandments, which are usually styled the moral law. The Ten Commandments are the sum and substance of it. There is, however, this difference between it and them: in it there is nothing but what is moral, but in them there is something that is positive.

The obligation of the law of nature results from both the nature of God and the nature of man and from the relation between God the Creator, proprietor, preserver, benefactor, and governor of man; and man the creature, the property, and the subject of God. The immediate ground of the obligation of the natural law on man is the sovereign authority of God, or His absolute right to command the perfect obedience of man. This sovereign authority of the Lord flows from the infinite supereminence, or supreme excellence, of His nature above the nature of man; from His being the Creator of man and man's being His creature; from His being the preserver and benefactor of man and man's being dependent on Him for life and all the comforts of life; and from His being, therefore, the sole proprietor and sovereign ruler of man and man's being His property and in absolute subjection to Him.

The obligation of the natural law on mankind, then, as resulting from the nature of God and from the relations between God and man, is such that even God Himself cannot dispense with it. It cannot cease to bind as long as God continues to be God and man to be man, God to be the sovereign Creator and man to be His dependent creature. Since the authority of that law is divine, the obligation flowing from it is eternal and immutable. It must continue forever without the smallest diminution, and that on all men, whether saints or sinners; at all times, from the moment of man's creation before the covenant of works, under the covenant of works, under the covenant of grace, and even through all eternity. Man has no being, no life, no activity without God. As long, therefore, as man continues in existence, he is bound to have no being but for God and no activity but such as is according to His will.

That fair copy of the natural law which had been transcribed into the nature of the first man in his creation was by the fall much obliterated, and it continues still to be, in a great degree, defaced and even obliterated in the minds of all his unregenerate offspring. And, indeed, if it was not in a great measure obliterated, what need could there be of inscribing it anew on the hearts of the elect? What occasion for such a promise as this: "I will put my laws into their mind, and write them in their hearts" (Heb. 8:10)? What necessity could there be of writing it in the Sacred Volume in order to make it known to men in all their generations? Indeed, so obliterated was it that the Lord saw it necessary to make it known to His people by both external and internal revelation.

But although this natural law inscribed on the heart of Adam was much defaced by the fall, yet it was not wholly obliterated. Some faint impressions or small relics of it remain still in the minds of all men. Indeed, with respect to its general principles and the immediate conclusions obviously deducible from them, it is not and it cannot be totally effaced; but with regard to such conclusions as are more or less remote, it is, by the darkness of the mind and the depravity of the heart of man, wholly perverted (Rom. 1:21, 32). The general principles that, in some measure, are still inscribed on the minds of men, even where they have not the benefit of the written law, are such as these: there is a God; that God is to be worshiped; that none are to be injured; that parents ought to be honored; that we should do to others what we would reasonably wish that they would do to us, etc. That such general principles as these are still in some degree engraved on the minds of all men is evident from these words of an apostle: "The Gentiles, which have not the law, do by nature the things contained in the law…. Which shew the work of the law written in their hearts, their conscience also bearing witness, and their thoughts the mean while accusing or else excusing one another" (Rom. 2:14–15). The same is also manifest from the laws that, in countries destitute of the light of revelation, are commonly enacted for encouraging virtue and discouraging vice and for preserving the rights of civil society. Men in heathen countries can have no standard for those laws but the relics of natural law, which all the descendants of Adam bring with them into the world.

The remains of the law of nature in the minds of men are commonly styled the light of nature and sometimes the light of reason. They are the dictates of natural conscience, and they contain those moral principles respecting good and evil that have essential equity in them. The law of nature, as engraved on the heart of Adam in his creation, should always be distinguished from the light of nature as now enjoyed. The former is uniform and stable, of universal extent, and of perpetual obligation; the latter, being that knowledge of the nature of God and of their own nature, as well as of the duties resulting from the relations between them that men since the fall actually possess, is greatly diversified in its extent and degree, according to their different opportunities, capacities, and dispositions. In some parts of the world where the light of nature is not assisted by the light of revelation, it does not appear superior to the sagacity of some of the inferior creatures. How far, then, must it be from being sufficient to guide men to true virtue and happiness or to afford them in their present depraved state proper views of the wisdom, power, justice, goodness, and mercy of God!

So much for the law of nature, which is the law of God in its primitive, simple, and absolute form.

◆ SECTION 2 ◆
The Law as Given to Adam under the Form of the Covenant of Works

The law of creation, or the Ten Commandments, was, in the form of a covenant of works, given to the first Adam after he had been put into the garden of Eden. And it was given him as the first parent and the federal representative of all his posterity by ordinary generation. An express threatening of death and a gracious promise of life annexed to the law of creation made it to Adam a covenant of works proposed; and his consent, which he as a sinless creature could not refuse, made it a covenant of works accepted. As formed into a covenant of works, it is called by the apostle Paul the law of works (Rom. 3:27)—that is, the law as a covenant of works. It requires works or perfect obedience on pain of death—spiritual, temporal, and eternal; and it promises to the man who performs perfect and personal obedience life—spiritual, temporal, and eternal. In the law, under the form of a covenant of works, then, three things are presented to our consideration: a precept, a promise, and a penal sanction.

1. *A precept requiring perfect, personal, and perpetual obedience as the condition of eternal life.* The law of creation requires man to perform perfect obedience and says, "Do." But the law as a covenant of works requires him to "do and live"; to do, as the condition of life; to do, in order to acquire by his obedience a title to life eternal. The command to perform perfect obedience merely is not the covenant of works, for man was and is immutably and eternally bound to yield perfect obedience to the law of creation though a covenant of works had never been made with him. But the form of the command in the covenant of works is perfect obedience as the condition of life. The law in this form comprised not only all the commandments peculiar to it as the law of nature but also a positive precept that depended entirely on the will of God. "The LORD God commanded the man, saying, Of every tree of the garden thou mayest freely eat: but of the tree of the knowledge of good and evil, thou shalt not eat of it: for in the day that thou eatest thereof thou shalt surely die" (Gen. 2:16–17). This positive precept was, in effect, a summary of all the commands of the natural or moral law; obedience to it included obedience to them all, and disobedience to it was a transgression of them all at once. The covenant of works, accordingly, could not have been broken otherwise than by transgressing that positive precept. The command requiring perfect obedience as the condition of life bound Adam and

all his natural posterity in him not only by the authority of God, his sovereign Lord and Creator, but by his own voluntary consent to perform that obedience.

The natural law, given in the form of a covenant of works to Adam and all his natural descendants, required them to believe whatever the Lord should reveal or promise and to do whatever He should command. All divine precepts, therefore, are virtually and really comprehended in it. "The law of the LORD is perfect" (Ps. 19:7). But if any instance of duty owed by man to God in any age of the church were not either directly or indirectly commanded in it, it would not be a perfect law. But since it is perfect, all duties and, among others, the duties of believing and repenting of sin are virtually commanded in it; they are required in its first commandment.[1]

Adam, it is true, was not actually obliged by it to believe in a Redeemer until, after he had sinned, a Redeemer was revealed to him. But the same command that required him to believe and trust the promise of God his Creator required him also to believe in God his Redeemer as soon as He should be revealed and offered to him. Nor was Adam required to repent of sin before sin was committed. But the same law that obliged him to abhor, watch against, and abstain from all appearance of evil bound him also to bewail and forsake sin whenever he found that he was guilty of it. Since the holy law is a perfect rule of all internal as well as external obedience, it cannot but require faith and repentance as well as all other duties. Without them, no other performances can please God (Heb. 11:6). Our blessed Lord informs us that faith is one of "the weightier matters of the law" (Matt. 23:23), and the apostle Paul says, "Whatsoever is not of faith is sin" (Rom. 14:23). Unbelief, which is a departing from the living God, is evidently forbidden in the first commandment of the law. Faith, then, as I said already, is required in the same command (Isa. 26:4; 1 John 3:23). And with regard to repentance, though

---

1. Westminster Larger Catechism 104.

neither the covenant of works nor of grace admits of it as any atonement for sin or any ground of title to life, yet on the supposition that sin has been committed, it is a duty enjoined in the first and, indeed, in every other precept of the moral law.

Although the law in its covenant form requires of all who are under it since the fall perfect obedience as the condition of life and full satisfaction for sin in their own persons, and at the same time, upon the revelation and offer of Christ in the gospel as Jehovah Our Righteousness, commands them to believe in Him as such; yet as is the case in various other instances of duty, it requires the one of these only on supposition that the other is not performed. The law as a covenant of works requires that all who are under it do present to it as the conditions of eternal life perfect obedience and complete satisfaction for sin, either in their own persons or in that of a responsible surety. So long, then, as a sinner, unwilling to be convinced of his sin and his want of righteousness, cleaves to the law as a covenant and refuses to accept and present in the hand of faith the spotless righteousness of the adorable Surety, that sinner continues "a debtor to do the whole law" (Gal. 5:3). He keeps himself under an obligation to do, in his own person, all that the law in that form requires and also to suffer all that it threatens. The righteous law, accordingly, goes on to use him as he deserves. It continues to proceed against him without the smallest abatement of its high demands, requiring of him the complete payment of his debt both of perfect obedience and of infinite satisfaction for his disobedience. As it accepts no obedience but that which is absolutely perfect or fully answerable to all its demands (Gal. 3:10–11), so the acceptance of a man's person as righteous according to it will depend on the acceptance of his obedience (Matt. 5:18; Rom. 10:5).

In consequence of God's having proposed the law in its covenant form to Adam, and of Adam's having, as the representative of all his natural descendants, consented to it, all the children of men, while they continue in their natural state, remain firmly, in the sight of God, under the whole original obligation of it, even those who, as members of the visible church, are under an external dispensation of the covenant of grace remain under all its obligation (Rom. 9:31–32). For though the law in its covenant form is broken, yet it is far from being repealed or set aside. The obligation of this covenant continues in all its force, in time and through eternity, on every sinner who is not released from it by God, the other party. The awful consequence is that every unregenerate sinner is bound at once to perform perfect obedience and also to endure the full execution of the penal sanction. The preceptive part of that divine contract continues to bind both by its original authority and by man's consent to it, which consent is no more his to recall, except he is freed from his obligation by the other contracting party. And now that the curse of the covenant is, in consequence of transgression, become absolute, it binds as strongly as even the precept.

The law, then, as a covenant of works, does, in the most authoritative manner, demand from every descendant of Adam who is under it perfect holiness of nature, perfect righteousness of life, and complete satisfaction for sin. And none of the race of fallen Adam can ever enter heaven unless he either answers these three demands perfectly in his own person or accepts by faith the consummate righteousness of the second Adam, who "is the end of the law for righteousness to every one that believeth" (Rom. 10:4).

2. In the law as a covenant of works there is also a promise, a gracious promise of the continuance of spiritual and temporal life and, in due time, of eternal life. This promise, which flowed solely from infinite benignity and condescension in God, was made and was to have been fulfilled to Adam and all his natural posterity on condition that he, as their representative, perfectly obeyed the precept. That a promise of life was made to the first Adam and to all his natural descendants in him on condition of his perfect obedience during the time of his probation is evident, for the Lord Jesus said, "If thou wilt enter into life,

keep the commandments" (Matt. 19:17). Again, "This do, and thou shalt live" (Luke 10:28). The apostle Paul also says, "Moses describeth the righteousness which is of the law, that the man which doeth those things shall live by them" (Rom. 10:5). The promise of life to Adam as the representative of his posterity was implied in the threatening of death. When the Lord said to him, "In the day that thou eatest thereof thou shalt surely die" (Gen. 2:17), it implied, "If thou eat not of it, thou shalt surely live." Besides, the tree of life, which was one of the seals of that covenant, serves to evince the same thing. It sealed the promise of life to Adam as long as he continued to perform perfect obedience.

It is evident that the infinitely great and sovereign Creator could be under no obligations to man, the creature of His power, but such as arose from the wisdom, goodness, and faithfulness of His own nature. It was therefore free to Him whether He would still, by absolute authority, command man to obey Him or enter into a covenant with man for that purpose; whether after perfect obedience to His law He would give man eternal life or annihilate him; and whether, if it should please Him to give it, He would bestow it on condition of man's obedience or make a free grant of it to him and confirm him in the eternal enjoyment of it, as He has done elect angels. It depended solely on the will of God whether there should be a covenant at all containing a promise of eternal life to man and, if a promise of it, whether that promise should be absolute or conditional. The promise of eternal life upon man's perfect obedience, then, flowed entirely from the good pleasure and free grace of God. Had Adam fulfilled the condition of life in the first covenant, the Lord, instead of having been a debtor to him for his obedience, would have been a debtor only to His own grace and faithfulness in the promise. It is manifest, then, that there could have been no real merit in the perfect obedience of man nor so much as the smallest proportion between it and the promised reward. Although Adam had performed the condition of that covenant, he could not have expected eternal life on any ground except this: that God had graciously promised it on that condition.

The peculiar form of the covenant of works, or that which distinguishes it from every other contract, does not consist in the connection between the precept and the promise but in the manner of that connection. Obedience to the precept is made to give a pactional title to the life promised.[2] Eternal life is made so to depend on personal and perfect obedience that without this obedience, that life cannot be obtained; it cannot be claimed on any other ground. But if the obedience be performed, the life promised becomes due in virtue of the covenant. This being the manner of the connection between the precept and the promise of the first covenant; when this covenant was broken, that connection was as far as ever from being dissolved. Eternal life, according to the covenant, will still follow upon perfect, personal, and continual obedience. It still continues true "that the man which doeth those things shall live by them." But since no such thing as perfect obedience is to be found now among any of the sons of men, no man can have a title to life, according to the promise of that covenant. Thus, the law has become weak not by any change in itself but because men have not yielded perfect obedience to it. The reason why it cannot now justify a man in the sight of God or satisfy him with eternal life is because he cannot satisfy it with personal and perfect obedience.

Although eternal life was in the covenant of works promised to Adam and his posterity on condition of his perfect obedience and that only, yet a man is to be counted a legalist or self-righteous if while he does not pretend that his obedience is perfect, he yet relies on it for a title to life. Self-righteous men have, in all ages, set aside as impossible to be fulfilled by them that condition of the covenant of works which God had imposed on Adam, and have framed for themselves various models of that covenant which, though they are

---

2. By "pactional title," Colquhoun means a right granted by pact or covenant.—Ed.

far from being institutions of God and stand on terms lower than perfect obedience, yet are of the nature of the covenant of works.

The unbelieving Jews who sought righteousness by the works of the law were not so very ignorant or presumptuous as to pretend to perfect obedience. Neither did those professed Christians in Galatia who desired to be under the law and to be justified by the law, of whom the apostle therefore testified that they had "fallen from grace" (Gal. 5:4), presume to plead that they could yield perfect obedience. On the contrary, their public profession of Christianity showed that they had some sense of their need of Christ's righteousness. But their great error was this: they did not believe that the righteousness of Jesus Christ alone was sufficient to entitle them to the justification of life, and therefore they depended for justification partly on their own obedience to the moral and ceremonial law. It was this, and not their pretensions to perfect obedience, that the apostle had in view when he blamed them for cleaving to the law of works and for expecting justification by the works of the law. By relying for justification partly on their own works of obedience to the moral and ceremonial laws, they, as the apostle informed them, were "fallen from grace"; Christ had "become of no effect" to them; and they were "debtor[s] to do the whole law" (Gal. 5:3–4). By depending for justification partly on their imperfect obedience to the law, they framed the law into a covenant of works, and such a covenant of works as could admit of imperfect instead of perfect works; and by relying partly on the righteousness of Christ, they mingled the law with the gospel and works with faith in the affair of justification. Thus, they perverted both the law and the gospel and formed them for themselves into a motley covenant of works.

The great design of our apostle, then, was to draw them off from their false views of the law, to direct them to right conceptions of it in its covenant form in which it can admit of no personal obedience as a condition of life but such as is perfect, and so to destroy their legal hope as well as to confute their wrong notions. By the reasonings of the apostle on this subject, it is manifest that every evangelical as well as every legal work of ours is excluded from forming even the smallest part of a man's righteousness for justification in the sight of God. It is evident that even faith itself as a man's act or work, and so comprised in the works of the law, is thereby excluded from being any part of his justifying righteousness.[3]

It is one thing to be justified by faith merely as an instrument by which a man receives the righteousness of Christ, and another to be justified for faith as an act or work of the law. If a sinner, then, relies on his actings of faith or works of obedience to any of the commands of the law for a title to eternal life, he seeks to be justified by the works of the law as really as if his works were perfect. If he depends, either in whole or in part, on his faith and repentance for a right to any promised blessing, he thereby so annexes that promise to the commands to believe and repent as to form them for himself into a covenant of works. Building his confidence before God on his faith, repentance, and other acts of obedience to the law, he places them in Christ's stead as his grounds of right to the promise, and so he demonstrates himself to be of the works of the law and to be under the curse (Gal. 3:10).

3. Last, in the law as a covenant of works, there is moreover a penal sanction, an express threatening of death: spiritual, temporal, and eternal. This dreadful threatening was annexed to the positive precept not to eat of the tree of the knowledge of good and evil, as comprehending all the precepts of the natural or moral law. "Of the tree of the knowledge of good and evil, thou shalt not eat of it: for in the day that thou eatest thereof thou shalt surely die" (Gen. 2:17). "The soul that sinneth, it shall die" (Ezek. 18:4). Seeing the natural law was promulgated to Adam, who, though a holy creature was yet a mutable creature and liable to fall away from God, not only was a promise of

---

3. Westminster Confession of Faith 11.1.

eternal life in case of obedience but a threatening of eternal death in case of disobedience superadded to it. Thus, it was turned into a covenant or law of works, of which the law of the Ten Commandments was, and is still, the matter.

Accordingly, in its covenant form it says to every man who is under it not only "Do and live" but "Do or die; do on pain of death in all its dreadful extent." This law of works has a twofold power: a power to justify persons if they yield perfect obedience, and a power to condemn them if in the smallest instance they disobey. It said to Adam, and it says to every descendant of Adam, "If you offend but in one instance, dying you shall die." It is to every sinner the ministration of condemnation and of death. That awful sanction is founded in the justice of God and is as much according to His mind and will as the precept of the law itself. His mind and will are unchangeable; consequently, no sooner did man become a sinner than he became subject to the first and the second death, which divine justice and faithfulness were bound to see inflicted on him. One single transgression has forever cut him off from all possibility of attaining life by the law. And since all have sinned, consequently, "by the works of the law shall no flesh be justified" (Gal. 2:16). The law of works has pronounced all the race of Adam guilty, has condemned them to eternal punishment, and has not made the smallest provision for their deliverance.

That penal sanction annexed to the law of the covenant was most reasonable. There were indeed many other motives that might have induced Adam to continue obedient, but as he was naturally a mutable creature and as yet was only in a state of probation, his Creator had sufficient reason to be jealous of him. The Lord, therefore, in order to guard His grace and condescension from being despised and trampled on, annexed such a penalty to His righteous law as, if duly considered, should serve to terrify man from violating His gracious covenant. Death, especially spiritual and eternal death, could not but appear to Adam, whose knowledge and holiness were perfect, to be of all objects the most horrible. Nothing could appear better calculated to deter him from transgressing the covenant than the awful consideration that as he was already bound by the precept to perform perfect obedience, so he should, if he disobeyed, be as firmly bound by the curse to suffer endless punishment. Besides, the punishment of death in all its dreadful extent and duration is no more than the smallest sin against the infinite Majesty of heaven justly deserves. It is due to the sinner, and immutable justice requires that every man should have all that is due to him. "The wages of sin is death" (Rom. 6:23).

It is evident, then, that the promise of life in case of obedience and the denunciation of death in the event of disobedience, annexed to the law of creation, made it to Adam a covenant of works proposed. Nothing further was necessary to complete this covenant with him, as the head and representative of his natural posterity, than his consent to each of those articles. Since he was created in the image of God, he could not but clearly discern the equity and advantage of that divine covenant and so approve and consent to it. His consenting to it, accordingly, is hinted in these words of Eve to the serpent: "We may eat of the fruit of the trees of the garden: but of the fruit of the tree which is in the midst of the garden, God hath said, Ye shall not eat of it, neither shall ye touch it, lest ye die" (Gen. 3:2–3).

Adam then consented to the precept, promise, and threatening of the first covenant. And in his consent to it, as well as in God's approbation of the tenor of it, the formal obligation of it consisted, as far as that was superadded to the previous obligations under which he lay by the law of creation. In consenting to the precept, he bound himself to perfect obedience as the condition of eternal life to himself and his posterity, as well as to believe whatever God should afterward reveal and to do whatever He should command. By consenting to the promise, he agreed that he would have eternal life on no other condition than that of personal and perfect obedience and that he would never have eternal life unless he performed and persevered in such obedience. In consenting to the threatening in case of disobedience, he bound himself to renounce, in that event, all his pretensions to life by that covenant; and he obliged himself to suffer the full execution of the penalty denounced. By thus approving of and consenting to that proposed contract, the form of it was completed, and the obligations of it became so firm that the one contracting party could not retract without the consent of the other.

Since Adam, in consenting to the penal sanction of the first covenant, bound himself and his natural posterity never to have eternal life but on condition of his perfect obedience; and since he failed in this obedience and so fell with all his natural descendants under the begun execution of the penalty, no sinner under that broken covenant is bound by it to seek eternal life by his own performances.

The penalty of the covenant to which Adam, as the representative of his posterity, consented is by his transgression now become absolute, and it binds the unregenerate sinner as firmly as the precept itself does. Instead, then, of obliging him to seek eternal life for his obedience, it binds him to suffer eternal death for his disobedience. His consent in the first Adam to the penalty he is not at liberty to recall except he is released by God, the other contracting party. He is therefore as firmly bound, according to the constitution of the covenant, to endure the full execution of the penalty, unless God Himself delivers him from it, as to yield perfect obedience to the command. The curse of the law is so bound on him that it would be a second breach of the covenant to seek to elude the execution of it, as long as he desires to continue under that covenant. But to seek eternal life by his own righteousness is to try to elude that execution.

No obligation, therefore, lies on a sinner under the covenant of works to seek eternal life for his own obedience; on the contrary, it is utterly unlawful for him to attempt this. That very contract which afforded man, while innocent, a prospect of life, now that he is guilty debars him from all expectation of it. The covenant of works left innocent man at liberty to expect life upon his perfect obedience but did not oblige him to seek it on that ground, but only on the ground of the faithfulness of God in the promise in which He graciously annexed eternal life to perfect obedience (Matt. 19:16–17). And if it did not oblige innocent man to seek life on the ground even of perfect obedience, how can it bind guilty man to seek it on the account of imperfect obedience?

The law as a covenant, indeed, leaves the sinner at liberty—nay, it commands him to receive the righteousness of the second Adam offered to him in the gospel and to seek as well as to expect eternal life on the ground of this consummate righteousness. But as long as he continues to reject this righteousness, the law continues its obligation on him both to perform perfect obedience and to suffer the infinite execution of the curse. The connection established by the covenant between perfect obedience and life and between the smallest instance of disobedience and death is immutable and eternal. And therefore, no sinner can otherwise be delivered from the bond of that covenant than by receiving and presenting to the law of it the perfect and glorious righteousness of the second Adam, which answers fully all its high demands (Rom. 10:4; 7:6, respectively). If he labors to escape the death threatened and to procure the life promised in it by his own righteousness, his labor is to no purpose but to increase his guilt and aggravate his condemnation (Rom. 9:30–32).

Before I conclude this section, it may be proper to remark that the moral law, in the revelation that is given of it in Scripture, is almost constantly set forth to us in its covenant form as proposed to the first Adam. And it appears that the infinitely wise and holy Lord God has left it on record in that form in order that sinners of mankind might be convinced by it not only of their sinfulness and misery under the dominion of it but of the utter impossibility of their ever obtaining justification and eternal life by any righteousness of their own (Rom. 3:20).

✦ SECTION 3 ✦

*The Law in the Hand of Christ the Blessed Mediator
as a Rule of Life to All True Believers*

The authority and obligation of the law of nature, which is the same as the law of the Ten Commandments, being founded in the nature of God, the almighty Creator and sovereign ruler of men, are necessary, immutable, and eternal. They were the same before the law received the form of a covenant of works. That they are after it has received this form, and that they are and will continue to be after it has dropped this form. It is divested of its covenant form to all who are vitally united to the last Adam, who have communion with Him in His righteousness and who are instated in the covenant of grace. But though it is to them wholly denuded of its covenant form, yet it has lost nothing of its original authority and obligation.

Now that it is taken in under the covenant of grace and made the instrument of government in the spiritual kingdom of Christ, it retains all the authority over believers that, as a covenant of works, it has over unregenerate sinners. It is given to believers as a rule to direct them and as an authoritative law to bind them to holy obedience. It has the sovereign and infinite authority of Jehovah as a Creator as well as a Redeemer to afford it binding force. His nature is infinitely, eternally, and unchangeably holy; and therefore His law, which is a transcript of His holiness, must retain invariably and eternally all its original authority (Lev. 11:44; 1 Peter 1:15–16). The law as a rule, then, is not a new preceptive law but the old law, which was from the beginning, issued to believers under a new form.

This law issues to true Christians from Christ, the glorious Mediator of the new covenant, and from God as their Creator, proprietor, benefactor, and covenant God. It proceeds immediately from Jesus Christ, the blessed Mediator between God and men. It is taken in under the covenant of grace, and in the hand of Christ, the Mediator of that covenant, it is given to all who believe in Him and who are justified by faith as the only rule of their obedience. The apostle

Paul accordingly styles it "the law of Christ" (Gal. 6:2). It is a law that Christ has clearly explained and that He has vindicated from the false glosses of the scribes and Pharisees, His new commandment that He has given and enforced by His own example and whose obligation on the subjects of His spiritual kingdom He has increased by His redemption of them from their bondage to sin and Satan. It is a law that He, according to the promise of His gracious covenant, inscribes by His Holy Spirit on their hearts; a law to which He calls His yoke and which, in comparison to the law of works, is a light and easy yoke (Matt. 11:29–30).

While the law as a rule of life to believers is issued forth immediately from Christ to them, it proceeds at the same time from God as their sovereign Lord, their Creator, proprietor, and covenant God in Him. God the Father says concerning Messiah, "Behold, I have given him for a witness to the people, a leader and commander to the people" (Isa. 55:4). All the sovereign authority of the Father, the Son, and the Holy Spirit is, according to the everlasting covenant, vested in Him as God-man, Mediator, and king of Zion. In Exodus 23:21, Jehovah gives this solemn charge to the Israelites in reference to Messiah, the uncreated angel of the covenant: "Beware of him, and obey his voice, provoke him not;… for my name is in him." It is as if He had said, "My essence, My sovereignty, My authority, My law are in Him; yea, all the fullness of the Godhead is in Him, and in Him only will obedience to My law be acceptable to Me." The name of the Father is so in Him that His voice in the law is the Father's voice, for it follows in verse 22, "But if thou shalt indeed obey his voice, and do all that I speak."

To the same purpose, the apostle Paul said of himself that he was "not without law to God, but under the law to Christ" (1 Cor. 9:21). To be "not without law to God" can mean no less than to be under the law of God. Therefore, to be under the law of Christ is the same as to be under the law of God. By being under the law as a rule in the hand of Christ or, which is the same thing, by being under the law to

Christ, believers are under the law of God. When they are under the law of the Ten Commandments as the law of Christ, they are under it as enforced by all the sovereign authority of God.

The original authority of the moral law is not in the smallest degree lessened by the believer's reception of it not as the law or covenant of works but as the law of Christ standing in the covenant of grace. Its original obligation proceeding from the infinite authority of the adorable Trinity is inseparable from it and cannot possibly be in the least impaired by its being conveyed to believers by and from the Lord Jesus. For He, equally with the Father and the Holy Spirit, is, in His divine nature, the eternal Jehovah, "the most high over all the earth" (Ps. 83:18). He is God over all, and the Creator of "all things…that are in heaven, and that are in earth, visible and invisible" (Col. 1:16). He is also "in the Father," and the Father is in Him (John 14:11). As God's authority to judge is not lessened by His having committed all judgment to the Son, so His authority to command is not and cannot be in the least diminished by His having given Christ for a "commander to the people" (Isa. 55:4).

That the holy law of God should be given to believers in and through the Mediator, and not immediately by God Himself, is necessary. When the divine law was at first given to man, he was the friend of God, and so he could receive the law immediately from Him in a manner consistent both with the honor of God and the safety of his own soul. But now that man has sinned against the Lord and has become an object of His infinite wrath and that God has assumed the character of an offended sovereign and an avenging judge, now that the law as a covenant of works has become the dreadful instrument of divine indignation on account of sin, the guilty sinner cannot regard either God or His righteous law but as an object of the greatest terror to him. It was requisite, then, that a mediator should interpose both between the offended Lawgiver and the sinner and also between the violated law and the sinner, who, by satisfying the justice of the one and by answering the demands of the other, might obtain free access for the guilty criminal to both.

Out of Christ the blessed Mediator, a holy God cannot, with the safety of His honor, have any dealing with a sinful creature; but in and by Christ He can, consistently with His own infinite honor and that of His holy law, issue forth His commandments to believers and receive their sincere obedience. Accordingly, the great Mediator, having admitted believers to communion with Himself in His surety-righteousness, writes, by His Spirit, the law on their hearts, and in His Father's name makes it the instrument of His government of them and the rule of their duty to Him. And as the same law is called the law of nature because in his creation it was inlaid in the nature of the first man, so it may be styled the law of renewed nature because in the hand of Christ and as standing under the covenant of grace, it is interwoven with the new nature of all who are "created" again in Him "unto good works" (Eph. 2:10).

Since it is only in Christ, then, that the offended Majesty of heaven can give His holy law to a sinner and that a sinner can with safety receive and obey such a law, it may well be called "the law of Christ" (Gal. 6:2). Considered as the law of Christ's justified, sanctified, and peculiar people, it is not the law of an absolute God or of God out of Christ, but the law of God in Christ. Were believers to keep the moral law only as the law of nature and without any relation to the Mediator, their obedience would be but natural religion. Were they to obey it merely as a covenant of works, their obedience would be but legal righteousness. But when they obey it in its relation to Christ and the covenant of grace, their conformity of heart and life to it is true holiness, acceptable to God by Jesus Christ (1 Peter 2:5).

The precepts of the law as a rule of life to true Christians are the same with those of the law as a covenant of works, and they require the same perfection of obedience. The Ten Commandments are the precepts of the divine law both as a covenant of works to the unregenerate and as a rule of duty to the saints. But while they are issued to believers with all the sovereign authority that originally belonged to them, the obligations under which believers lie to yield obedience to them are greatly increased by the grace of the Redeemer and the mercies of redemption.

If the saints are obliged as creatures, they are still more firmly bound as new creatures to keep those commandments. If they were formerly under firm obligations to obey them in their covenant form as the precepts of God out of Christ, they are now under additional obligations to yield obedience to them as the commands of God as their own God and Father in Christ. Does the grace displayed in the first covenant oblige all who are under that covenant to perform perfect obedience? The exceeding riches of grace in the second covenant lay all who are instated in it under additional ties to give perfect obedience. If sinners under the covenant of works are bound to yield perfect obedience *for* life, believers within the bond of the covenant of grace are under still higher obligations to perform perfect obedience *from* life and for the glory of Him who, by fulfilling all the righteousness of the law in its covenant form, has merited eternal life for them.

The law as a rule, then, enforced by all the sovereign authority of God, both as Creator and Redeemer, requires believers to perform not sincere only but perfect and perpetual obedience. The great Redeemer gives this high command to all His redeemed: "Be ye therefore perfect, even as your Father which is in heaven is perfect" (Matt. 5:48). Accordingly, real believers, instead of resting satisfied with sincere obedience to that law, consider their want of absolute perfection in obedience as their sin and bewail it as such.

True Christians, and none else, are under the law as a rule in the hand of Christ. The apostle Paul exhorted the brethren in the churches of Galatia thus: "Bear ye one another's burdens, and so fulfil the law of Christ" (Gal. 6:2). The endearing relations in which believers stand to Christ and to God in Him, as well as the inestimable blessings of salvation conferred on them and the exceeding great and precious promises given them, all require and enforce their obligation to abound in holy obedience to the law as a rule (1 Peter 2:4–5, 9; Titus 2:11–14; 2 Cor. 7:1, respectively). Believers before the incarnation of Christ were as much under the binding force of it as believers now are (Luke 1:73–75).

The great design of God in giving this law in the hand of Christ to His people is not that by their obedience to it they may procure for themselves a right to eternal life, but that it may direct and oblige them to walk worthy of their union with Christ, of their justification in Him, of their legal title to and begun possession of life eternal, and of God Himself as their God in Him. Their conformity of heart and life to its commands, instead of procuring their title to salvation, is a principal part of their salvation already begun and a necessary preparative for the consummation of it through eternity (Heb. 12:28; 1 Peter 2:9).

The law as a rule of life to believers, especially in this view of it, is very different from the law as a covenant of works. The precept of the law as a covenant is "Do and live," but the command of the law as a rule is "Live and do"; the law of works says, "Do or you shall be condemned to die," but the law in the hand of Christ says, "You are delivered from condemnation; therefore do." The command of the former is "Do perfectly that you may have a right to eternal life," but that of the latter is, "You already have begun possession of eternal life, as well as the promise of the complete possession of it, therefore do in such a manner as to advance daily toward perfection." By the former, a man is commanded to do in his own strength, but by the latter he is required to do in the strength that is in Christ Jesus. The Lord Jesus says to every believer, "My grace is sufficient for thee: for my strength is made perfect in weakness" (2 Cor. 12:9); therefore, do. The commandments of the law, both as a covenant and as a rule, are materially but are not formally the same.

Although the law as a rule of duty to believers requires perfect obedience from them, yet it admits of God's accepting their sincere obedience performed in faith, though it is imperfect. It admits of His accepting this obedience not indeed as any part of their justifying righteousness, not as the foundation of His acceptance of their persons as righteous, but as the fruit and evidence of their being vitally united to His beloved Son as Jehovah their Righteousness, and of their being already accepted in Him (Eph. 1:6; Heb. 13:16).

Since true believers are already irrevocably interested in the covenant of grace, in the righteousness of Christ, and in the favor of God; and since they have in Christ and on the ground of His righteousness imputed to them a complete security against eternal death and a full title to eternal life, the law as the law of Christ has no sanction of judicial rewards or punishments. It has no promise of eternal life or threatening of eternal death annexed to it. The form of the covenant of works, indeed, is eternally binding on all who live and die under that violated covenant, but because Christ, as last Adam, has answered all the demands of it for believers, they are delivered from the law in that form (Rom. 7:4–6).

The law that believers are under is the law of Christ and of God in Christ, which has no promise of eternal life to them for their obedience to it. The promise of eternal life to the saints is the promise of the covenant of grace, or the gospel, and not of the law as a rule of duty. Eternal life is promised to them not in consideration of their sincere obedience to the law as a rule of life but on account of Christ's perfect obedience to it as a covenant of works received by faith and imputed by God. It is promised to them not as a reward of debt for their sincere obedience but as "the gift of God…through Jesus Christ our Lord" (Rom. 6:23). The righteousness of Jesus Christ imputed to them gives them a perfect title to life; they are already heirs of it "and joint-heirs with Christ" (Rom. 8:17). They have begun possession of it and have the gracious promise of the gospel that they shall, in due time, attain the perfect and everlasting possession.

There is therefore no need that a promise of eternal life should be annexed to the law as a rule of duty to be fulfilled to believers on the ground of their obedience to that law. And, indeed, it cannot be annexed to it, for since the law as a rule cannot require less than perfect obedience and since believers cannot in this life yield perfect obedience to its precepts, it cannot justify them or promise life to them for their obedience. Neither can they begin to perform even sincere obedience to it until, in union with Christ, they are already justified and fully entitled to life eternal. Accordingly, we are informed in Scripture that believers are justified by grace and by no law or work of a law, whether it is of the law as a covenant or the law as a rule. "That no man is justified by the law in the sight of God, it is evident" (Gal. 3:11); and "Christ is become of no effect unto you, whosoever of you are justified by a law" (Gal. 5:4). "Therefore we conclude that a man is justified by faith without the deeds of the law" (Rom. 3:28).[4] No promise of life, then, is made to the sincere obedience of believers to the law of Christ; otherwise, their title to life would be founded not entirely on the righteousness of Christ imputed to them but partly, if not wholly, on works done by themselves.

As no promise of eternal life belongs to the law as a rule of duty to believers, so no threatening of eternal death belongs to it. Not that the law considered as a covenant of works is stripped of its sanction; the penal sanction of it in that form is eternal and must be eternally endured by all who die under it. But because the whole penal sanction of it was wholly endured by Christ, the surety of those who believe on Him, and because His infinite satisfaction for all their sins is placed to their account—that law, being satisfied, cannot now condemn them. And as the law in its covenant form cannot condemn them or require from them a double payment for the same debt, so neither can the law in the hand of Christ, as a rule. No divine law can condemn them. "There is therefore now no condemnation to them which are in Christ Jesus" (Rom. 8:1).

---

4. The original word used for *law* in these passages I used the freedom to translate literally, that the apostle's meaning may more clearly appear.

Believers are perfectly and irreversibly justified, and therefore, though their iniquities deserve eternal wrath, yet they can no more make them actually liable to that wrath. It is the peculiar privilege of believers only, who are already justified and so set forever beyond the reach of condemnation, to be under the law in the hand of Christ. But were a threatening of eternal death annexed to the law as a rule in His hand, every time that the believer transgressed this law it would lay him anew under condemnation, and as he every moment falls short of perfection in his obedience, he must inevitably be every moment under condemnation to eternal wrath. But instead of this, he always continues in a state of justification and "shall not come into condemnation" (John 5:24). "Whom [God] did predestinate, them he also called: and whom he called, them he also justified: and whom he justified, them he also glorified…. Who shall lay any thing to the charge of God's elect? It is God that justifieth. Who is he that condemneth?" (Rom. 8:30, 33–34). "Their sins and their iniquities will I remember no more" (Heb. 8:12).

Though the law as a rule of duty, then, standing under the covenant of grace as the instrument by which the Lord Jesus rules the subjects of His spiritual kingdom has lost nothing of its original authority to direct and bind them, even to perfect obedience, yet it has no promise of eternal life to them for their obedience and no threatening of eternal death for their disobedience. Therefore, as the law in its covenant form can neither justify nor condemn believers, so neither can the law as a rule of life.[5]

But though the law as a rule of duty to believers has no sanction of judicial rewards and punishments, yet it has a sanction of gracious rewards and paternal chastisements. A promise of gracious rewards, or rewards of grace, to believers in the way of their obedience is annexed to the law in the hand of Christ. In order to dispose and encourage them to obedience, God promises, on Christ's account,

---

5. Westminster Larger Catechism 97.

gracious rewards to them, such as the light of His gracious countenance, sensible and comfortable communion with Him, peace and joy in the Holy Ghost, the assurance of their personal interest in Christ, freedom from trouble of mind, hope in their death, and degrees of glory in eternity, corresponding probably to the degree of their holy activity in time (Ps. 19:11; 2 Cor. 1:12; 2 Tim. 4:7–8).

To the law as a rule in the hand of Christ belongs also a threatening of paternal chastisements. In order to deter believers from disobedience, as well as to promote in them the mortification of sin, the Lord threatens that although He will not cast them into hell for their sins, yet He will permit hell, as it were, to enter their consciences; that He will visit them with a series of outward afflictions; that He will deprive them of that sensible communion with Him which they sometime enjoyed; and that He will afflict them with bitterness instead of sweetness and with terror instead of comfort (Ps. 89:30–33; 1 Cor. 11:30–32; Heb. 12:6–11). These chastisements are, to a believer, no less awful and much more forcible restraints from sin than even the prospect of vindictive wrath would be. A filial fear of them will do more to influence him to the practice of holiness than all the slavish fears of hell can do. A fear, lest he should be deprived of that sweetness of communion with God with which he is favored, will constrain him to say to his lusts, as the fig tree in Jotham's parable, "Should I forsake my sweetness, and my good fruit, and go to be promoted over the trees?" (Judg. 9:11). "Shall I leave the spiritual delight which I have had in communion with my God and Savior and have fellowship with you?" Or if, for his iniquities, he is already under the dreadful frowns of his heavenly Father, his recollection of the comfort which he formerly enjoyed and of which he is now deprived will make him say, "I will go and return to my first husband; for then was it better with me than now" (Hos. 2:7).

It is plain that no sanction but this is suitable to the happy state of believers. They, in union and communion with the blessed Redeemer, are justified, adopted, sanctified, and instated in the covenant of grace in which they "should not perish, but have everlasting life" (John 3:16; see also 10:28). As long, indeed, as they are imperfect in holiness and their temper and practice subject in change, such promises and threatenings are necessary. But it is manifest that their necessity is occasioned by the remainders of sin in the saints, who require to be treated as children underage. It is necessary in their state of imperfection that they be influenced to obedience by the promises and threatenings of the law of Christ, for though their being excited to obedience by these promises and threatenings is neither servile nor slavish, yet it is childish. It is not suitable to the state of one who has come to the "measure of the stature of the fullness of Christ" (Eph. 4:13). When believers become perfect, they will perform obedience as freely as the angels in heaven do, without being in the least influenced to it by promises or threatenings. And the nearer they come to perfection in holiness, the freer and more disinterested will their obedience be. But as long as they are in a state of imperfection, it is their duty, in order to advance in holiness, to have respect in their obedience to what the law of Christ promises and threatens to them.[6]

• REFLECTIONS •

It appears evident from what has been said that though the Ten Commandments are the substance of the law of nature, yet they do not contain the whole of this law. The law of nature, inscribed on the heart of man in his creation, had a penal sanction. Although a penal sanction, as is evident from the case of glorified saints and confirmed

---

6. Promises of gracious rewards and threats of paternal chastisements properly belong to the covenant of grace, which has no proper penalty, rather than to the law as a rule. They are implied in the blessings promised in that covenant, or at least are means of accomplishing the promises of it. But seeing the law as a rule is received into the covenant of grace as the instrument of Christ's government of His spiritual subjects, those promises and threats may, I humbly apprehend, be said, though not with strict propriety, to belong or be annexed to the law in that form.

angels who are and who will remain eternally under the law of nature, is not inseparable from that law, yet such a sanction belongs to it.

The devout and attentive reader may hence discern the difference between heathen morality, pharisaic righteousness, and true holiness. Heathen morality is external obedience to the law of nature and may be termed *natural religion*. Pharisaic righteousness is hypocritical obedience to the law as a covenant of works and is usually called *legal righteousness*, or *the works of the law*. True holiness is spiritual and sincere obedience to the law as a rule of life in the hand of the blessed Mediator and is commonly called *evangelical holiness*, or *true godliness*. True believers are the only persons who obey the law in its relation to Christ and to the covenant of grace, and their acts of obedience are the only spiritual sacrifices acceptable to God by Jesus Christ (1 Peter 2:5). The holy Lord God does not account Himself glorified by any obedience from the sons of men except that which they perform to Him as in Christ. For it is the will of the Father, the almighty Creator and sovereign ruler of the world, "that all men should honour the Son, even as they honour the Father" (John 5:23) "and that every tongue should confess that Jesus Christ is Lord, to the glory of God the Father" (Phil. 2:11).

It may be justly inferred from the preceding doctrine that the distinction of the divine law, especially into the law as a covenant of works and as a rule of life, is a very important distinction. It is, as the attentive reader has seen, a scriptural distinction; and it is necessary in the hand of the Spirit to qualify believers for clearly understanding the grace and glory of the gospel, as well as the acceptable manner of performing every duty required in the law. To distinguish truly and clearly between the law as a covenant and the law as a rule is, as Luther expressed it, "the key that opens the hidden treasure of the gospel." No sooner had the Spirit of truth given Luther a glimpse of that distinction than he declared that he seemed to be admitted into paradise and that the whole face of the Scripture was changed for him. Indeed, without a spiritual and true knowledge of that distinction, a man can neither discern, nor love, nor obey acceptably the truth as it is in Jesus (Eph. 4:21). Nay, if the law as a covenant were not to be distinguished from the law as a rule in the hand of the Mediator, it would inevitably follow that believers are still under the law as a covenant of works; that they ought still to regard God not as their gracious God and Father but as their angry and avenging judge; and that their sins are still to be considered as transgressions only of the covenant of works and as rendering them, notwithstanding their justification, actually subject to the curse and revenging wrath of God—contrary to Scripture (Rom. 6:14; 7:1–6; 8:1–2) and to our confession of faith.[7]

As an evidence that all unregenerate persons are under the dominion of the law as a covenant of works, the natural bent of their hearts in all their views respecting the means of salvation is to the way of that covenant. They all desire to be under the law of works. All who have embraced either one or another of the false religions that are in the world agree at least in this principle: it is by doing that men are to live. Hence, when the Lord opens the eyes of a man to see that horrible gulf of sin and misery into which the first Adam plunged him, he is strongly inclined to exert himself for deliverance in the way of the covenant of works. He struggles hard to forsake his sins and to perform his duties, hoping that by his own performances he will become so righteous as to pacify the wrath of God and to procure for himself eternal life. Ah, ignorant, proud, vain attempt! This, however, he resolutely persists in doing until he is made to despair of ever being able to procure salvation for himself in the way of that covenant. Indeed, this natural bent of the depraved heart toward the way of the law as a covenant, together with deep ignorance of the high demands of the law in that form, is the source of all the self-righteousness that is in the world. To take sinners off from this to a cordial reliance only on the righteousness of the second Adam for all their title to salvation is a special part of the Holy Spirit's work in

---

7. Westminster Confession of Faith 19.1, 6.

conviction and conversion, and to do it requires a greater exertion of His almighty power than even to create a world.

From what has been said, we may also see that there are two sorts of sinners who offend more especially against the law in its covenant form—namely, legalists and antinomians. Legalists, on the one hand, transgress against it by seeking to be justified by their own pretended obedience to it. Antinomians, on the other hand, offend against it by despising the divine authority and obligation of it. The former transgress against the form of the law as a covenant by depending on their own obedience for justification; the latter offend against the matter of it, or the Ten Commandments, as vested with all the infinite authority that belongs to it, by disregarding that high authority. Legalists contend that believers are under the law even as it is the covenant of works; antinomians, on the contrary, assert that believers are not only not under it as a covenant but not under it even as a rule of duty. These two assertions are not more contrary to one another than they both are to the truth as it is in Jesus. In the Scriptures, we are informed that believers are delivered from the law as a covenant of works but that they are under it and delight to be under it as a rule of life. Indeed, to affirm that they are freed from it in its covenant form implies that they are under it in another form.

Does the law in its covenant form command every sinner under it who hears the gospel to believe and repent? Then it is of inexpressible importance to every sinner to believe that it does. If the law as a covenant of works does not require of every sinner under it who hears the gospel faith and repentance, it will follow that faith and repentance, as acts or works, cannot be excluded from being grounds of a sinner's justification in the sight of God, since on that supposition they cannot be denominated works of the law. Under this character, all the sinner's works of obedience are, in Scripture, excluded from being causes of his justification before God (Gal. 2:16). Doubtless, if the moral law, or law as a covenant, taken into the administration of the covenant of grace does not require faith and repentance, then there must be a new law to command them. Besides, if faith and repentance, which, as some have said, contain all that is necessary to salvation, are commanded only by a new and gospel law, then the moral law is unnecessary—and so a wide door will be opened to gross antinomianism. Sinners, then, are commanded by the moral law as a covenant, and by no other law, to believe and repent; and saints are commanded by the moral law as a rule of life, and by no other, to advance in the exercise of faith and repentance.

To conclude, is it so that the moral law has lost nothing of its original authority and obligation by being, to believers, divested of its covenant form? Then the supposition that the sovereign authority of God in it is laid aside or that the original obligation of it is, in the least degree, weakened by its being issued to believers as the law of Christ, is utterly groundless. Such a supposition reflects great dishonor on the glorious Mediator, for is not our Lord Jesus, equally with the Father and the Holy Spirit, Jehovah, the Most High over all the earth (Ps. 83:18)? Does not all the fullness of the Godhead dwell in Him bodily (Col. 2:9)? Is not the name, or infinite authority of God, in Him (Ex. 23:21)? Is it not by Him that all things were created and that they all consist (Col. 1:16–17)? How then is it possible that the original and infinite authority of the divine law can, in the smallest degree, be lessened by its issuing to true believers from Him who is God over all, the great God our Savior?

CHAPTER 2

The Law of God as Promulgated to the Israelites from Mount Sinai

After the Israelites, the peculiar people of God, had become grossly ignorant of the precepts and penalties of His righteous law during their long continuance and grievous bondage in Egypt, He graciously condescended to reveal it to them in express terms and with awful solemnity from Mount Sinai.

In this publication of His law to them, He summed it up in ten commandments, and therefore it is commonly styled the law of the Ten Commandments. While it is largely set forth and explained in the whole Word of God, it is briefly comprehended in ten words or commandments (Deut. 10:4). It was God in the person of the Son who, from the top of Mount Sinai, spoke these words. For we read that the prophet whom Jehovah was to raise up to the children of Israel of their brethren like unto Moses was "the angel which spake to him in the mount Sina" (Acts 7:38). And the apostle Paul said, "See that ye refuse not him that speaketh"—namely, "Jesus the mediator of the new covenant"—"For if they escaped not who refused him that spake on earth, much more shall not we escape, if we turn away from him that speaketh from heaven" (Heb. 12:24–25). After the Son of God, in the hearing of all the assembly of Israel, had spoken those commandments out of the midst of the fire, He wrote them on two tablets of stone. Moses informs us that "the tables were written on both their sides; on the one side and on the other they were written" (Ex. 32:15). They were filled with writing on both sides in order, perhaps, to teach us that when this law is written on the hearts of believers, they are sanctified wholly (1 Thess. 5:23) and that nothing must be either added to the words of the law or taken away from them. It is remarkable that the Ten Commandments were, by the finger of God, written on tables of stone twice.

After the first two tables had been broken by Moses beneath the mount, the Lord was graciously pleased to write on two other tables the same words that He had written on the first (Ex. 34:1). His writing of the law twice, without the smallest variation, and that on tables of stone, was doubtless intended to represent to us, as well as to the Israelites, the immutable authority and eternal obligation of that law. When the moral law was promulgated to Israel from Mount Sinai or Horeb, we are informed that it was given them in the form of a covenant. Moses said to them, "The LORD our God made a covenant with us in Horeb" (Deut. 5:2). "Take heed unto yourselves, lest ye forget the covenant of the LORD your God, which he made with you" (Deut. 4:23). Hence, the tables of stone are styled the tables of the covenant, and the words engraved on them the words of the covenant.

The Ten Commandments, accordingly, were published from Sinai in the form of a covenant, or federal, transaction. The Sinai transaction was a mixed dispensation. In it, the covenant of grace was repeated and published; the covenant of works was awfully displayed in subservience thereto; and a national covenant between God and the Israelites was also made as an appendage to the covenant of grace. Accordingly, the law of the Ten Commandments was thence promulgated by the Son of God, the glorious Mediator, as a rule of life to believers in a manner suited to the covenant of grace. The same law was repeated and displayed to the Israelites in the form of the covenant of works, and it was published to them as the matter of a national covenant, or covenant of peculiarity, between God and them. I shall endeavor briefly to consider the moral law in each of these views.

✦ SECTION 1 ✦
*The Covenant of Grace and the Ten Commandments
as the Rule of Duty to Believers according to
That Covenant, as Published from Mount Sinai*

The covenant of grace, both in itself and in the intention of God, was the principal part of the Sinai transaction. It was therefore published first, as appears from these words in the preface standing before the commandments: "I am the LORD thy God" (Ex. 20:2). These gracious words, in which Jehovah exhibited Himself to the Israelites as their God, were spoken to them as His peculiar people, the natural seed of Abraham, and as typical of all His spiritual seed (Gal. 3:16–17). To this gracious offer or grant, which Jehovah made of Himself to them as their God and Redeemer, the Ten Commandments were annexed as a rule of duty to them as His professed people, and especially to true believers among them as His spiritual seed. In virtue of His having engaged to answer for them all the demands of the law as a covenant of works, He repeats and promulgates it to them as a rule of life in the covenant of grace. Instead of saying to them, "Keep My commandments, that I may become your God"; He, on the contrary, said to each of them, "I am the Lord thy God; therefore, keep My commandments."

This is not the form of the law as it is the covenant of works but the form of it only as the law of Christ and as standing in the covenant of grace. But more particularly: that, in the Sinai transaction, the covenant of grace, with the law annexed to it as a rule of life, was repeated and delivered to the Israelites appears evident to me from the following considerations:

1. The Ten Commandments are founded on these words of the preface: "I am the LORD thy God, which hath brought thee out of the land of Egypt, out of the house of bondage" (Ex. 20:2). The inestimable privilege here exhibited is made the foundation of the duty required. Jehovah, the Son of God and the messenger of the covenant

of grace, spoke those words to the members of His visible church, the natural posterity of Abraham. He declares that He is their God by virtue of this covenant made with Abraham: "I will establish my covenant between me and thee and thy seed after thee…to be a God unto thee, and to thy seed after thee" (Gen. 17:7). He also affirms that He is their God who has brought them out of the land of Egypt, according to the promise He made to Abraham when, in the most solemn manner, He renewed the covenant with him. "Afterward shall they come out with great substance" (Gen. 15:14). He first avouches Himself to be their God and Redeemer and then commands them to perform all their duties to Him. This was the very form of His covenant with Abraham. "The LORD appeared to Abram, and said unto him, I am the Almighty God; walk before me, and be thou perfect" (Gen. 17:1), as if He had said, "I am a God all-sufficient for you both to uphold and protect you and to provide all good things for you. Walk therefore before My face and be perfect."

But the covenant made and renewed with Abraham, and also with Isaac and Jacob, was the covenant of grace, a covenant to be believed and embraced by faith. When the covenant made with the Israelites at Sinai was afterward renewed with them in the land of Moab, we are told it was in order that the Lord might be unto them a God, as He had sworn to their fathers, "to Abraham, to Isaac, and to Jacob" (Deut. 29:12–13). The covenant of grace, then, which had been made with Abraham was the very covenant that was expressed in the preface to the Ten Commandments and repeated from Mount Sinai to the Israelites. Besides in the Sinai transaction, Jehovah exhibited Himself to Israel not only as their God and Redeemer but as a God who promised to forgive iniquity (Ex. 34:7); to circumcise the heart to love Him (Deut. 30:6); to take them for His inheritance, to lead them, instruct them, and keep them as the apple of His eye (Deut. 32:9–10); and to dwell and walk among them (Ex. 29:45–46; Lev. 26:12). These clearly are promises of the covenant of grace.

2. They with whom Jehovah covenanted at Sinai are styled in Scripture the people of God, on whom He was to have mercy (Hos. 2:23); a peculiar treasure to Him above all people (Ex. 19:5); His first-born, precious in His sight and honorable (Ex. 4:22); and the seed of Abraham, to whom the promises were made (Gal. 3:16). These descriptions of ancient Israel, given of them as a people in covenant with God, refer evidently to the covenant of grace.

3. God commanded that the two tables of stone on which He had written the Ten Commandments the second time be laid up in the ark. Accordingly, after the first two tables, which had been hewn as well as engraved by God Himself, had been broken beneath the mount, the second, which were hewn by Moses, the typical mediator, were deposited in the ark (Deut. 10:3, 5). This represented that after the divine law as a covenant of works had been broken, it was to be fulfilled by Christ the true Mediator and to be laid up as fulfilled and honored in Him (Isa. 42:21). Because the fulfilling of the law written on those tables by obedience and suffering was the proper condition of life in the covenant of grace made with the second Adam, as the representative of His spiritual seed (Matt. 3:15), they are called "the tables of the covenant," and the ark in which they were deposited, "the ark of the covenant" (Heb. 9:4). And because the law as a rule of life, in which Jehovah testified His will to His people, was written on them, and also because they were a testimony of His gracious covenant with that people, they are styled the "two tables of testimony" (Ex. 31:18), and the ark into which they were put, "the ark of the testimony" (Ex. 25:22).

Moreover, the tables of the law in the ark were covered and hid by the mercy seat, or propitiatory cover. This prefigured that the violated law should be so covered by the divine Surety, who was to fulfill all the righteousness of it for believers, as never to appear any more to condemn them (Rom. 8:33–34). It was after the Lord had renewed with the believing Israelites the covenant of grace that He said to Moses,

"Come up to me into the mount, and be there: and I will give thee tables of stone, and a law, and commandments which I have written; that thou mayest teach them" (Ex. 24:12). It was after that, too, that He commanded Moses to make the ark and the mercy seat in order not only to keep the tables safely but to cover and remove the form of the covenant of works, which had been on the commandments engraved on them, that believers might not perceive it. And it was also after that solemn transaction that Moses was enjoined to lay up the tables in the ark and under the mercy seat to signify that as the ark with the mercy seat was an eminent type of Christ, so the law is in Christ to believers and in His hand is issued forth as from the mercy seat to them, or from God as pacified toward them. It is manifest, then, that the covenant of grace, with the law annexed to it as a rule of life, was published from Mount Sinai.

4. The same also appears evident if we consider that the covenant made with the Israelites at Sinai could not be the covenant of works. God could not consistently, either with His own honor or with the nature of the covenant of works, renew or make again that covenant with persons who, by breaking it in the first Adam, had already subjected themselves to the penalty of it. He could, indeed, display it in its terror before condemned sinners but could not again make it with them. Neither could He renew it with the Israelites in particular without disannulling the covenant of grace made with Abraham in which He graciously promised to be a God to him and to his seed after him, for a future covenant of works made with the seed of Abraham would annul the former covenant of grace made with him as their representative.

But this covenant was not, and could not be, annulled by the transaction at Sinai; for the apostle Paul says that "the covenant, that was confirmed before of God in Christ, the law, which was four hundred and thirty years after, cannot disannul, that it should make the promise of none effect" (Gal. 3:17). Since the covenant made with the Israelites at Sinai, then, did not and could not so disannul the covenant of grace made with Abraham and his seed, especially his believing seed after him, as to make the promise of no effect, it could not be the covenant of works. It was, therefore, the covenant of grace that was repeated and offered to his posterity on that solemn occasion; and it was the law, standing in that gracious covenant as the rule of their obedience, that was promulgated to them.

5. That in the transaction at Sinai the covenant of grace was published to the Israelites is also evident from this: that after Moses had taken the book of the covenant and read it in the audience of the people, he took half of the blood of the sacrifices that had on that solemn occasion been slain and sprinkled it on the people and said, "Behold the blood of the covenant, which the LORD hath made with you concerning all these words" (Ex. 24:8). An apostle informs us that Moses, on that great occasion, sprinkled with the blood the book of the covenant as well as all the people (Heb. 9:19). It would seem that he laid the book on the altar before he sprinkled the altar with the other half of the blood. Now according to the same apostle, it was the first testament, or Old Testament dispensation of the covenant of grace, that was thus dedicated with the blood of the sacrifices (Heb. 9:18–20). It was therefore the covenant of grace, according to the Jewish dispensation of it, that was delivered from Mount Sinai. Moreover, the blood sprinkled by Moses was typical of the blood of Christ, and the sprinkling of that, both on the altar and on the people, was figurative of the sprinkling of this: both on the altar of His divine nature for the satisfaction of justice and on His people for the justification of their persons and the sanctification of their natures. But it was the New Testament dispensation of the covenant of grace that the blood of Christ confirmed, which is therefore called "the blood of the everlasting covenant" (Heb. 13:20), and it is according to the covenant of grace, and that only, that the blood of Jesus is sprinkled, either for pardon or for purification.

6. The promulgation of the ceremonial law formed a part of the transaction at Sinai, and that law had no reference but to the covenant of grace. When it was enacted to regulate the worship of the Israelites, it was so framed as to prefigure the Messiah in His obedience and suffering and also the privileges and duties of believers in every future age, according to the covenant of grace (Col. 2:17; Heb. 10:1). The sacrifices enjoined by that law did not make atonement for sin in any other point of view than as types of the sacrifice of Christ. Hence, the burnt sacrifice is said to have been "an offering…of a sweet savour," or for a savor of rest to the Lord (Lev. 1:9). But it could not be a sacrifice of a grateful odor to Him from any value or virtue in itself, but only from its being a figure of the sacrifice of Christ, with which, as an atonement for the sins of His people, God is infinitely well pleased (Heb. 9:9–14; 10:4).

The sacrifices that the Israelites were enjoined to offer had indeed influence to remove typical or ceremonial guilt and prevent temporal punishment, but they had not the smallest efficacy to remove real or moral guilt from the conscience. But though they themselves could procure only a figurative pardon, they served to prefigure our great Redeemer, who "by one offering…hath perfected for ever them that are sanctified" (Heb. 10:14). And it was only when an Israelite presented his sacrifice in the faith of the great atonement to be according to the covenant of grace, made by the sacrifice of Christ, that he received a real and full remission of sin.

7. Last, circumcision and the Passover, the two sacraments of the covenant of grace as formerly made with Abraham, Isaac, and Jacob, were appended to the transaction at Sinai (John 7:22–23; Deut. 16:1–8, respectively). They were added to it as seals of the covenant of grace in order to confirm the interest and the faith of believers in that covenant, and by a divine appointment they continued to be the signs and seals of it during the whole period of the Jewish dispensation. But the sacraments of the covenant of grace could not, as sealing ordinances,

be appended to any other covenant. The covenant of grace, then, with the moral law standing in it as a rule of life to believers, was promulgated from Mount Sinai to the Israelites and was, both in itself and in God's intention, the principal part of the transaction at Sinai.

It will be proper here to observe that although believing and unbelieving Israelites in the Sinai transaction were under the covenant of grace, yet they could not both be under it in the same respects. The believers among them were internally and really under it and under the moral law as a rule of life, as all true believers in every age are (Rom. 6:14; 1 Cor. 9:21). But the unbelievers were only externally, in respect of their visible church-state, under it (Rom. 9:4) and under the law as a rule of duty.

• SECTION 2 •
The Moral Law in the Form of a Covenant of Works as Displayed to the Israelites on Mount Sinai

The violated covenant of works, as I observed above, was not and could not be made or renewed with the Israelites at Sinai, for it was a broken covenant; and besides, it was a covenant between God and man as friends, whereas now man has become the enemy of God. But though it was not renewed with them, yet it was, on that solemn occasion, repeated and displayed to them. It was not proposed to them in order that they might consent, by their own works, to fulfill the condition of it; but it was displayed before them in subservience to the covenant of grace, that they might see how impossible it was for them as condemned sinners to perform that perfect obedience which is the immutable condition of life in it. Although the Lord knew well that they were far from being able to yield perfect obedience, yet He saw proper to set forth eternal life to them on these terms (Lev. 18:5; Deut. 27:26) and so to speak to them in a strain adapted to their self-righteous temper.

For previous to the giving of the law to them at Sinai, they were so ignorant of the perfection and vast extent of that holy law, as well as of their own utter inability to perform the smallest acceptable obedience to it; and at the same time, they were so full of self-confidence as to say to Moses, "All that the LORD hath spoken we will do" (Ex. 19:8). God therefore displayed on Mount Sinai the law of the Ten Commandments as a covenant of works in subservience to the covenant of grace. He displayed it in that form in order that the people might, by contemplating it, see what kind and degree of righteousness it required as the condition of eternal life, and that by means of it, finding themselves utterly destitute of perfect righteousness, they might be impelled to take hold of the covenant of grace in which the perfect righteousness of the second Adam is provided and exhibited for the justification of all who believe.

Now, that the law of the Ten Commandments as a covenant of works was repeated and displayed on Mount Sinai in subservience to the covenant of grace appears evident:

1. From the thunderings and lightnings, the noise of the trumpet and the mountain smoking, the thick darkness and the voice of the living God, speaking out of the midst of the fire on that awful occasion (Ex. 20:18; Deut. 5:22–26). These terrible emblems signified the vindictive and tremendous wrath of God that is due to all the race of Adam for their breach of the covenant of works by transgressing the law of that covenant (Gal. 3:10). They also represented the extreme danger to which every sinner who continues under the law in its covenant form is exposed as being liable, every moment, to the eternal execution of its dreadful curse. This awful display of the law as a covenant of works, though it was not the principal, yet it was the most conspicuous part of the Sinai transaction, for "the people saw the thunderings, and the lightnings, and the noise of the trumpet, and the mountain smoking" (Ex. 20:18). "And so terrible was the sight, that Moses said, I exceedingly fear and quake" (Heb. 12:21).

Now the covenant of works was displayed in this tremendous form before the Israelites in order that self-righteous and secure sinners among them might be alarmed and deterred from expecting justification in the sight of God by the works of the law and that, convinced of their sinfulness and misery, they might be persuaded to flee speedily to the blessed Mediator and to trust in Him for righteousness and salvation. That terrible display, accordingly, contributed in some measure to humble them, to lessen that self-confidence which they had formerly discovered, and to show them their need of the divine Redeemer and of union with Him by faith, in order to their being qualified for performing acceptable obedience. This appears from their own words to Moses after the dreadful sight that they beheld: "Speak thou unto us all that the LORD our God shall speak unto thee; and we will hear it, and do it" (Deut. 5:27). Standing afar off, they do not say, as they did before the publication of the law at Sinai, "All that the LORD hath spoken we will do" (Ex. 19:8); but, "We will hear it, and do it." We will first hear or believe, and then do. For speaking in this strain, the Lord commended them thus: "They have well said all that they have spoken. O that there were such an heart in them" (Deut. 5:27–29).[1] They said well in that they made hearing or believing the principle of acceptable obedience (Heb. 11:6). The law then, as it is the covenant of works, entered at Sinai "that the offence might abound" not in the life by the commission of it but in the conscience by conviction (Rom. 5:20); it entered that it might be their "schoolmaster to bring [them] unto Christ, that [they] might be justified by faith" (Gal. 3:24).

2. That the law as a covenant of works was displayed on Mount Sinai appears also from this: the Ten Commandments, written on tables of stone and so given to Moses on Sinai are called, by the apostle Paul, "the ministration of death, written and engraven in stones" (2 Cor. 3:7). Now it is manifest that these commandments are no otherwise the ministration of death than as they are in the form of the covenant

---

1. Hearing is applicable to the words of the gospel, as well as to those of the law.

of works. In this form they were delivered to Moses to be deposited in the ark in order to prefigure the fulfilling of them by Messiah, the surety of a better covenant (Heb. 7:22), and the concealing of that form, or the removal of it from them, to all who should believe in Him.

3. The moral law, as it was delivered from Mount Sinai, is in Scripture expressly called a covenant. These are the two covenants: the one from Mount Sinai (Gal. 4:24). The law, in that promulgation of it, was such a covenant as had the appearance, through misapprehension of its design, of disannulling the covenant of grace made with Abraham. "The covenant," says the apostle Paul, "that was confirmed before of God in Christ, the law, which was four hundred and thirty years after, cannot disannul, that it should make the promise of none effect" (Gal. 3:17). The law included a way of obtaining a title to the heavenly inheritance, typified by that of Canaan, so very different from that of the promise made to Abraham as to be incompatible with it. "For if the inheritance be of the law, it is no more of promise: but God gave it to Abraham by promise" (Gal. 3:18). The covenant of the law from Mount Sinai, then, was the covenant of works, which contains a method of obtaining the inheritance inconsistent with that of the promise, but which cannot disannul the promise or covenant of grace. Besides, Moses, speaking of that law under the denomination of a covenant, affirms that it was not made with the patriarchs or displayed publicly before them. "The Lord our God made a covenant with us in Horeb. The Lord made not this covenant with our fathers, but with us" (Deut. 5:2–3). This covenant displayed on Sinai, then, was not the covenant of promise made with the fathers of the Israelite people.

4. The covenant of works is, in the New Testament, introduced and illustrated from the law as given by Moses. Our blessed Lord, in replying to one who asked Him what good thing he should do that he might have eternal life, said, "If thou wilt enter into life, keep the

commandments"; namely, "Thou shalt do no murder, Thou shalt not commit adultery, Thou shalt not steal, Thou shalt not bear false witness, Honour thy father and thy mother" (Matt. 19:17–19). These being some of the commandments promulgated from Mount Sinai, our Lord repeats them to him in the form of the covenant of works. And the apostle Paul, when mentioning the promise of the covenant of works, says, "Moses describeth the righteousness which is of the law, that the man which doeth those things shall live by them" (Rom. 10:5). In expressing also the penal sanction of that covenant, he says, "As many as are of the works of the law are under the curse: for it is written, Cursed is every one that continueth not in all things which are written in the book of the law to do them" (Gal. 3:10; see also Deut. 27:26). That a conditional promise (Lev. 18:5), then, and a dreadful curse (Deut. 27:26), as well as the Ten Commandments were published to the Israelites is plain; and it is no less evident that, according to our apostle in the passages cited above, they are the *form* of the covenant of works.

5. That the law in the form of a covenant of works was displayed on Mount Sinai appears, likewise, from the opposition between the law and grace often mentioned and inculcated in the New Testament. We there read that, "The law was given by Moses, but grace and truth came by Jesus Christ" (John 1:17), and that, "The law is not of faith: but, the man that doeth them shall live in them" (Gal. 3:12). But it is in its covenant form only that the law in Scripture is contrasted with grace.

6. In the Sinaitic transaction, the hewing of the latter tables of stone by Moses, before God wrote the Ten Commandments on them, might be intended to teach sinners that they must be convinced of their sin and misery by the law as a covenant of works before it can be written legibly on their hearts as a rule of life.

7. Last, the same also appears from these words of the apostle Paul cited above: "These are the two covenants; the one from the mount

Sinai, which gendereth to bondage" (Gal. 4:24). The covenant that genders to bondage is the covenant of works, made with Adam as the head and representative of all its natural posterity and displayed on Mount Sinai to the Israelites. This covenant genders to bondage for, according to the apostle, the children of it, or they who are under it are excluded from the heavenly inheritance, as Ishmael was from Canaan the typical and earthly inheritance. "Cast out the bondwoman and her son: for the son of the bondwoman shall not be heir with the son of the freewoman" (Gal. 4:30). The generating of bond children, excluded from the heavenly inheritance, is a distinguishing property of the covenant of works, and it cannot be a property of the covenant of grace under any of its dispensations. It is the covenant of works only that has a tendency to beget a servile and slavish frame of spirit.

It is evident, then, that the covenant of works was displayed on Mount Sinai. It was there displayed, together with the covenant of grace, in order to subserve the latter and particularly to represent to the Israelitish church that the discharging of the principal and penalty of the covenant of works was to be required of Messiah, the surety of elect sinners, as the proper condition of the covenant of grace.

Although the Sinai transaction was a mixed dispensation, yet the covenant of grace and the covenant of works were not blended together in it. The latter, as well as the ceremonial law, was added to the former and was added to it in order that the Israelites might be so convinced of their sinfulness and misery as to see their extreme need of embracing the promise, or covenant of grace. "God," says the apostle Paul, "gave [the inheritance] to Abraham by promise. Wherefore then serveth the law? It was added because of transgressions, till the seed should come to whom the promise was made" (Gal. 3:18–19). The promise made to Abraham and his seed we have found in the preface to the Ten Commandments. To this promise, or covenant of grace, then, was the law or subservient covenant of works added. It formed no part of the covenant of grace, which had been a covenant entirely to the patriarchs before that was added to it at Sinai, and it is a covenant entirely to believers under the gospel after that is removed from it. For our apostle says, "It was added…till the seed should come."

Accordingly, the Ten Commandments, as promulgated from Mount Sinai, must be considered at least in a twofold point of view—namely, as the law of Christ, or the law as a rule of life to believers; and as the law as it is the matter of a covenant of works to unregenerate sinners. This, I humbly apprehend, is intimated to us by their having been twice written on tables of stone by God Himself (Ex. 32:16; 34:1) and by the double accentuation of them in the sacred original.

In the Sinai transaction, then, the promise, or covenant of grace, was published to the Israelites; and the law, or covenant of works, also as subservient to it. The former was and still is a covenant to be believed or embraced by faith; the latter was a covenant to be done or fulfilled. The apostle Paul, accordingly, contrasts the one with the other thus: "The law is not of faith: but, the man that doeth them shall live in them" (Gal. 3:12). The covenant to be embraced by faith was given to the fathers of the Israelites as well as to themselves, but concerning the covenant to be done Moses said to them, "The LORD made not this covenant with our fathers, but with us" (Deut. 5:3). And again, "The LORD spake unto you out of the midst of the fire.… And he declared unto you his covenant, which he commanded you to perform, even ten commandments" (Deut. 4:12–13). Although the same covenant of works that was made with Adam was displayed from Mount Sinai, yet it was for a very different purpose. God's design in making this covenant with Adam was to have that righteousness which was due to Him from man, but His great design in displaying it to Israel at Sinai was that they, by contemplating it, might see what kind and degree of righteousness it was by which they could be justified before God and that, finding themselves wholly destitute of that righteousness, they might be excited to take hold of the covenant of grace in which a perfect righteousness for justification is graciously provided.

Should the attentive reader now ask, "Seeing the covenant of grace and also that of works were both repeated from Mount Sinai, were not the Israelites under both these covenants at one and the same time?"

I would answer that they could not be under both at the same time and in the same respects. The believers among them, as I hinted above, were internally and really under the covenant of grace and only externally under that terrible display of the covenant of works as it was subservient to that of grace (Gal. 3:24); whereas the unbelievers were externally, and by profession only, under that dispensation of the covenant of grace (Rom. 9:4) but were internally and really under the covenant of works (Rom. 4:14).

◆ SECTION 3 ◆

The Law Promulgated from Mount Sinai to the
Israelites as the Matter of a National Covenant
between God and Them

When we consider God as delivering to the Israelites at Mount Sinai not only the moral law but the ceremonial and judicial laws as appendages to it and as requiring them to perform obedience to these as the condition of their happy entrance into Canaan, and especially of their peaceful and continual residence in it as a nation, we are to regard those laws as the matter of a national covenant, or covenant of peculiarity, between Jehovah and them. To consider Jehovah, the Son of God, as the king or sovereign of Israel as a nation or political body is perfectly consistent with our viewing Him likewise as their God and Redeemer. And to regard His law, promulgated from Mount Sinai to them, as the rule of their obedience considered as a nation is consistent enough with viewing it, at the same time, as a covenant of works and as a rule of duty to believers in the covenant of grace.

In the Sinaitic transaction, then, the eternal Son of God is to be considered as the monarch or king of the Israelites (1 Sam. 12:12), and they are to be viewed as a nation or political community under a theocratic government. As their king, He enacted and proclaimed laws, exacted tribute, disposed of offices in the state, made war and peace, defended His people from their enemies, and punished with death those of His subjects who refused allegiance to Him. He gave the moral law to them as the primary rule of the obedience that He required in this covenant (Deut. 4:13). He gave them also the ceremonial and judicial laws as appendages to it; and these were reducible to one or another of its precepts. The ceremonial institutions that in the sacred history are frequently called statutes were, for the most part, reducible to precepts of the first table; and the judicial laws that, in the same history, are often styled judgments were mostly reducible to precepts of the second table. Some of the judicial institutions, however, were appendages to precepts of the first table.

Now, as the moral law required Israel to perform obedience both to the ceremonial and the judicial precepts, so, while the ceremonial institutions were to regulate them in their ecclesiastical capacity, the judicial precepts were to direct them in their civil capacity as a nation under the immediate government of God as their king. The laws, then, that Jehovah prescribed to the Israelites, by which He was to govern them as His subjects, were chiefly the judicial laws. And seeing these are all reducible to precepts of the moral law, they required internal as well as external obedience, the obedience of the heart as well as of the life. They directed and bound every Israelite in the inward man as much as in the outward.

The sum of the duty required in the moral law is love. "Thou shalt love the LORD thy God with all thine heart, and with all thy soul, and with all thy might" (Deut. 6:5). "Thou shalt love thy neighbour as thyself" (Lev. 19:18). Remarkable are these words of Moses to Israel: "Know, therefore, that the LORD thy God, he is God, the faithful God, which keepeth covenant and mercy with them that love him and keep his commandments to a thousand generations; and repayeth them that hate him to their face, to destroy them: he will not be slack to him that hateth him, he will repay him to his face" (Deut. 7:9–10). One of the precepts of the second table of the moral law to which the judicial precepts were reducible is, "Thou shalt not covet" (Ex. 20:17). Seeing God was a spirit under the old as well as He is under the new dispensation, He, as the king of Israel, required more from them than mere external obedience to His commands. Loyalty even to a mere earthly prince comprises inward respect as well as outward adherence to Him and His laws.

The conditions, then, of that national covenant which God made with the Israelites at Sinai were the obedience both of the heart and of the life to all His commands and, more immediately, to those of His judicial law. "And it shall come to pass, if ye shall hearken diligently unto my commandments which I command you this day, to love the LORD your God, and to serve him with all your heart and with all your soul, that I will give you the rain of your land in his due season" (Deut. 11:13–14).

The promises of that national covenant were promises of temporal good things to the Israelites, both as a body politic and as individuals, and of these in subservience to their enjoyment of religious privileges. The inheritance of the earthly Canaan as typical of the eternal inheritance was given to Abraham by promise, by an absolute promise. "For if the inheritance be of the law," says the apostle, "it is no more of promise: but God gave it to Abraham by promise" (Gal. 3:18). God promised freely the land of Canaan to Abraham and his seed as an inheritance, and therefore the promise of it was not a conditional but an absolute promise. Accordingly, it is called "the land of promise" (Heb. 11:8–9).

The typical inheritance of Canaan, then, was not of the law—that is, it was not given to Abraham and his seed on condition of their obedience, as if that had founded their title to it—but it was given to them by an absolute promise. In the Sinai transaction, Jehovah promised to Israel as a nation, in reference to Canaan, that they should easily subdue the nations of Canaan; that their land should abound with milk and honey, corn and wine, and everything else conducive to their external prosperity; that under the divine protection they should enjoy a long and peaceable possession of that country; that God would multiply them as the sands of the sea and as the stars of heaven; that He would render them valiant in battle and victorious over their enemies; that He would save them from famine, pestilence, and the other plagues which He had inflicted on the Egyptians; and that He would favor them with the symbols of His peculiar presence. These were the leading promises of the Sinaitic covenant considered as a national covenant, and they were all exhibited to the Israelites in a conditional form. This will appear evident if the following passages are considered: Exodus 23:22–31; Leviticus 26:3–13; Deuteronomy 7:12–24; 11:13–17; and 28:1–13.

But conditions are of two sorts, antecedent or consequent: antecedent when the condition is the cause of the thing promised or is that which gives a pactional title to it; consequent when the condition is annexed to the promise as an adjunct to the thing promised or as a qualification in the party to whom the promise is made.[2]

Now in the latter sense, the obedience of the Israelites to the precepts, especially of their judicial law, was a condition of those promises. It was not a cause why the good things promised were bestowed on them, but it was a qualification in them, or an adjunct, that was required to attend the blessings promised and freely conferred. Accordingly, Moses said to Israel, "The LORD hath avouched thee this day to be his peculiar people, as he hath promised thee, and that thou shouldest keep all his commandments" (Deut. 26:18). Had the good things promised to the Israelites been suspended on their obedience as the cause of them, or that which was to give a pactional title to them, such promises would have been inconsistent with the

---

2. See Ball on the covenant. [John Ball, *A Treatise on the Covenant of Grace* (London: G. Miller for Edward Brewster, 1645), 133.]

absolute promise given them in Abraham, their illustrious progenitor. As the Israelites, even in their civil capacity, were a typical people and their obedience a typical obedience, so their obedience was to be so connected with their temporal privileges as to resemble the obedience of God's spiritual Israel in its connection with their spiritual privileges under the gospel.

True believers among the children of Israel were the only persons who performed sincere obedience to the law of that covenant. The unbelievers yielded only an external and hypocritical obedience, and that merely to the letter of the law. As long, however, as they continued to yield even an external obedience, the promises of temporal good things were fulfilled to them, for the Lord loved them "for the father's sakes" (Rom. 11:28). And therefore He favored them with many external benefits. He also conferred favors on them for the sakes of those among them who were the objects of His everlasting love (Isa. 6:13; 2 Cor. 4:15). And so great was His love of true holiness that He rewarded that external obedience, which was only the shadow of it, with those external benefits that were shadows of good things to come.

The penal sanctions of that national covenant were, for the most part, temporal punishments. These were denounced to the Israelites not only as a nation but as individuals. The punishments that the Lord threatened against the violations of that covenant by Israel as a community were chiefly these: famine, pestilence, and various other diseases; want of success in war; a smiting of their land with barrenness; a casting of them out of that promised land; and a dispersing of them among the heathen (Deut. 4:25–28; 11:17; 28:15–68; 29:22–28). The punishments that He threatened to inflict on the individual who would disobey the law of that covenant were such as these: that He would "set [his] face against that man, and will cut him off from among his people," and that He would "blot [him] out of [His] book" or out of the register of the living (Lev. 20:3; Ex. 32:33; see also Lev. 17:10; 20:2–6; 23:29).

So much the law of God promulgated from Mount Sinai in its threefold character: as a rule of life to believers, as a covenant of works, and as the matter of a national covenant between God and the Israelites.

✦ REFLECTIONS ✦

What has been advanced in this and the two preceding sections may assist in guiding us to the meaning of what the apostle Paul says in Hebrews 8:6–10 concerning the old and new covenants. His design in this epistle to the Hebrew Christians was to show them the preference of the new dispensation of the covenant of grace, which has taken place since the death of Christ, to that old dispensation of it, which had been established at Sinai and had continued until His death. This he illustrates not by stating the difference between the covenant of works and the covenant of grace, but by showing the difference between the old dispensation, or former manner of administration of the covenant of grace, and the new dispensation of the same covenant. The former of these dispensations he styles the first or old testament, and the latter the new. The covenant of grace, according to the old dispensation of it, was published from Mount Sinai, and at the same time, the law was given to the Israelites as the substance of a national or political covenant between God and them.

Now the apostle, in stating the difference between the old and new dispensations of the covenant of grace, affirms that the new dispensation, or testament, is better than the old and that the promises of the new are better than those of the old. They are comparatively better than the spiritual promises of the old dispensation, or testament, since in them the grace of God is held forth in more fullness, evidence, and spiritual efficacy to all nations than in those of the old.[3] And they are absolutely better than the temporal promises of that national covenant which the Lord made with Israel as a political body.

---

3. Westminster Confession of Faith 7.6.

Since the land of Canaan had been given to the posterity of Abraham by promise, or as an inheritance, the apostle might, with strict propriety, call even the national covenant that had been made with that people a testament and might show the preference of the new testament to it as well as to the old testament, or old dispensation of the covenant of grace. He seems in Hebrews 8:9 especially to have stated the contrast between the new testament and that national covenant. From the sixth verse to the end of the chapter, the original word that we render *covenant* the Geneva translators render *testament,* which seems to me more suitable to the apostle's argument, as well as to the analogy of faith, than to translate it *covenant.* For one and the same covenant of grace was made with believers at Sinai and is made with believers now, though under different dispensations, each of which is called a *testament.* That gracious covenant as published to Israel from Mount Sinai was a testament, for it consisted of absolute grants and promises. Hence, our apostle expressly styles it a testament and "the first testament" (Heb. 9:18–20). The promises of it were turned into a testament, for the spiritual blessings promised were, as they now are, gifts of sovereign grace.

From what has been said, we may also learn the meaning of these words above cited: "The law was given by Moses, but grace and truth came by Jesus Christ" (John 1:17). The law that was given from Mount Sinai by the ministry of Moses, considered as the matter of the covenant of works, was a ministry of rigor and of terror in opposition to the gospel dispensation, which is called *grace*; it was a ministration of condemnation and of death. Considered as a rule of duty in the covenant of grace and in the hand of Moses the typical mediator, it was a ministration of shadows as opposed to truth. The gospel, or New Testament dispensation of the covenant of grace, is styled "grace and truth" (John 1:14, 17). It is grace, for it is a clear and efficacious exhibition of the covenant of grace to sinners of mankind. It is truth, as opposed not only to falsehood but to shadows. While Jesus Christ has brought to His church the clearest discoveries of redeeming grace, He Himself is the substance of all the Jewish types and the accomplishment of all their predictions and promises. Moses was the minister of the law; Christ is the author of grace and truth. All the promises and blessings of salvation flow from His grace and are performed by His truth.

Must all the obedience required in the law as a rule of life be performed to the Lord as our God and Redeemer? Then in order to perform spiritual and acceptable obedience to the Ten Commandments, a man must trust in the Lord Jesus for all his salvation and trust that God in Christ is His redeeming God, or that Christ is his Redeemer, and God in Christ is his covenant God. No obedience to those commands is acceptable but that which flows in the channel of the covenant of grace and is performed to God in Christ as our covenant God. The only way to yield evangelical and spiritual obedience is, first, to accept cordially the offer of Christ to trust that God in Christ is our God and then to attempt universal obedience to Him as such. We cannot otherwise fear this glorious and fearful name "THE LORD THY GOD" (Deut. 28:58). We are not to do in order to believe, but to believe in order to do. We are to trust in Christ and in the promise in order to be strengthened for obedience to the precept, for acceptable obedience can never be performed but in the strength of our almighty Redeemer. "Without faith" in Him as the principle of obedience, "it is impossible to please [God]" (Heb. 11:6).

To serve the Lord by keeping diligently His holy commandments is a most reasonable service. Instead of requiring obedience from us by His mere will, without assigning any other reason, He condescends to enforce His commands by the most engaging and endearing motives. He exhibits Himself to us as Jehovah, the infinite, eternal, and unchangeable one who has His being of Himself and from whom all being is derived; who is supereminent in every adorable perfection; and at the same time is our Creator, preserver, and governor. Our obedience, therefore, is not only due to Him but is infinitely reasonable. Besides, He makes a grant of Himself to us as our

God, our God in covenant, related to us by an everlasting covenant that is exhibited in the gospel to us so that we may so take hold of it as to take possession of Him as our God and portion. He also presents Himself to us as our redeeming God who, in the person of the Son, redeems us from all our iniquity, who delivers us from our spiritual thraldom and purifies us to Himself a peculiar people zealous of good works (Titus 2:14). How delightful to reflect that He incites us to obedience not merely by His sovereignty over us but by the attracting consideration that He is our God, our redeeming God who has obtained eternal redemption for us! When the believer considers what the great Redeemer is to him and what He has done and is doing for him, should not his heart overflow with adoring gratitude, and should not he express his gratitude by a voluntary and cheerful obedience to all His commands? Can anything be more reasonable?

The children of fallen Adam are so bent on working for life that they will on no account cease from it till the Holy Spirit so convinces them of their sin and misery as to show them that Mount Sinai is wholly on fire around them and that they cannot with safety remain a moment longer within the limits of it. Strange indeed it is that sinners, already condemned by the law of works, should, nevertheless, imagine a probability—yea, a certainty—of obtaining eternal life by their own works according to that very law. The depraved sons of Adam think, like Samson, to rouse themselves and walk as in former times, as if their strength were yet in them; and multitudes never perceive that is gone till after they have been seized in virtue of that violated law and bound with chains of eternal darkness (see Judg. 16:20). And, oh, what addition to the anguish of damned souls will it be to reflect that they dreamed of attaining life by a law that, to a sinner, is and cannot but be a "ministration of death" (2 Cor. 3:7); and that, by supposing in themselves an ability still to answer the demands of the law, they have rendered it so much the more able to condemn them!

One reason, therefore, why the Lord displayed the law as a covenant of works on Sinai was that self-righteous Israelites and all pharisaic professors to the end of time might see that as they have sinned and so have not performed perfect obedience, it is absolutely impossible for them to attain justification and eternal life on the footing of their own works (Rom. 3:20). The law was there displayed in its covenant form in order to discover sin and condemn for it and so to stir up secure sinners to inquire after the perfect fulfillment of it by the second Adam (Deut. 27:26), for until self-righteousness is overthrown, a man will never submit to the righteousness of Jesus Christ.

We may hence learn the great difference between performing duties in the way of the covenant of works and in that of the covenant of grace. According to the first covenant, sinners perform duties in order that these may entitle them to life; but, according to the second, saints perform them because they already have a title to life. According to the former, unregenerate men do them in their own strength; but according to the latter, regenerate persons perform them in the strength of grace derived from the second Adam. The motives of obedience, under the covenant of works, are the slavish fear of hell and the servile hope of heaven; whereas the motives of duty in the covenant of grace are love and gratitude to God not only as the Creator and preserver of His people but as the God and Redeemer of His people (2 Cor. 5:14–15).

CHAPTER 3

The Properties of the Moral Law

The peculiar and distinguishing qualities of the moral law are these:

1. It is universal, or of vast extent. It extends to all men in every age, place, and condition and to all their inclinations, thoughts, words, and actions. "Now we know," says the apostle Paul, "that what things soever the law saith, it saith to them who are under the law: that every mouth may be stopped, and all the world may become guilty before God. Therefore by the deeds of the law there shall no flesh be justified in his sight" (Rom. 3:19–20). While it binds all the human race, at all times and in all places and conditions, it reaches to all the dispositions, thoughts, and purposes of the heart as well as to all the words and actions of the life. It extends to every motion and affection of the soul and to every part and circumstance of human conduct. The divine law is a rule for the heart as well as for the life of every descendant of Adam. "Thy commandment," says David, "is exceeding broad" (Ps. 119:96). No finite understanding can reach the boundary of it or find out how comprehensive it is. It extends to countless multitudes of things in every moment and in every possible circumstance. The moral law, indeed, is summed up in the Ten Commandments, but it extends itself, notwithstanding, through the whole Word of God. So extensive are those commandments that everything which He requires may be reduced to one or another of them.

2. It is perfect. "The law of the LORD," says David, "is perfect, converting the soul" (Ps. 19:7). So perfect is it that it binds everyone to full

conformity in the whole man to the righteousness of it and to entire obedience forever so as to require the utmost perfection of every duty and to forbid the least degree of every sin (Matt. 5:21–48; James 2:10).[1] It requires all the duty that a man owes to God, to himself, and to his neighbor; and it demands perfection of obedience. No partial or defective obedience can be sustained. The smallest degree of imperfection renders a person obnoxious[2] to the curse, so that salvation by the law is absolutely unattainable because no man since the fall can perform the perfect obedience that it demands. The perfection of every grace and of every act of obedience is required in it. Nothing must be taken from it or corrected in it, and nothing is to be added to it (Deut. 4:2).

The Lord Jesus explained the law, but He did not in the smallest degree either correct or enlarge it. He and His apostles taught nothing but what Moses and the prophets had previously indicated (Matt. 7:12; Acts 26:22). He said, indeed, to His disciples, "A new commandment I give unto you, that ye love one another" (John 13:34). This command, however, is not new as to the substance of it, for it is a summary of the second table of the law; and therefore it is called "an old commandment which ye had from the beginning" (1 John 2:7). But it is called new because it is enforced by the new motive and example of the immense love of Christ in dying for us. This is evident from His words that immediately follow: "As I have loved you, that ye also love one another" (John 13:34). Christ also commands us to deny ourselves and to take up our cross and follow Him, but these duties are comprised in that of loving God supremely.

The prayer, likewise, that our Lord taught His disciples contains no petitions but what the saints under the Old Testament were taught to present to Jehovah (Isa. 63:16; Pss. 57:11; 143:10–12; Prov. 30:8; Pss. 25:11; 16:1, respectively). Indeed, such is the perfection of the divine law that it cannot require or sustain anything short of

---

1. Westminster Larger Catechism 99.
2. Archaic use, meaning "exposed" or "deserving." —Ed.

obedience absolutely perfect. It requires not only that there be no direct violation of any of its precepts but that there be no appearance of transgressing any of them—no consent of the heart, no inclination or affection to the smallest violation of any, no secret delight in evil or desire that it were lawful—but on the contrary, that there be a supreme delight in the purity and perfection of every one of its commands. This law is despised and dishonored if it is not acknowledged to be so perfect that nothing can be accepted by it but that which is in all respects perfect. It demands perfection in the principles, in the parts, in the degrees, and in the perpetuity of obedience. In a word, such is the perfection of it that it was sufficient to be the rule even of the consummate righteousness of Jesus Christ Himself.

3. This law is also spiritual. The Lawgiver is a spirit, the God of the spirits of all flesh, and He beholds all the inclinations and affections of the soul as well as all the deeds of the body. His law therefore is spiritual (Rom. 7:14), requiring internal as well as external obedience. It reaches the understanding, will, and affections, with all the other faculties of the soul, as well as all the gestures, words, and actions of the body. It extends not only to external appearances, words, and works but to the dispositions, thoughts, principles, motives, and designs of the heart and requires the spiritual performance of both internal and external obedience (Lev. 19:17; Matt. 22:37–39; Heb. 4:12). It requires that every duty proceed from spiritual principles such as union with Christ, faith, love, and every right habit of the soul, so that it is performed in a spiritual manner—that is, according to a spiritual rule and in the exercise of the graces of the Spirit—and that it is directed to spiritual ends, the glory of God in Christ and the eternal enjoyment of Him. Every man is commanded by it thus to mind the things of the Spirit and so to live and walk in the Spirit (Rom. 8:5; Gal. 5:16).

4. It is a holy law. "The law," says the apostle Paul, "is holy, and the commandment holy" (Rom. 7:12). The moral law is a fair transcript

of the infinite holiness of God's nature and an authoritative declaration of His will; it binds all the children of Adam to perfect holiness of heart and of life. It enjoins everything that is holy, everything that is conformable to those moral attributes and actions of God that are patterns for our imitation. Since it is intrinsically pure and holy, it gives no just occasion to the least motion of sin in the heart; but on the contrary, it discovers, forbids, and condemns every inordinate affection, every unholy desire. It is the immutable and eternal standard of all true holiness, whether of the heart or of the life; and while it is both the rule and the reason of holiness, its direct tendency is to encourage and advance it in every regenerate soul. All the precepts of it are perfectly holy, every way becoming for an infinitely holy God to publish and rational creatures to obey. The divine law is so holy that it calls for spotless obedience not only in the words and actions of the life but in all the inclinations, thoughts, and motions of the heart. It reaches not only to the streams of actual transgression but to the fountain of original sin and calls for perfect holiness of nature as well as of life. Hence, the apostle Paul, as soon as he discerned the holiness of it, considered the first motions of irregular desire, even before the will actually consented to them, as sinful and bitterly bewailed them as well as firmly resisted them (Rom. 7:7).

5. Moreover, it is perfectly just and equal (Rom. 7:12). This righteous law is exactly suited to our frame as reasonable creatures and to our condition in this world. It requires nothing from us but what we owe to God, to ourselves, and to our neighbor and what we, in the first Adam, had sufficient ability to perform. Accordingly, the holy psalmist says, "The statutes of the LORD are right, rejoicing the heart" (Ps. 19:8). "I will praise thee with uprightness of heart, when I shall have learned thy righteous judgments" (119:7). The law of God is just and right. Its demands are infinitely equitable. And therefore, to fret against any command of it or to wish that it were in the smallest degree relaxed is unjust and is a breach of the whole law. Seeing it requires nothing but what we already owe to God and nothing but

what we are under infinite and immutable obligations to pay to Him. Our obedience to it, supposing that obedience were perfect, could never merit the smallest blessing from Him. Were we, indeed, to perform but a single act of obedience more than we owed to God, we would thereby merit some recompense from Him. But this is impossible for us ever to do. It is not the obedience even of a true believer that merits the blessings of salvation for him, but only the meritorious righteousness of Christ imputed to him.

6. The law is good, as well as holy and just (Rom. 7:12). The commandments of it are so good that they require nothing but what is good in itself and good for the observers of them. "In keeping of them there is great reward" (Ps. 19:11). They enjoin nothing but what is conducive to the happiness of both the souls and the bodies of men. "Great peace," says the psalmist, "have they which love thy law: and nothing shall offend them" (119:165). The apostle Paul also says, "Glory, honour, and peace, to every man that worketh good, to the Jew first, and also to the Gentile" (Rom. 2:10). And again, "We know that the law is good, if a man use it lawfully" (1 Tim. 1:8). The chief ingredient in the happiness of Adam in innocence was his having this law inscribed on his heart. And no man since the fall begins to be either good or happy till this promise begins to be fulfilled to him: "I will put my laws into their minds, and write them in their hearts" (Heb. 8:10). It is this that makes a man a good man and capable of performing good works. As the law, then, is good, desirable, and excellent, it is most unreasonable, as well as sinful, not to love it and not to delight in performing universal obedience to it.

7. Last, this law is of perpetual obligation. The precepts of it are indispensable and perpetual (Ps. 119:89). They continue to direct and oblige all men to perfect obedience not only through all time but through all eternity. "It is easier for heaven and earth to pass, than one tittle of the law to fail" (Luke 16:17). "Till heaven and earth pass, one jot or one tittle shall in no wise pass from the law, till all be fulfilled"

(Matt. 5:18). The law as a covenant of works will continue not only through time but through eternity to bind all who live and die under that covenant, and the law as a rule of life will continue binding on the spiritual seed of the second Adam through time and eternity. It is an immutable and an eternal law. "Every one of thy righteous judgments," says David, "endureth for ever" (Ps. 119:160).

⬧ REFLECTIONS ⬧

Is the law of the Lord perfect, and does it require that our obedience be perfect in its principles, parts, degrees, and continuance? It is impossible, then, that sincere obedience can entitle a sinner to eternal life. A man's faith may be sincere, but if it is not perfect it cannot be a proper condition of life; it cannot procure for him a right to eternal life. His repentance also may be deep and sincere, but if it is not absolutely perfect, it cannot afford him the smallest title either to the progress or the consummation of life eternal.[3] His obedience, in general, may be sincere, yet if it is not absolutely perfect, it cannot give him the smallest degree of title to eternal salvation. These cannot entitle him in the smallest degree to life, either according to the law as a covenant of works or as a rule of life. They are necessary as parts of salvation and as means of attaining complete salvation, but they cannot be the grounds of a man's title to salvation. Nothing can be the ground of a believer's title to salvation but the perfect righteousness of Jesus Christ, received by faith and imputed to him for justification.

Is the moral law of perpetual obligation? Then it follows that, as a covenant of works, it retains and will continue throughout eternity to retain its whole authority and obligation over every sinner of mankind who lives and dies under it. In its covenant form, it stands in full force and can never be repealed. It will continue throughout

---

3. This is not to be understood as implying that the law, either as a covenant or as a rule, requires either perfect or imperfect faith and repentance as the *proper* condition of eternal life; but only that no instance of personal obedience, however *sincere* that obedience may be, can ever entitle a sinner to life eternal.

all eternity to hold the finally impenitent under both its commanding and its condemning power. They shall remain forever under an infinite obligation both to yield perfect obedience to its righteous precepts and to give infinite satisfaction for their disobedience of them.

There is no possible way in which a sinner can be freed from the perpetual obligation of the law as a covenant but by presenting, in the hand of faith to it, the infinitely perfect and meritorious righteousness of the second Adam as a full answer to all its high demands. When this glorious righteousness is received by faith and graciously imputed to a man, the law in its covenant form is fully satisfied with respect to him, and in that form it has nothing more to demand from him. He now passes from the obligation of the covenant of works and comes under the perpetual obligation of the law as a rule of duty in the covenant of grace, and he will remain under its infinite obligation through all eternity.

Even the angels in heaven are under a law as their eternal rule of duty (Ps. 103:20). And if the holy angels are not without law to God, surely glorified saints will be under the law to Christ as the eternal rule of their obedience. And so ardent will their love of this holy and righteous law be that they will account it their highest honor and their greatest happiness to continue eternally under the obligation of yielding perfect obedience to it. No man sincerely loves it, even in an imperfect degree, but the man who hopes to be under the eternal obligation of it.

CHAPTER 4

The Rules for Understanding Aright the Ten Commandments

To understand aright the perfection, spirituality, and great extent of the divine law is necessary to qualify believers for delighting in it after the inward man and for performing acceptable obedience to all its precepts. The holy psalmist, therefore, prayed thus: "Give me understanding, and I shall keep thy law; yea, I shall observe it with my whole heart" (Ps. 119:34). "I am a stranger in the earth: hide not thy commandments from me" (119:19).

Seeing that the Ten Commandments contain very much in a few words, which cannot but render it more difficult to apprehend their full meaning, the rules to be carefully observed for understanding them aright are chiefly the following:

1. Where a duty is required, the contrary sin is forbidden (Isa. 58:13); and where a sin is forbidden, the contrary duty is required (Eph. 4:28). Every command forbids the sin that is opposite to, or inconsistent with, the duty which it requires. The duties required in the law cannot be performed without abstaining from the sins forbidden in it, and the sins forbidden cannot be avoided unless the contrary duties are performed. We must not only cease to do what the commands forbid but do what they require; otherwise, we do not obey them sincerely. A negative holiness is far from being acceptable to God. Every affirmative precept includes a negative one, and every negative command contains an affirmative. Every precept, whether affirmative or negative, has two parts: it requires obedience and

forbids disobedience. The fourth commandment, for instance, while it requires us to "remember the sabbath day, to keep it holy" (Ex. 20:8), forbids us to profane that holy day. The Lord Jesus, accordingly, comprehends all the negative as well as affirmative precepts in these two great affirmative commandments: to love God and our neighbor. It is also remarkable that where a promise is annexed to a precept, the contrary threatening is included (Ex. 20:12; Prov. 30:17); and that where a threatening is annexed to a prohibition, the contrary promise is implied (Ps. 24:4–5; Jer. 18:7–8).

2. Where a duty is required, every duty of the same kind is also required; and where a sin is forbidden, every sin of the same sort is prohibited. Under one duty, all of the same kind are commanded; and under one sin, all of the same sort are forbidden. When the Lord commands us to have no other gods before Him, He requires us to know and acknowledge Him to be the only true God and our God, and to love, worship, and glorify Him accordingly. When He commands us to "remember the sabbath day, to keep it holy" (Ex. 20:8), He requires us to engage in prayer, praise, hearing the word, receiving the sacraments, and all the other duties of that holy day.

Where a duty is commanded, the avowing of that duty is required likewise. Believing in Christ and a profession of faith in Him are enjoined in the same commandment (Rom. 10:10). Where the duties of children to parents are commanded, not only are all the duties of inferiors to superiors in every other relation required but also all the duties of superiors to inferiors. On the other hand, when the Lord forbids us to kill, He forbids us also to strike or wound our neighbor or to harbor malice and revenge against him (Matt. 5:21–22). When He forbids us to commit adultery, He at the same time prohibits fornication, incest, and all impure imaginations, affections, and purposes (vv. 27–28). Where great sins are expressly forbidden, all the lesser sins of that sort are forbidden; and they are prohibited under the names of the grosser sins in order to render them more detestable and horrible in our view and also to show us how abominable even the very least of them is in the sight of an infinitely holy and righteous God.[1]

3. That which is forbidden is at no time to be done, but that which is required is to be done only when the Lord affords opportunity. What God forbids is sin and is never to be done (Rom. 3:8); what He requires is always our duty (Deut. 4:8–9), and yet every particular duty is not to be performed at all times (Matt. 12:7). That which is forbidden is at all times sinful and therefore ought never, on any pretense whatsoever, to be done (Gen. 39:9).

That which is required, as it is always our duty, so it is to be performed as often as opportunity is afforded and as it does not interfere with the performance of our other duties. We are commanded, for instance, to honor our parents; but unless they are alive or present with us, we do not have the opportunity of performing this duty. In the third commandment, we are required to use, in a holy and reverent manner, the names and ordinances of God, especially in all our acts of worship; but we cannot, and should not, be every moment employed in acts of immediate worship, for we are commanded to abound in the performance of other duties equally necessary.

Although the affirmative part of every precept is of as high authority and binding force as the negative part, yet it does not bind us to the performance of every particular duty at all times. It obliges us to be always in a suitable frame for our present duty but not to be always in the actual performance of every duty. It binds us to the performance of a particular duty every time that we are called to perform that duty, every time in which the performance of it can

---

1. Instead of attempting an explanation of each of the Ten Commandments, which would increase too much the size of this volume, I refer the devout reader to Boston's excellent exposition of them in his sermons on our Westminster Shorter Catechism. [Thomas Boston, *An Illustration of the Doctrines of the Christian Religion, with Respect to Faith and Practice, upon the Plan of the Assembly's Shorter Catechism,* in *The Complete Works of Thomas Boston,* ed. Samuel M'Millan (1848; repr., Grand Rapids: Reformation Heritage Books, 2023), 2:84–374.]

glorify God and the omission of it dishonors Him. There is, however, one affirmative precept that binds us to perform the duty required at all times—namely, the commandment to love the Lord our God with all our heart, with all our soul, with all our strength, and with all our mind (Deut. 6:5; Matt. 22:37–39). There is no state, nor time, nor place in which we can be exempted from the duty of loving God supremely.

4. Whatever we ourselves are commanded to be, do, or forbear, we are obliged to do all that it is possible for us to do, according to our places and stations in society, to make others around us to be, do, or forbear the same. We are strictly bound, according to our different stations, to endeavor that every duty is performed and every sin is forborne by all to whom our influence can extend (Gen. 18:19; Lev. 19:17; Deut. 6:6–7). Accordingly, in the fourth commandment, are these words: "The seventh day is the sabbath of the LORD thy God: in it thou shalt not do any work, thou, nor thy son, nor thy daughter, thy manservant, nor thy maidservant, nor thy cattle, nor thy stranger that is within thy gates" (Ex. 20:10). Here, the duty of both the servant and the stranger is required of the master.

Whatever sin is forbidden to us also forbids us to partake with others in it, either by example, advice, connivance, or by giving them occasion to commit it. "Be [not] partaker of other men's sins; keep thyself pure" (1 Tim. 5:22). However free of personal transgressions we may pretend to be, yet we are transgressors of the law as far as, by connivance or otherwise, we are partakers of the sins of others (Eph. 5:11). Whatever duty others around us are commanded to perform, we are required, by advice, encouragement, prayer, and other helps, to assist them in performing it (2 Cor. 1:24). How much iniquity, alas, do many even of the saints themselves commit by not attending more than they usually do to this rule!

5. The same duty is required and the same sin is forbidden, in different respects, in several and even in all the divine commands. The

transgression of one precept is virtually a breach of all. They are so intimately connected together that if the divine authority is disregarded in any one of them, it is slighted in all (Col. 3:5; 1 Tim. 6:10; James 2:10; 1 John 4:20). The first commandment, for example, is so closely connected with all the other precepts that it is obeyed in all our obedience or disobeyed in all our disobedience to any one of them. Obedience or disobedience to it is virtually obedience or disobedience to the whole law.

6. Where a duty is required, the use of all the means of performing it aright is required; and where a sin is forbidden, every cause, and even every occasion of it, are prohibited. When chastity in heart, speech, and behavior is required, temperance and diligence in our lawful employments, as means of preserving it, are, at the same time, enjoined. On the other hand, when the Lord forbids the profanation of the Sabbath, at the same time He forbids all the employments and recreations by which men profane that holy day. When He forbids uncleanness, at the same time He prohibits drunkenness, gluttony, idleness, or whatever else may be an incitement to that sin. Where He forbids murder, He also prohibits the wrath, malice, and revenge that prompt men to commit that crime (Matt. 5:21–22; 1 John 3:15). When children are commanded to honor their parents, parents are, in the same command, enjoined to regard their children with parental affection and to bring them up in the nurture and admonition of the Lord (Eph. 6:4).

7. No sin is at any time to be committed in order to avoid or prevent a greater sin. We must not "do evil, that good may come" (Rom. 3:8) The very least sin ought not, on any account whatever, to be committed. None of the dispensations of adorable providence lays a man under a necessity of sinning. "Let no man say when he is tempted, I am tempted of God: for God cannot be tempted with evil, neither tempteth he any man" (James 1:13). As no man is allowed by the law, so none is necessitated by the providence of an infinitely holy and

righteous God to commit one sin in order to prevent another. We are commanded in the law not only to abstain from all evil but even "from all appearance of evil" (1 Thess. 5:22). But while no sin must be committed in order to prevent a greater sin, some duties required should, as was observed above, give place to other duties.

8. The commandments of the second table of the law must give place to those of the first when they cannot both be observed together. Our love of our neighbor, for instance, ought to be subjected to our love of God; and we are enjoined to hate—that is, to love in a less degree—father and mother for Christ when our love of them comes at any time in competition with our love for Him (Luke 14:26). When our love for our nearest relations and dearest friends becomes inconsistent with our love for Christ, the former must yield to the latter. We must prefer Christ, and God in Christ, to all the other objects of our esteem and affection (Matt. 10:37). When the commands of our superiors among men are at any time contrary to the commandments of the Lord, then we are to "obey God rather than men" (Acts 5:29). But although our natural duties to men, required in the second table of the law, must give place to our natural duties to God, required in the first (Acts 4:19), yet the positive duties enjoined in the first table must yield to the natural duties required in the second when they cannot both be performed at the same time (Hos. 6:6).

9. In our obedience, we should have a special and constant respect to the scope and final end at which the Lord aims by all the commandments in general, or by any one of them in particular. The great end at which God aims in general, in subordination to His own manifested glory, is perfect holiness of heart and life in His people, even as He Himself is holy (2 Cor. 7:1; 1 Peter 1:15). Whatever obedience, therefore, He enjoins, He requires that it be absolutely perfect; and whatever obedience we perform, we are bound to aim at perfection in it (Phil. 3:14) and to assure ourselves that in proportion as we fall short of perfection, we sin and come short of His glory.

This rule, in the hand of the Spirit of truth, is of special use to teach both sinners and saints the true meaning of every divine precept. The aim of God in each of His commandments is perfection of holiness, of conformity "to the image of his Son, that he might be the firstborn among many brethren" (Rom. 8:29). And the perfection in obedience that He requires is, as has been hinted above, a perfection of principle that our obedience proceed from "a pure heart, and of a good conscience, and of faith unfeigned" (1 Tim. 1:5; see also Matt. 5:48); a perfection of the parts of it, so that it is universal in respect of all the commands, or of all things written in the book of the law; a perfection of degrees, that every part of it be raised to the very highest degree of conformity to the holy law; and a perfection in respect of duration, that from the beginning to the end of our life we continue "in all things which are written in the book of the law to do them" (Gal. 3:10).

10. Last, the beginning and the end as well as the sum of all the commandments is love. "Love is the fulfilling of the law" (Rom. 13:10). "The end of the commandment is [love]" (1 Tim. 1:5). As all the blessings of God to His people flow from and are comprised in His love to them, so all the duties of man to God are comprehended in love to Him. The love of God to man is the sum of the gospel; the love of man to God is the sum of the law. Love to God as our God is the sum of what is required in the first table of the law; love to our neighbor is the whole of what is enjoined in the second. The former is called "the first and great commandment," and the latter is "like unto it" (Matt. 22:38–39). These two commandments are so closely connected together that obedience to the one cannot be performed without obedience to the other. We cannot love God supremely unless we love our neighbor as ourselves; nor can we love our neighbor, who was made in the image of God, as ourselves except we love God, who created him in His own image, with supreme affection (1 John 4:20). All the duties required in the first table of the law are but the native expressions of supreme love to the Lord our God; and

all the duties enjoined in the second are only the genuine expressions of sincere love to our neighbor.

·REFLECTIONS·

Now is it so that our love of our neighbor is to be subjected or subordinated to our love of God? We may hence learn how we ought to love God and how to love our neighbor. We must love God more than we love ourselves and love our neighbor as ourselves. We are bound to love the Lord our God supremely, or with all the powers of our souls, and to love our neighbor coordinately, or as ourselves. To love the Lord our God, according to the commandment, with all our heart is to love Him with a perfect degree of sincerity (Rom. 12:9). To love Him with all our soul is to love Him spiritually and affectionately, and that in a perfect degree, and to express our ardent affection to Him by every instance of obedience in which any faculty of our souls can be exercised. To love Him with all our strength is to love no other amiable object as much as Him, and none but in Him and for Him, or in subordination to Him (Luke 14:26). And to do it with all our mind is to regard Him with an intelligent love or a superlative esteem, and to love Him principally for His own infinite amiableness, as manifested especially in the person and work of our adorable Redeemer (Song 1:3; Phil. 3:8).

The highest degree of love, then, of which man, even in his state of innocence, was capable is due to our God; but a lesser degree of it is due to ourselves and our neighbor. To love our neighbor as ourselves is to love him in the same manner as we ought to do ourselves. A lawful and regular love of ourselves is here implied, for it is made the pattern according to which we ought to love others. This regular self-love is a habitual desire and endeavor always to aim at the happiness of our souls and bodies in subordination to the glory of God. To love, then, our neighbor as ourselves is to love him as constantly, as sincerely, as tenderly, as ardently, as actively, and as inviolably as we love ourselves (Eph. 5:29). This love of our neighbor should be expressed by our doing to him all that we would, from a well-informed judgment, have him to do to us in the same relations and circumstances. We are required to love all men with a love of benevolence and beneficence, but the saints not only with a love of benevolence but with a love of complacence and delight (Ps. 16:3). This love of God and of our neighbor must flow "out of a pure heart, and of a good conscience, and of faith unfeigned" (1 Tim. 1:5). And when it proceeds from these principles, it is "the fulfilling of the law" (Rom. 13:10), the essence of true holiness, and "the bond of perfectness" (Col. 3:14). Reader, trust in the Lord Jesus with all your heart for all His salvation to yourself, in particular, and especially for purity of heart and peace of conscience, and then your faith will work by love.

It is evident from what has been said that we were all born into the world utterly destitute of conformity to the holiness of God's law. We were born in iniquity and conceived in sin (Ps. 51:5). We came into the world entirely destitute of the moral image of God and wholly under the dominion of natural depravity (Job 11:12). The holy law commands us to love God supremely, but by nature we love ourselves supremely. It enjoins us to love our neighbor as ourselves, but we, on the contrary, hate our neighbor, especially in relation to the momentous concerns of his immortal soul. The law requires us to delight supremely in the Lord our God, but instead of this we delight only in sin, or at least in that which is not God. We are commanded in the law to "do all to the glory of God" (1 Cor. 10:31; see also Rom. 3:20–23), but we are naturally disposed to do all to our own glory. These corrupt propensities are native in the heart of every descendant of Adam and are directly contrary to the holy nature and law of God (Ps. 53:1–3). So great is the contrariety between the holy nature of God as expressed in His law and the nature of a sinner that God is said to hate sinners (Ps. 5:5), and sinners to hate Him (Rom. 8:7). And no man has attained a true conviction of his sin but he whom the Holy Spirit has made to see and feel that by nature he is a hater of God and of the whole revealed character of God.

Hence, it is manifest also that the very best actions of unconverted persons are sinful in the sight of God. Such persons, indeed, do many things that are materially good but nothing that is formally good—nothing from a good principle, in a good manner, or to a good end. All that they do is done, either directly or indirectly, in opposition to the holy commandments of the Lord, and so it is sinful and hateful to Him (Prov. 15:8; Rom. 8:8; Heb. 11:6). How then can such performances atone for their past transgressions and entitle them to the favor of God and eternal life? Ah, how deep the infatuation, how great the folly of relying on our own righteousness for a title to our eternal salvation!

From what has been said, it is evident that it is a righteous thing with God to require of unregenerate sinners what they cannot perform. He commands them to love Him with all their hearts and so to perform perfect and perpetual obedience to His righteous law, but in their state of unregeneracy they have no moral ability to perform a single duty according to the commandment (Rom. 5:6). It is infinitely just, however, that the Lord should require of sinners what they are unwilling and so unable to perform and that He should condemn them to death, in all its latitude and extent, for not performing it. For nothing can be more just and reasonable than that they should yield perfect obedience to His righteous law. He gave them, in the first Adam, sufficient ability to perform perfect obedience, and they chose to deprive themselves of it by their transgression in him as their federal representative (Eccl. 7:29; Rom. 5:12, 19). Besides, they have no inability but what is voluntary. They love the depravity of their hearts and choose to commit iniquity. Indeed, if the Lord could not justly require of sinners what they cannot perform, it would inevitably follow that they could have no need either that the Son of God should fulfill all righteousness for them or that His Holy Spirit should implant holiness in them. To say, then, that God cannot justly require sinners to perform that obedience to Him which of themselves they are unable to perform tends to undermine, at once, both the law and the gospel.

To conclude, we may hence see that no influences of the Holy Spirit but such as are irresistible will suffice to convert a sinner to God and to the love and practice of sincere obedience to His law. So strong and inveterate is the corruption that is in the hearts of unregenerate sinners that elect sinners do resist the saving operation of the Spirit as much and as long as they can; and were it not that the adorable Spirit is infinitely efficacious in His operation, they would all so resist Him as to hinder Him from converting them. An infinitely powerful operation of the Holy Spirit, such as will be sufficient to conquer all the resistance made to it by sinners, is necessary to change their natures and to make them willing to believe in Jesus Christ and return through Him to God as their God. Accordingly, the Holy Spirit, in converting sinners, is in Scripture represented as putting His laws into their minds and writing them in their hearts (Jer. 31:33; Heb. 10:16), as creating them in Christ Jesus unto good works (Eph. 2:10), as quickening and raising them up from the dead (Eph. 2:1, 5–6), and as opening their eyes and calling them out of darkness into His marvelous light (1 Peter 2:9). Hence, they are said to be born of the Spirit (John 3:8), to be new creatures (2 Cor. 5:17; Gal. 6:15), and to walk in newness of life (Rom. 6:4). This great and wonderful change is indispensably necessary to true conversion. Happy, inexpressibly happy, are you, reader, if you are a subject of it! No sooner do you begin to experience this happy change than you begin so to believe the gospel as to have communion with the second Adam in His righteousness and salvation and so to obey the law as to walk worthy of the Lord to all pleasing.

CHAPTER 5

The Gospel of Christ

The word *gospel* signifies good news, or glad tidings of salvation, to lost sinners of mankind through that "Saviour, which is Christ the Lord" (Luke 2:10–11). The term in Scripture is used in a twofold sense. It is taken in a lax and general meaning and also in a strict and proper acceptation.

First, it is employed in a lax and general acceptation. The gospel, in its lax, large, or general meaning, is the doctrine of Christ and His apostles, which, strictly speaking, is a mixture both of law and gospel. It is used sometimes to denote the history of the birth, life, death, resurrection, and ascension of Christ (Mark 1:1); sometimes the New Testament dispensation of the covenant of grace (2 Tim. 1:10); sometimes the preaching of the word of Christ, particularly of the doctrines and offers of salvation through Him (1 Cor. 9:14); and more frequently, the whole system of revealed truth (Mark 1:14).

The whole of divine truth, comprising both the law and the gospel strictly taken, is in Scripture called *the gospel*; for in publishing it, the law must be preached in subservience to the gospel in its strict acceptation. The law as a covenant of works must be preached to unregenerate sinners in order to convince them of their sin and misery and to impel them to accept the compassionate Savior offered to them in the gospel. The law as a rule of life must be preached to believers in order to excite them to trust at all times in Christ for new supplies of sanctifying grace and to advance in holy conformity to Him. Since the law in its covenant form is of special use in the dispensation of the gospel; since the law as a rule of duty stands in the covenant of grace and is to the spiritual seed of Christ the only rule of acceptable obedience; and since the gospel, strictly taken, is the center in which all the lines of revelation meet, the whole of divine revelation is denominated *the gospel*. The law, as far as I know, is never in Scripture contrasted with the gospel in this large acceptation of the word but is rather comprised in it.

Some have thought that whatever is in the Old Testament is law and that whatever is in the New is gospel. But this is such a mistake as reveals great ignorance of the sacred oracles. The law and the gospel, in their strict and proper sense, are intermingled with each other both in the Old Testament and in the New. Moses and the Prophets often published the gospel as well as the law. Christ and His apostles, on the other hand, frequently preached the law together with the gospel. As Moses wrote of Messiah (and so published the gospel, though he principally promulgated the law to the Israelites), so the Lord Jesus and His apostles explained and urged the law, though they chiefly employed themselves in preaching the gospel.

If by the gospel we mean the whole of that doctrine which was delivered by our Lord and His apostles, it is manifest that the duties of the law are more clearly explained and more strongly enforced in the gospel than ever they were by Moses and the Prophets. And therefore, this part of the gospel may well be styled "the commandment of us the apostles of the Lord and Saviour" (2 Peter 3:2) and "the perfect law of liberty" (James 1:25). An apostle informs us that the new covenant or testament was established or brought into the form of a law on better promises (Heb. 8:6).

The gospel, in its large acceptation, contains the purest and fullest system of morals that has ever been presented to the world. It reveals the infinitely glorious perfections of God, for He who "is in the bosom of the Father, he hath declared him" (John 1:18). It affords, at the same time, plain and affecting discoveries of a future state. "Our Saviour Jesus Christ," says the apostle Paul, "hath abolished death, and hath brought life and immortality to light through the gospel" (2 Tim. 1:10).

The gospel, in this point of view, contains precepts, all the precepts that the Lord ever gave to the children of men and all the precepts that are to be found in the whole compass of divine revelation and summed up in the Ten Commandments. It comprehends not only the commands to believe, to repent, and to perform new obedience but all the other commandments of God to men, so that every precept in the Word of God is a precept of the gospel in its lax and general meaning. Accordingly, the apostle Paul informs us that "the Lord Jesus shall be revealed from heaven with his mighty angels, in flaming fire taking vengeance on them that know not God, and that obey not the gospel of our Lord Jesus Christ" (2 Thess. 1:7–8). He also says of them who heard the gospel from himself and the other apostles that "they have not all obeyed the gospel" (Rom. 10:16). And the apostle Peter says, "If [judgment] first begin at us, what shall the end be of them that obey not the gospel of God?" (1 Peter 4:17). By *the gospel* in these passages is meant the whole Word of God, comprehending both the law and the gospel strictly so called. If, therefore, we exhort one another to obey the precepts of the gospel, we certainly should, in order to prevent error, inform each other at the same time that we do not mean the gospel in its strict sense, which contains no precepts, but the gospel in its lax and general acceptation, which comprises all the precepts which the Lord has given to the sons of men.

Second, the term in Scripture is also used in its strict and proper meaning. *The gospel* strictly taken signifies "good news, glad tidings, or a joyful message." It is the joyful tidings of a free salvation through Jesus Christ to sinners of mankind (Matt. 11:5; Luke 2:10–11; Rom. 10:15), or it is a revelation and exhibition of the covenant of grace to men. The gospel reveals to us what the Father, the Son, and the Holy Spirit have done for us; what inestimable blessings they have provided for us and are willing to impart to us; how fully and freely these are offered to us; and how they are to be received and enjoyed as gifts of infinitely free and sovereign grace. Now *the gospel*, in this point of view, comprises the following particulars:

1. It contains the doctrines of grace, or the doctrinal declarations of God concerning the redemption of lost sinners; concerning His counsel of peace and also His covenant of grace in the source, the parties, the making, the conditions, the promises, and the administration of it; concerning the Lord Jesus, the only Mediator of it, in His person, offices, relations, and estates; concerning the Holy Spirit as the quickener, enlightener, sanctifier, and comforter of elect sinners according to it; and concerning the inestimable blessings promised in it. This is the sum of all the doctrinal declarations of the glorious gospel. It is a declaration or publication of the free grace of God to sinners of mankind, manifested in His redemption of them by Jesus Christ; and it is the best tidings that ever have reached their ears. It is by His gospel that the great Redeemer "mayest say to the prisoners, Go forth; to them that are in darkness, Shew yourselves" (Isa. 49:9). By enabling convinced and disquieted sinners to believe with application to themselves the doctrines of the gospel, He gives "them beauty for ashes, the oil of joy for mourning, and the garment of praise for the spirit of heaviness" (Isa. 61:3). That joyful message Christ was anointed to preach, angels brought to the shepherds; and the apostles, evangelists, and ministers of Christ published to the world.

The gospel, then, is glad tidings of good things. No tidings were ever as joyful as those that are announced in the gospel, and no benefits were ever as good as those that are exhibited in it. At the same time, no man will ever love or so much as understand rightly a single doctrine of the gospel unless he sees and feels that as a sinner he is utterly undone. It is to men as sinners that the word of this salvation is sent. No doctrine deserves to be called gospel but that which makes the adorable Redeemer "all in all" (Eph. 1:23), the "Alpha and Omega" (Rev. 22:13) in the redemption of a sinner. Of such high importance is the doctrine of our Redeemer's divine sonship that the evangelist Mark begins his account of the gospel (Mark 1:1) and the apostle Paul began his ministry of it with that grand article (Acts 9:20). And so fundamental is the doctrine of Christ's consummate righteousness for the justification of believers that the same apostle says of the gospel that "it is the power of God unto salvation to every one that believeth…. For therein is the righteousness of God revealed from faith to faith" (Rom. 1:16–17). The word of the gospel which the apostle Peter spoke to the Gentiles that they might believe was the doctrine of peace by Jesus Christ, with remission of sins through His name, to be received by faith (Acts 10:36; 15:7). The gospel, in this point of view, differs so much from the law as a covenant as to be the very reverse of it.

2. The gospel strictly taken comprises also all the promises of the covenant of grace as included in the great and comprehensive promise of eternal life. Every promise of that gracious covenant belongs to the gospel. The gospel, in the proper acceptation of it, consists of free and absolute promises of grace and glory; or it includes a free and gracious promise of justification and eternal life through our Lord Jesus Christ. It contains the promises of faith and repentance and, indeed, of all the other blessings of the everlasting covenant. The gospel after the fall was revealed in the form of a free and absolute promise of a Savior with salvation in Him to lost sinners of mankind. It was then promised that the seed of the woman would bruise the head of the serpent (Gen. 3:15). The gospel was preached to Abraham also under the form of an absolutely free promise: in thee and in thy seed shall all the nations of the earth be blessed (see Gen. 12:3; 22:18; Gal. 3:8). In the gospel, salvation from sin, from the curse of the law, and from the wrath of God, as well as restoration to fellowship with God, conformity to Him, and the eternal enjoyment of Him are graciously promised in Christ to all who cordially believe in Him. The Lord promises in His gospel that He will give His Holy Spirit to elect sinners to quicken their dead souls; to enlighten their dark minds; to enable them to believe in Jesus; to repent of their sins after a godly

sort; to love, obey, and enjoy Him now; and to attain the perfect fruition of Him forevermore. In the gospel, as preached under the Old Testament, were promises of the coming of Messiah in human nature; and in the same gospel, as preached under the New, are promises of the coming of the Spirit, or of Christ's coming in a greater measure of spiritual influences. These promises are, in the gospel, presented or offered to sinners in common and are made and performed to such sinners as believe.

The gospel, in this its strict and proper sense, seeing it is the form of Christ's testament, which consists of absolute and free promises of salvation by Him, contains no precepts. It commands nothing. It does not enjoin us even to believe and repent, but it declares to us what God in Christ as a God of grace has done and what He promises still to do for us and in us and by us. Every requirement of duty, all precepts, those to believe and repent not excepted, belong to the moral law that binds the new duty on us the moment that the gospel exhibits the new object. Indeed, if but a single instance of duty owed by the reasonable creature to God were not, either expressly or by consequence, commanded in the moral law, that divine law would be so far defective; it would not be a perfect law. But in the Oracles of Truth we read that "the law of the Lord is perfect" (Ps. 19:7) and that His "commandment is exceeding broad" (119:96).

The divine law then, being perfect, cannot but reach to every condition of the creature and require of him every duty. When therefore God in the gospel graciously promises to give elect sinners faith, repentance, and eternal life, the law that commands every duty obliges them, in common with all other sinners who hear the gospel, cordially to believe and trust and plead those promises. It binds them to trust those promises especially and to receive the fulfillment of them in the order in which the gospel exhibits them; to exercise faith in order to the exercise of true repentance; and to exercise faith and repentance daily in order to be prepared for the consummation of eternal life. While every divine promise, then, belongs to the gospel of God, and none of them to His law, every divine precept is contained in His law, and none of them in His gospel strictly taken.

3. The gospel, in its proper acceptation, contains likewise God's gracious offers of Christ in His person, righteousness, fullness, offices, and relations and of Himself in Christ to sinners of mankind in common (Isa. 42:6–7; 55:4; John 3:16; 6:32). It also comprehends His offer of all His promises in and with Christ to sinners indefinitely (Acts 2:39; 2 Cor. 1:20; Heb. 4:1). Hence, we commonly style these offers gospel offers because they form a main and special part of the gospel. "This is the record," says the apostle John, "that God hath given to us eternal life, and this life is in his Son" (1 John 5:11). That God has given to us an offer of eternal life in and with His Son is the record which He has given of His Son. It is the sum, or at least a leading part, of the testimony of God concerning His Son. As the gospel, then, cannot be published faithfully unless the unlimited offer is declared to all who hear it, so it cannot be cordially believed except the gracious offer, and all that is offered, is accepted and received as a gift of infinitely free grace.

While all duties are commanded in the law, all privileges and blessings are offered in the gospel. While the former are required of all, the latter are presented to all. Christ and all the blessings of His great salvation are in the gospel offered freely, fully, presently, and particularly, and that to sinners of mankind in common; and as they are offered, so must they be received by sinners. The ministers of the gospel are authorized by the Lord Jesus to "preach the gospel to every creature" (Mark 16:15)—that is, to publish the full and free offer of Himself and of His righteousness and salvation to every rational creature, every son and daughter of Adam to whom they may have access to speak. And it is, indeed, good tidings of great joy which shall be to all people that "unto us" sinners of the human race this "child is born," this "son is given" (Isa. 9:6). The receiving of Christ by faith supposes a previous offering or giving of Him to hearers of the gospel in order to afford them a warrant to receive Him. As the raining of the manna about the camp of Israel in the wilderness is called a giving of it prior to their eating of it, so the gospel offer of Christ is styled a giving of Him previous to a sinner's reception of Him by faith (John 6:31–32). Indeed, it is as necessary a part of the glorious plan of salvation by Jesus Christ that He be given in offer before believing as that He be given in possession in and after believing.

4. Last, the gospel strictly taken includes God's infinitely gracious and tender invitations to sinners of mankind in common to accept His offers of a Savior and of salvation by Him. In the gospel He graciously calls and with inexpressible earnestness entreats men to come as sinners and receive all that He has offered to them on the warrant of His authentic offer of it. He earnestly invites and urges them to believe that the Lord Jesus Christ, with His righteousness and salvation, is graciously offered to them and so to trust in Him for all their salvation (Prov. 8:4; 9:4–5; Isa. 55:1–3; Matt. 11:28–30; Rev. 3:17–20; 22:17). Those invitations, when considered as calls to perform the duties of believing and repenting, belong to the law; but when viewed as expressions of the readiness or willingness of God to bestow salvation on sinners and as affording them an additional warrant to trust in the compassionate Savior for it, they form a part of the gospel. No man believes the gospel cordially until, convinced of his sinfulness and misery, he believes with application to himself those invitations and, on the warrant of them, trusts in the Lord Jesus for all salvation to himself in particular. For the gracious invitations of the gospel, equally as the direct offers of it, are addressed to every sinner of mankind who hears the joyful sound of it. As for the commands to believe and repent, they, as I hinted above, belong entirely to the law. These commands, when given to unregenerate sinners, belong to the law as a covenant of works; and when given to believers to persevere in believing and repenting, they belong to the law as a rule of life.

The gospel in its proper acceptation (as comprising the doctrines, promises, and offers of a free salvation, with invitations to accept these offers) is in Scripture styled "the gospel of God" (Rom. 1:1; 15:16; 2 Cor. 11:7). He devised and appointed it in all its parts. It contains the declarations and promises of His redeeming mercy, the gracious offers of Himself in Christ to sinners of mankind to be their God and Father, and it affords the most illustrious displays of all His perfections and especially of His glorious grace in the salvation of such as believe. It is also called "the gospel of Christ" (Rom. 1:16). He is the glorious author, the principal messenger and preacher, the blessed subject and end of it in whom all its doctrines and promises are yea and amen, to the glory of God (2 Cor. 1:20).

It is denominated "the gospel of the grace of God" (Acts 20:24), for it proceeds from His free favor and goodwill to men. It manifests the exceeding riches of His grace and the kindness of His love, and it is the means by which He graciously communicates the undeserved blessings of salvation to sinful men.

"The gospel of peace" is another of its characters (Eph. 6:15). It flows from God as reconciled in Christ and reconciling sinners to Himself. By means of it, the peace of God is published to men, and it is the means of reconciling their hearts to Him as the God of peace and to one another as friends and children and heirs of Him.

It is also called "the gospel of your salvation" (Eph. 1:13), for it reveals, promises, and offers salvation. And in the hand of the adorable Spirit, it is the instrument of applying the great salvation of Jesus Christ to the souls of lost sinners.

It is styled likewise "the gospel of the kingdom" (Matt. 4:23), for it is issued from the royal authority of Christ, the King of Zion; is proclaimed in His church; and is the means of bringing rebels and enemies, first, into His kingdom of grace and afterward into His kingdom of glory.

Another of its qualities is that it is a "glorious gospel" (1 Tim. 1:11). It affords the most illustrious displays of the infinitely glorious perfections, purposes, favors, mercies, and truths of God in Christ; the brightest discoveries of the glory of Him who is the brightness of the Father's glory and the express image of His person; and it is the means of His bringing many sons and daughters to glory.

In a word, it is called "the everlasting gospel" (Rev. 14:6). It continues to be preached, heard, and believed from the beginning to the end of time; and the inestimable blessings exhibited in it will continue to be enjoyed by the saints through all eternity.

✦ REFLECTIONS ✦

From what has here been advanced, it will be obvious to the attentive reader that there is a great difference between the gospel in itself and in its dispensation by Jesus Christ. If the gospel is considered in its large acceptation or as dispensed by the Lord Jesus, the messenger of the covenant, legal precepts and threatenings are comprised and dispensed in it. A dreadful sanction is contained in it in order that none may presume to turn the grace of it into licentiousness. On the other hand, if it is viewed in itself, or in its strict and proper meaning, it has neither precepts nor threatenings, but, as was observed above, it is an exhibition of the covenant of grace to sinners of mankind, or good tidings of great joy to all people.

Such expressions as the following are gospel in the strict sense of the word: Christ "was delivered for our offences, and was raised again for our justification" (Rom. 4:25). "Unto you is born this day in the city of David a Saviour, which is Christ the Lord" (Luke 2:11). "My Father giveth you the true bread from heaven" (John 6:32). "This is the promise that he hath promised us, even eternal life" (1 John 2:25).

But on the other hand, such expressions as these are gospel considered in its dispensation to the sons of men: "Believe on the Lord Jesus Christ, and thou shalt be saved" (Acts 16:31). "He that believeth and is baptized shall be saved; but he that believeth not shall be damned" (Mark 16:16). "He that believeth on the Son hath everlasting life: and he that believeth not the Son shall not see life; but the wrath of God abideth on him" (John 3:36). In these and similar passages, the command to believe on the Lord Jesus and the denunciation of divine wrath against all who believe not do not belong to the gospel in itself, or strictly taken, but they belong to the external dispensation of it to sinners. In the dispensation of the gospel, the law and the gospel are dispensed together. The law is promulgated in subservience to the gospel, and therefore it is included in the dispensation of the gospel. The gospel strictly taken is one thing, and the precept and threatening in the dispensation of it is another.

Do we read in Scripture that unbelievers obey not the gospel? We are not from this to suppose that the gospel in its proper meaning is a law, but in all such passages it is to be understood not in its strict but in its large acceptation as comprising both law and gospel.

Does the gospel in its large or extended sense include the law, the same law that was given to man at the beginning? Hence, it is manifest that Christ as Mediator gives no new law, either to saints or sinners, under the gospel. He indeed said to His disciples, "A new commandment I give unto you, That ye love one another; as I have loved you, that ye also love one another" (John 13:34). But this is not the command of a new law and on that account styled new, for it is "an old commandment which ye had from the beginning" (1 John 2:7; see also 2 John 5). But it is called new because it is a most excellent one; because it is more clearly and fully explained than before; because it is to be kept in a new manner, or "in newness of spirit, and not in the oldness of the letter" (Rom. 7:6); and because it is enforced by a new motive and pattern.

For Christ says, "As I have loved you, that ye also love one another" (John 13:34). He does not here say to His disciples, "Ye shall love your neighbor merely as yourselves," but "as I have loved you." The Lord Jesus, then, has not purchased or published a new law of grace to sinners in which faith, repentance, and sincere obedience to it are made the conditions of justification and eternal life. There is a deep silence throughout the Oracles of Truth with regard to any new law of easier terms or any new conditions of justification and salvation. We read, indeed, that Christ, the last Adam, "[fulfilled] all righteousness" (Matt. 3:15) for His spiritual seed and that by His "obedience…shall many be made righteous" (Rom. 5:19). But nowhere in the Word of God do we read that He purchased a new law of grace for them, according to which they might fulfill a justifying righteousness for themselves and according to which sincerity might be accepted instead of perfection of obedience.

Hence, it is also manifest that if any good quality or work of ours were made the condition of our justification or title to eternal life, this would turn the covenant of grace exhibited in the gospel into a covenant of works. The covenant of grace revealed and offered to sinners in the gospel is the only covenant according to which a sinner can be justified and entitled to life eternal. It is absolutely impossible that he can be justified according to the broken covenant of works. But were any graces, acts, or works of his the proper conditions of his justification, the covenant of grace would be as much a covenant of works as ever the covenant made with Adam was. The condition of Adam's covenant was perfect obedience, and according to this imaginary law of easier terms, the conditions of the covenant of grace are sincere faith and sincere obedience.

But it was far easier for Adam in his state of innocence to perform the condition of perfect obedience than it is for an impotent sinner or even for the holiest saint to perform that of sincere faith and obedience. The terms of the new covenant, according to that scheme, would, instead of being milder, be more rigorous and difficult than those of the old. The condition of the one covenant would be works as well as that of the other, for works are still works whether they are perfect or sincere. All indeed who, according to the covenant of grace, attain justification are justified by faith, but it is one thing to be justified by faith as merely the instrument of justification and another to be justified for faith as an act or work affording a title to justification. It is one thing for faith as an act of obedience, and as being seminally all sincere obedience, to give a title to justification, and a very different thing for faith as a means or instrument to receive a title to it. Faith, according to the gospel, gives no manner of title to the smallest blessing of the everlasting covenant, but it receives the surety-righteousness of the second Adam, which gives a full title to every one of them (Rom. 5:18). It gives possession of nothing in that gracious covenant, but it takes possession of everything.

From what has been said, we may see when a man's obedience to the law is evangelical. His obedience is spiritually good and acceptable to God, or, in other words, is evangelical, when he performs it from faith and love, from union with Christ and justification for his righteousness as the principles of it; when he performs it not to the law as a covenant of works, but to the law in the hand of Christ as a rule of duty; when he yields it not for life but from life; not in the strength of nature nor of grace already received but in the strength of "the grace that is in Christ Jesus" (2 Tim. 2:1), trusting that Christ, according to the promise, affords him continual supplies of grace; and when he performs it chiefly for the glory of Christ and of God in Christ. It is evangelical obedience when a man performs it not to recommend him to the favor of God but in the faith of God's favor; not that it may be his justifying righteousness but that it may be a continued expression of adoring gratitude for the gift of his Redeemer's righteousness; not that it may dispose the Lord to become his God but because He is already his God and Father. Such obedience only as that is agreeable to the gospel of Christ.

Is the whole of Christ's salvation offered in the gospel to sinners? Then salvation from the law as a covenant of works is tendered to them. In the declarations and offers of the blessed gospel, the consummate righteousness of Jesus Christ, which has not only answered all the demands of the law as a covenant but has magnified the law and made it honorable (Isa. 42:21), is presented to them. In the gospel they are also invited to receive the gift of that glorious righteousness, against which the utmost rigor of the violated law can offer no objection because it is the righteousness of Him who is God as well as man. When they are enabled to accept the gift of it and to rely with humble confidence on it for all their title to justification and eternal life, it is imputed to them; and they are so justified in the sight of God as to be set free from all the demands of the law in its covenant form. And when by means of the gospel they are thus delivered from the dominion of the law as a covenant, they are, in consequence, saved from the dominion of sin. Well may the glorious gospel, then, be styled "the gospel of your salvation" (Eph. 1:13), for by being in the hand of the Holy Spirit, the means of delivering us from the law in its covenant form, which is "the strength of sin" (1 Cor. 15:56), it becomes the means of our salvation from the power of sin.

Are the offers and invitations of the gospel addressed to all in common who are the hearers of it? Then no man believes the gospel with his heart unto righteousness except he believes the declarations, offers, and invitations of it with application to himself. As long as a sinner refuses to believe these with application or to believe that they are addressed to him in particular, he continues to reject the compassionate Savior and make God a liar (1 John 5:10–11). Whatever his profession of religion may be, he remains under the dominion of unbelief and under condemnation to eternal punishment. The gospel is the doctrine of free and sovereign grace, and it is to be preached to every creature descended from Adam. The righteousness and salvation revealed and offered in it, then, are free to every human creature to whom it is preached; and it is the first or principal duty of every sinner of the human race to accept the gracious offer and to rely on the righteousness of the divine Redeemer for all his title to eternal life. It is only they, therefore, who receive Christ Jesus and trust in His name who shall have life through His name; and it is only they who "receive abundance of grace and of the gift of righteousness" that "shall reign in life by one, Jesus Christ" (Rom. 5:17).

To conclude, is the reader desirous to know whether he is experimentally acquainted with the grace of the gospel or not? Let him pray that the Lord may examine and prove him, and then let him put such questions as these to himself: Do I know spiritually and believe cordially the doctrines of this glorious gospel? Do I spiritually discern the excellence and suitableness of the plan of redemption exhibited in the gospel, and do I heartily approve, as far as I know them, all the parts of that wonderful scheme? Do I heartily comply with the invitations and accept the offers of the gospel? Do I frequently endeavor to embrace and trust the promises of it, and do I place the confidence of my heart in the Lord Jesus for all the salvation that is offered and promised in it? Do I so love the gospel as to delight in reading, hearing, and meditating on it? Do I love and admire the gospel because it is the doctrine, the only doctrine, "which is according to godliness" (1 Tim. 6:3) or because it is the only mirror in which believers so contemplate the glory of God in the face of Jesus Christ as to be "changed into the same image from glory to glory, even as by the Spirit of the Lord" (2 Cor. 3:18)? And do I find that under the transforming and consoling influence of the gospel that I, in some measure, "delight in the law of God after the inward man" (Rom. 7:22) and run in the way of all His commandments (Ps. 119:32)?

If the reader can answer these questions in the affirmative, he may warrantably conclude that he has attained, in some happy measure, that supernatural and experimental knowledge of the glorious gospel which is the beginning of eternal life in the soul and is inseparably connected with evangelical holiness in all manner of conversation; and his duty is, in the faith of the promise, to grow daily in grace and in the knowledge of our Lord and Savior Jesus Christ and never to be moved away from the hope of the gospel.

But if he cannot answer as much as one of them in the affirmative, he ought to conclude that he is yet a stranger to the grace of the gospel; and instead of yielding to despair he should, without delay, come as a sinner to the Lord Jesus, who is given for a light to the Gentiles, that He may be God's salvation unto the end of the earth. And on the warrant of the unlimited grant, he should trust in Him for all the salvation promised in the gospel.

CHAPTER 6

The Uses of the Gospel and of the Law in Subservience to It

The gospel, in its strict and proper sense, is of great and manifold use to both sinners and to saints. I shall here point out only some of its uses.

⁜ SECTION 1 ⁜
The Principal Uses of the Gospel

The gospel in its strict acceptation is, in the hand of the Holy Spirit, of special use for the following reasons:

1. To reveal Christ and God in Him as reconciled and as reconciling sinners of mankind to Himself. The great use of the gospel is to make Christ known to lost sinners as the only and the all-sufficient Savior; to reveal Him to them in His infinitely glorious person as God-man and Mediator; in His surety-righteousness for their justification before God; in His immeasurable fullness of the Spirit for their sanctification and consolation; and in His saving offices and endearing relations to all who believe in Him. It serves to represent to them how Jesus has loved them, what He has done and suffered for them, and what blessings of salvation He has purchased for them and is ready to dispense to them (1 Cor. 1:24; 2:2; 1 Tim. 3:16). It is of use also to reveal to them God as reconciled in Him and as reconciling them to Himself by Him (2 Cor. 4:3–6; 5:18–20).

Hence, the manifold doctrines, offers, and promises of the gospel are in Scripture styled "the manifold wisdom of God" (Eph. 3:10).

They clearly show that God has devised the scheme of our redemption with such astonishing wisdom; that our salvation is all of grace and all of merit, all of mercy and all of justice; that our iniquities are forgiven, and yet the punishment due for them is inflicted; that the ungodly who believe are justified, and yet ungodliness is condemned; and that salvation is freely bestowed; and, after all, that the demands of law and justice are fully answered.

2. It is the gospel that also discloses to sinners the covenant of grace into which the Father and the Son as last Adam, with the infinite approbation of the Holy Spirit, have entered for the salvation of such sinners as believe. Sinful men cannot be otherwise saved than by being enabled to take hold of that everlasting covenant by faith as to come into the bond of it. This, however, they cannot do unless they are made so to know it as to discern spiritually the reality, glory, and suitableness of it to their miserable condition as lost sinners. But it is the gospel only, coming to them "in demonstration of the Spirit and of power" (1 Cor. 2:4), that reveals this gracious covenant to them and shows them how they may be so instated in it as to possess and enjoy the blessings of salvation. They could never, according to the plan established in the counsel of peace, have known that eternal contract but by the revelation of it in the everlasting gospel. It is by the gospel, accompanied with the illuminating influences of His Holy Spirit, that the Lord Jesus, the messenger of the covenant, shows elect sinners His covenant (Ps. 25:14).

3. It serves, likewise, the highly important purpose of discovering to sinners their warrant to trust in Christ Jesus for complete salvation. In the blessed gospel, Christ, and God in Christ, are freely offered to sinful men, and men are graciously invited as sinners to receive the offer and to entrust the whole affair of their salvation to Christ and to God in Him (Isa. 55:1–4; John 6:32). By the gospel, they are informed that the Lord Jesus offers Himself with all the inestimable blessings of the everlasting covenant to them and that He graciously

invites and urges them as sinners to accept Him as their all-sufficient Savior and to place the confidence of their hearts in Him for salvation from sin and wrath. Were they to not know that a divine warrant is thereby afforded them to receive and trust in the Savior for their salvation, it would be as great presumption in any of them as it would be in a fallen angel to attempt trusting that He would save him. But by the declarations, offers, calls, and promises of the word of grace, an ample warrant is afforded them as sinners of mankind to trust in the divine Savior and so to take possession of His great salvation. And it is by the gospel, accompanied by the illuminating grace of the Holy Spirit, that their warrant is revealed, that their full right of access to the compassionate Savior is disclosed to them, and that He manifests Himself to be so near them as to be within their reach (Rom. 10:6–8). Oh, how great is the importance and utility of the gracious offers and invitations of the blessed gospel to convinced and despondent sinners! By these, under the illuminating influences of the adorable Spirit, they see that it is lawful and warrantable for them to come as sinners and to entrust, with humble and strong confidence, the eternal salvation of their souls to the Lord Jesus.

4. The gospel is the means that the Holy Spirit employs for communicating the grace of Christ to elect sinners in order to produce that change of their state and of their nature to which they have been chosen. It is by means of the gospel that, in the moment of regeneration, the Spirit of Christ and His grace enter and take possession of the hearts of God's elect. Sinners who are born again are born "not of corruptible seed, but of incorruptible, by the word of God, which liveth and abideth for ever" (1 Peter 1:23). Hence, the psalmist, directing his speech to the Messiah, says, "The LORD shall send the rod of thy strength out of Zion: rule thou in the midst of thine enemies. Thy people shall be willing in the day of thy power" (Ps. 110:2–3). The gospel, accordingly, is called "the spirit [which] giveth life" (2 Cor. 3:6); "the grace of God that bringeth salvation" (Titus 2:11); and "the

power of God unto salvation" (Rom. 1:16). By the gospel, God exerts the exceeding greatness of His power in quickening and converting sinners to Himself. It is by means of it that He enlightens their minds, renews their wills, rectifies and sanctifies their affections, and so makes them partakers of a new and holy nature. Hence, the apostle Paul styles it "the law of the Spirit of life in Christ Jesus," which made him "free from the law of sin and death" (Rom. 8:2).

5. The gospel is also the instrument by which the Holy Spirit implants the principle and habit of true faith in the hearts of elect sinners. "Faith cometh by hearing, and hearing by the word of God" (Rom. 10:17). The Spirit renders the reading and, especially, the hearing of the gospel effectual means of working faith in the hearts of sinners, by which they believe with application the gracious offers of Christ, and of His righteousness and fullness, and trust in Him for salvation to themselves in particular. It is by means of the gospel, which the apostle Paul styles "the word of faith" (Rom. 10:8), that the Spirit of Christ implants and increases precious faith in the souls of His elect (John 20:31). Is it then the believer's desire that he may make swift progress in the habit and exercise of that living faith by which he gives glory to God and receives grace and glory from Him? Let him, in humble reliance on the promise and on the Spirit of faith, read, hear, and meditate frequently on the glorious gospel.

6. It is by means of the gospel that the Holy Spirit continues to apply Christ, with His righteousness and fullness, to the hearts of believers for increasing their sanctification and consolation. They are said in Scripture to be sanctified "through thy truth" (John 17:17–19), to be clean through the word that Christ has spoken to them (John 15:3), and to have their hearts purified by faith (Acts 15:9). The apostle Paul presented this prayer for the saints at Ephesus: "That Christ may dwell in your hearts by faith…that ye might be filled with all the fulness of God" (Eph. 3:17, 19). And he informed them that they were "built upon the foundation of the apostles and prophets" (Eph.

2:20). It is in proportion, then, as the saints are enabled to believe with application to themselves the offers and promises of the gospel and to trust in Jesus Christ for salvation that they advance in holiness and comfort. And it is "in the unity of the faith, and of the knowledge of the Son of God" that they all come "unto a perfect man, unto the measure of the stature of the fullness of Christ" (Eph. 4:13).

7. The gospel is a means of increasing the knowledge, of restraining the depravity, and of reforming the external conduct of many unregenerate sinners and so of qualifying them for being, in various respects, serviceable to the people of God around them. It is often a means, under the restraining influence of the Holy Spirit, of rendering many unregenerate men less hurtful and more useful to the saints of God than otherwise they would be. As the gospel is a special means of the renewing influences of the Spirit in holy men, so is it of His restraining influence on hypocrites and wicked men (Matt. 13:20–22; Heb. 6:4–5; 2 Peter 2:20). Now this restraining or providential influence is of inexpressible importance to the saints. For as no saint could continue to live in communion with Christ and with other saints without sanctifying grace, and that daily communicated to him, so neither could he live among sinners unless restraining influences were afforded to them. He ought, therefore, in a very high degree, to esteem and love the gospel not only because it is the means of special grace to himself but because it is the vehicle of common influence to the unregenerate around him.

8. Last, it is by means of the gospel that the glory of Christ, and of God in Him, is manifested to men and angels. It is in and by the gospel that the brightest displays "of the glory of God in the face of Jesus Christ" are graciously afforded (2 Cor. 4:6; see vv. 4–7). In the gospel, like in a mirror, the glory of the Lord Jesus and of all the divine perfections—as harmonizing and mingling their refulgent beams in the redemption of sinners by Him—is seen, contemplated, and adored (2 Cor. 3:18). It is the gospel strictly taken that, under the illuminating

influences of the blessed Spirit, serves to discover to the eye of faith "the glory as of the only begotten of the Father" (John 1:14), "the brightness of his glory, and the express image of his person" (Heb. 1:3). There the glory of the great Redeemer's person and work shines forth in the view of holy angels and redeemed men with the most resplendent luster. Hence, the gospel is called "the glorious gospel of Christ, who is the image of God" (2 Cor. 4:4) and "the glorious gospel of the blessed God" (1 Tim. 1:11). While the Lord affords far more illustrious displays of His infinite glory in redemption than in any other of His works, all the transcendent displays of it in redemption that He makes are in and by the gospel.

✦ SECTION 2 ✦

The Uses of the Moral Law in Its
Subservience to the Gospel

The law, both as a covenant of works and as a rule of life, is, in the hand of the Holy Spirit, of special use, and that both to sinners and to saints. Though righteousness and eternal life cannot, since the fall, be obtained by a man's own obedience to the moral law because "by the works of the law shall no flesh be justified" (Gal. 2:16), yet it is of manifold use to men. "The law is good," says the apostle Paul, "if a man use it lawfully" (1 Tim. 1:8)—that is, if he uses it suitably to the design for which it is given him and to the state in which he is, either as an unbeliever or as a believer or, in other words, if he improves it as a covenant for urging him to receive Jesus Christ and improves it as a rule for directing him how to walk in Christ.

The law is of use to men in general:

1. To discover to them the holy nature and will of God, or to show them the infinite holiness and rectitude of His nature and will. Jehovah said to the Israelites in the wilderness, "I am the LORD your God: ye shall therefore sanctify yourselves, and ye shall be holy; for I am holy" (Lev. 11:44). "The law is holy," says the apostle Paul, "and the commandment holy, and just, and good" (Rom. 7:12).

2. It serves to inform them of their duty to God, to themselves, and to others around them and to oblige them, by His sovereign authority, to perform it. "He hath shewed thee, O man, what is good; and what doth the LORD require of thee, but to do justly, and to love mercy, and to walk humbly with thy God?" (Mic. 6:8).

3. It is of use, likewise, to restrain men from much sin. By its peremptory commands and awful threatenings, it serves in some measure to keep them in awe and to frighten them from committing many external acts of sin in which they otherwise would freely indulge themselves. It is of use, by its terrible denunciations, to curb those who, destitute of every good principle, would rush forward to all manner of sin, and to deter them, through fear of punishment, from many gross enormities. In this view, it serves as a curb to hold sinners within the limits of external decency and to prevent the world from becoming a scene of robbery and blood. Accordingly, our apostle says "that the law is not made for a righteous man, but for the lawless and disobedient, for the ungodly and for sinners, for unholy and profane, for murderers of fathers and murderers of mothers" (1 Tim. 1:9–10).

4. The law conduces also to excite and encourage sinners to the practice of virtue from the consideration that even the external resemblance of true virtue will often be rewarded with exemption from many outward calamities and with the possession of many outward advantages (Isa. 1:19). Nay, it tends to impel sinners to virtuous actions, even from the consideration that in the event of their performance of them and afterward of their dying in an unregenerate state, their punishment in hell will be more tolerable than if they had not performed them. Although sinners cannot by their obedience to the law procure for themselves a title to heaven (yea, and though they should never be driven by the law from themselves to Christ for righteousness and salvation but should die under condemnation) yet the more external obedience they yield to the law, the lighter will their punishment be (Luke 12:47–48). They cannot, by their obedience to the law, merit

even the lowest place in heaven, but they can by it obtain for themselves an exemption from the lowest place in hell.

5. Moreover, it is of special use to convince sinners of their sinfulness and misery and also of their utter inability by any righteousness and strength of their own to recover themselves from their state of sin and misery. "What things soever the law saith, it saith to them who are under the law: that every mouth may be stopped, and all the world may become guilty before God. Therefore by the deeds of the law there shall no flesh be justified in his sight: for by the law is the knowledge of sin" (Rom. 3:19–20). And again, "But sin, that it might appear sin, working death in me by that which is good; that sin by the commandment might become exceeding sinful" (Rom. 7:13).

The precepts of the law serve to convince men of their sins of omission, and the prohibitions of it to convince them of their sins of commission. There are various evils that men would never have known to be sins unless the holy law of God had discovered the sinfulness of them. Accordingly, our apostle says, "I had not known sin, but by the law: for I had not known lust, except the law had said, Thou shalt not covet" (Rom. 7:7). While the precepts of the law are of use to convince sinners of the reality and sinfulness of their sins, the threatenings of it are employed to discover to them the tremendous wrath and curse of God due to them for their transgressions (Gal. 3:10). And by disclosing to them the deep depravity of their nature, the precepts and threatenings of the law serve, in the hand of the Spirit, to convince them of their utter inability to recover themselves and so to humble them under a painful sense of their sinfulness and misery (Rom. 3:9).

6. Last, the law serves to show them their extreme need of Christ and of His righteousness and salvation. "Wherefore then serveth the law?" asks our apostle. "It was added because of transgressions, till the seed should come to whom the promise was made" (Gal. 3:19). It awakens their consciences to a conviction of their guilt and to a dread

of everlasting punishment, and so discovers to them their absolute need of Christ and His perfect righteousness for their justification in the sight of God (Gal. 3:24; Rom. 10:4, respectively). Thus, the moral law is of use to men in general.

It is of special use to unregenerate sinners.

1. Under the awakening influences of the Holy Spirit, it serves as a covenant of works to convince them of sin and to show them that as they are sinners and so cannot perform perfect obedience to entitle them to life, it is absolutely impossible for them ever to attain to justification and salvation by their own performances. "By the deeds of the law," says the apostle Paul, "there shall no flesh be justified in his sight: for by the law is the knowledge of sin" (Rom. 3:20). "I was alive without the law once: but when the commandment came, sin revived, and I died" (Rom. 7:9).

2. It reveals the wrath of God against them for their innumerable transgressions of it, and so impresses them with fear of eternal punishment. "The law worketh wrath" (Rom. 4:15). It condemns every sinner who is under it to death in all its direful extent, and so it awakens his conscience to expect infinite and insupportable wrath as the just recompense of disobedience to its righteous precepts. Hence, the law, in this point of view, is called "the ministration of death" (2 Cor. 3:7). Thus, as a scourge, it troubles and torments the consciences of impenitent sinners and renders them uneasy in a course of sin.

3. The law is of use, likewise, to urge or drive them to Jesus Christ, the only Savior of lost sinners. Seeing it is the means of convincing sinners of their sinfulness, misery, and utter inability to recover themselves, it drives them from confidence in themselves to the Lord Jesus for "righteousness and strength" (Isa. 45:24). And thus it is their schoolmaster to bring them to Christ, that they may be justified by faith (Gal. 3:24). By demanding perfect holiness of nature, perfect obedience of life, and complete satisfaction for sin, which none of the

children of Adam is able to afford, the law shuts them up to see their need of Christ, who has fully answered all these demands for those who believe in Him (Rom. 10:4). It serves as a looking glass in which they may contemplate the exceeding sinfulness and demerit of their sins in order that, despairing of life by their own works, they may be necessitated to flee speedily to Jesus Christ, who has fulfilled a perfect righteousness for their justification.

4. It serves, at the same time, to convince them that they have those characters of sinfulness and misery under which the offers and invitations of the gospel are addressed to men. The offers and calls of the gospel are addressed to men as unjust, ungodly; as sinners, enemies, and persons without strength; as lost, dead in trespasses and sins, simple ones, scorners, fools, stouthearted, and far from righteousness; as backsliders and prisoners; as laboring and heavy laden, thirsting for happiness of any kind, spending their money for that which is not bread and their labor for that which satisfies not, disobedient, gainsaying, rebellious, etc. Now the law, under the illuminating influences of the Holy Spirit, is of use to show sinners that these are their very characters and therefore that they are the very persons to whom the Savior is offered and whom are invited and commanded to receive Him with His righteousness and salvation. In this view, it is eminently subservient to the gospel.

5. Last, the law serves to render those of them inexcusable who, turning a deaf ear to its dictates respecting their sinfulness and misery, refuse to accept the offer of a Savior and of salvation by Him (Rom. 1:20; 2:15). And it not only leaves all who reject the divine Redeemer without excuse and under its dreadful curse, but it dooms them to greater, to redoubled condemnation. "He that believeth on the Son hath everlasting life: and he that believeth not the Son shall not see life; but the wrath of God abideth on him" (John 3:36). "He that despised Moses' law died without mercy under two or three witnesses: of how much sorer punishment, suppose ye, shall he be

thought worthy, who hath trodden under foot the Son of God, and hath counted the blood of the covenant, wherewith he was sanctified, an unholy thing, and hath done despite unto the Spirit of grace? For we know him that hath said, Vengeance belongeth unto me, I will recompense, saith the Lord" (Heb. 10:28–30).

The law is of special use, likewise, to regenerate persons or true believers, and that both as a covenant of works and as a rule of duty.

In its covenant form, it serves to show them what Christ, the second Adam, did and suffered in their stead. By requiring from all who are under it perfect holiness of nature and perfect obedience of life with complete satisfaction for sin as the conditions of eternal life, it teaches believers what the Lord Jesus, in the greatness of His astonishing love, condescended to become, to do, and to suffer for them. They may see in it as in a glass that He did infinitely more for them than any mere man or angel could ever have done (Rom. 8:3–4; Gal. 3:13–14; Phil. 2:8). Thus, the law, in subservience to the gospel, teaches believers indirectly what the gospel teaches them in direct terms. It is of use also to show them under what infinite obligations they lie to the Lord Jesus for having fulfilled all the righteousness of it in their stead. Though they are not under the law in its covenant form to be either justified or condemned by it, yet it is of special use to them to teach them how much they are bound to love and serve Christ who, by obeying the precepts and enduring the penalties of it in their stead, has brought in everlasting righteousness for their justification. And so it is a means of exciting their gratitude to Christ and also to God, who so loved them as to send Him to answer all its demands for them (2 Cor. 9:15; Col. 1:12–14).

The law as a rule of life is also of great use to believers. For although, as I already observed, they are not under it as a covenant of works, either to be justified by it for their obedience or to be condemned by it for their disobedience, yet they are under it as the rule of their new obedience, and they count it their exalted privilege and pleasure to be so (1 Cor. 9:21). Now in this point of view, it serves in the following ways, under the illuminating influences of the Holy Spirit:

1. To show them how far they are from perfection of holiness. In order to render them humbler and more contrite; to cause them to renounce, in a higher degree, all confidence in their own wisdom, righteousness, and strength; and to trust constantly and only in the Lord Jesus for all their salvation, the law discovers to them the sin that dwells in them and that cleaves to all their thoughts, words, and actions. It is of great use to teach them the need that they have to be more humble, penitent, and holy. And so it serves, in a high degree, to promote their sanctification and their desire to attain perfection of holiness (Rom. 7:22–24; Phil. 3:10–14). As it requires them to be holy in a perfect degree (Matt. 5:48), it shows them that their want of perfect conformity to it is, every moment, their sin and that they ought continually to press on toward perfection and long for heaven, where their holiness and happiness will be perfect (2 Cor. 5:2–4; Phil. 1:23).

2. It serves, under the witnessing of the Spirit, to evidence to their consciences the reality of their sanctification. The holy law serves as a touchstone by which believers may try, and so discover, their begun conformity to the image of the Son of God, the firstborn among many brethren. Comparing their hearts and lives with that standard, they sometimes perceive that though they are far from having a perfection of the degrees, yet they have a perfection of the parts of sanctification; and so the law as a rule conduces, in the hand of the Holy Spirit, to promote their comfort as well as their holiness. "Our rejoicing is this," says an apostle, "the testimony of our conscience, that in simplicity and godly sincerity, not with fleshly wisdom, but by the grace of God, we have had our conversation in the world" (2 Cor. 1:12). As a covenant of works, the law is the instrument of the Spirit, as a Spirit of bondage, for convincing and alarming secure sinners; but as a rule of

life in the hand of the blessed Mediator, it is a means employed by the Spirit, as a Spirit of adoption, for comforting and encouraging true saints. Their habitual desire and endeavor from faith and love, and for the glory of God, to keep all the commandments of it are good evidence to them that they are the children of God and are conformed to the image of His Son.

3. It is of great use to show believers what duty they owe to their God and Redeemer and to direct them how to perform it. Christ, whom the Father has given for "a leader and commander to the people" (Isa. 55:4), gives to believers that law to be the rule of their obedience, to inform them what grateful service, what holy obedience they owe to Him and to God in Him, and to direct them in the course of their obedience. Accordingly, the holy psalmist says, "Through thy precepts I get understanding: therefore I hate every false way. Thy word is a lamp unto my feet, and a light unto my path" (Ps. 119:104–5). The law as a rule directs them how to express their gratitude to the Lord Jesus for fulfilling it for them in its covenant form (Rom. 8:3–5). It enjoins them to show their love and thankfulness to Him by a growing conformity of heart and life to it as the rule of their obedience (John 14:15; Rom. 12:1–2; 1 Tim. 1:5). While it shows them what is good and what is evil, what they ought to do and what they ought to forbear, it guides them in the exercise of their graces and in the performance of their duties. No sooner does the law as a covenant urge men to Christ for deliverance from the dominion of it in that form than Christ leads them back to the law as a rule for the regulation of their heart and conduct, in order that they may express their gratitude to Him for His perfect obedience to it as a covenant in their stead by their sincere obedience to it as a rule (John 14:15).

4. Finally, it serves the highly important purpose of binding or obliging the saints to all their various duties. The law as a rule of life to believers comes invested with infinite authority and therefore lays them under infinite obligations, even to perfect obedience. Seeing

they do not cease to be creatures by becoming new creatures, they are, and ever will be, obliged to yield personal obedience to the moral law as a rule of life, and that by the sovereign authority of the Father, the Son, and the Holy Spirit, their Creator. But this divine authority, as was hinted above, issues to them from the Lord Jesus, the great Mediator, who has created as well as redeemed them and who has "all the fulness of the Godhead" dwelling in Him bodily (Col. 2:9). They therefore receive the law at His mouth. And surely the law can lose nothing of its original authority by being conveyed to them in such a glorious channel as the hand of Christ, for not only is He Himself God over all, but all the sovereignty and authority of the infinitely glorious Godhead are in Him as Mediator (Ex. 23:21). The Lord Jesus, therefore, instead of dissolving, or in the smallest degree weakening, does greatly strengthen the original obligation of the moral law.[1] Indeed, it is only to God as in Christ, only according to the law as in the hand of Christ, and only by a real believer in Christ that the smallest acceptable obedience can be performed. The law as a rule in the hand of Christ, then, is of special utility to believers inasmuch as it shows them how high their obligations are to the love and practice of holiness. And thus it eminently subserves the gospel, that "doctrine which is according to godliness" (1 Tim. 6:3).

⋅ REFLECTIONS ⋅

From the foregoing detail, it will be obvious to the devout reader that the law as a covenant is of standing use in the effectual vocation of sinners to Christ. The Holy Spirit makes the offers and calls of the gospel effectual to no sinner without setting home the law as a covenant of works to their minds and consciences. Sinners may be drawn to the Savior by a discovery of His redeeming love (Hos. 11:4), and so may be effectually called without legal terrors; but no man is persuaded and enabled to come to Him without a true conviction of sin

---

1. Westminster Confession of Faith 19.5.

and of the want of righteousness. But it is by the law in its covenant form that sinners are convinced of sin and of their need of a perfect righteousness to free them from eternal death and to entitle them to eternal life. Thus, the law is of standing use to them to show them their extreme need of the compassionate Savior and of His perfect righteousness and so to "break up [the] fallow ground" of their hearts (Jer. 4:3; see also Hos. 10:12). In this way, the fiery law continues, by the almighty agency of the Spirit, to subserve the merciful design of the blessed gospel.

Hence, we may also learn how much conviction of sin and of righteousness by the law is requisite to true conversion. Such a measure of it in adult persons is necessary as will suffice to make them sensible that they are sinners in heart and in life; that they are already undone and that their misery under the curse of the law is inexpressible; that they have no righteousness to answer the just demands of the broken law; and that they are so dead in sin as to be totally unable to save themselves or so much as to prepare themselves for salvation. Such a measure as this is requisite because, without it, they would not see their absolute need of the Lord Jesus to save them either from their sin or their misery, nor would they desire above all things a personal interest in Him and His great salvation. Not that it is requisite as a federal condition of their being graciously received by Christ, but only as an excitement to urge them to flee speedily for refuge to Him.

From what has been said, we may also infer that a minister of the gospel may often preach the law to his hearers and yet not deserve to be called a legal preacher. He cannot preach the gospel faithfully and successfully unless he preaches the law in subservience to it. If he is a faithful and able minister of the New Testament, he will preach the law as a covenant of works and will press it on the consciences of secure sinners and self-righteous formalists. He will denounce the tremendous curse of it on those who continue under it and who rely securely on their own works for a title to eternal life in order to tear away every pillow of carnal security on which they repose themselves and to show them the vanity of every lying refuge. In proportion also as he is faithful, he will preach the law as a rule of life to them who believe. He will press on them the spiritual performance of every duty and a holy abhorrence of every sin. He will exhort them to perform all their duties from evangelical principles in a holy manner and to holy ends. Now if he preach the law in that manner, no man will be disposed to fix the odious character of a legal preacher on him but one who either is grossly ignorant or is an enemy both of the law and of the gospel.

Does the law in its covenant form require of everyone who is under it that he keep its commandments perfectly as the condition of eternal life? Then it is vain for him to say, "I endeavor, or I do all that I can, to keep them." It is not endeavors to obey but perfect and perpetual obedience that will satisfy the precepts of the righteous law. It is not said, "Cursed is everyone who does not endeavor to continue in all things," but "Cursed is every one that continueth not in all things which are written in the book of the law to do them" (Gal. 3:10). It is the man "which doeth those things," not the man who endeavors to do them, that "shall live by them" (Rom. 10:5).

Many flatter themselves that their state is good and their salvation sure because they do not live securely in a course of sin but, on the contrary, endeavor to keep the commandments as well as they can and because God is so merciful that He will surely pardon the sins that the infirmity of their nature renders unavoidable. This is a common but a very dangerous—yea, a fundamental—error; for it proceeds on the supposition that the righteous law can accept of defective or imperfect obedience and that divine justice can dispense with the punishment of sin. No man under the law as a covenant can be accepted for endeavoring to keep the precepts of it as well as he can. The law does not say, "Labor to obey" but "Do it" and "Do it perfectly and perpetually; do it without the smallest failure." The least deficiency in obedience will subject a man to the curse. The self-righteous sinner, then, would do well to consider that he is under a law that demands absolute perfection of obedience on pain of death in all its dreadful extent and that, if he has transgressed but in a single instance, he is thereby exposed to the eternal execution of its righteous and tremendous penalty. "Tell me," says our apostle, "ye that desire to be under the law, do ye not hear the law?" (Gal. 4:21). Do you not hear that it requires perfect obedience of you, on pain of the curse? And if it demands perfect obedience and, at the same time, complete satisfaction for sins that are past, what will you do, who cannot give to it either the one or the other? What will you do in the prospect of death and of judgment, who have no communion with the second Adam in His righteousness? Alas, your own righteousness is far, very far, from being commensurate with the perfect rule of that holy and righteous law by which all your thoughts, words, and actions are then to be tried!

Again, does the law, as a covenant of works, demand from everyone who is under it infinite satisfaction for sin as well as perfect obedience? Or does it demand from every unregenerate sinner perfection of suffering as well as of doing? Then, though a descendant of fallen Adam could say that he never had, in his own person, transgressed the law and that he would to the end of his life continue "in all things which are written in the book of the law to do them" (Gal. 3:10), yet even this perfect obedience of his would not suffice to fulfill the law and so entitle him to eternal life according to the covenant of works. For the law as a covenant would still demand from him full satisfaction for the sin that he committed in the first Adam, and satisfaction for sin cannot be given by obeying the precept but by suffering the penalty of the law in that form.

Ever since the fall, the law and the justice of God demand not only full payment of the original debt of perfect obedience but complete payment, likewise, of the debt of infinite satisfaction for the offense given by sin to the infinite Majesty of heaven (Gen. 2:17). Nay, in the order of law and justice, the debt of full satisfaction ought to be discharged previous to that of perfect obedience. The infinitely righteous Jehovah will first be pacified by a complete satisfaction to His justice for the infinite insult offered to His glorious majesty by transgression before He can consistently, with the honor of His character and government, be pleased with any degree of obedience from the sinner. If a sinner, then, hopes for eternal life on the ground of his own righteousness, he must first give infinite satisfaction for all his innumerable crimes and then begin and complete a course of perfect obedience as the condition of life. He must first of all make complete satisfaction to the penalty of the righteous law before his obedience to the precept can be acceptable to God. But is this possible? Is it possible for one who is to continue through all eternity to be a sinner as well as a sufferer? Is it possible for a sinner, first, to endure the whole of infinite punishment or eternal wrath and, after endless torments shall have been completely endured, to return and, under the dominion of sin, to perform perfect obedience as the condition of eternal life? Oh, that self-righteous and secure sinners would consider, before it is too late, how impossible it will be for them ever to obtain eternal life by their own righteousness and that they would, by faith, submit themselves to the righteousness of Jesus Christ, by which He has magnified the law and made it honorable!

Moreover, it appears from what has been said that when our apostle asserts, in his epistles to the Romans and Galatians, that no man can be justified before God by the works of the law, by *the law*, he does not mean the law merely as promulgated from Sinai or the law of Moses as such, for those churches consisted chiefly of Gentile converts who had no concern with the law of Moses merely as such. Before their conversion they were heathens and were under the law, not as delivered from Sinai, but as the law of nature and as a covenant of works made with Adam, and with them in him. As therefore no Jews can be justified by the works of the moral law as a covenant displayed on Mount Sinai, so no Gentiles can be justified by the works of the moral law as a covenant made with Adam. They among the Gentiles who have been redeemed are said to have been redeemed from the curse of the law (Gal. 3:13); that is, of the moral law in its covenant form as given to Adam.

Once more, is it by the law as a covenant that sinners are convinced of misery as well as of sin? Then how great is the misery, and how intolerable will the punishment be, especially of those under the gospel who obstinately continue in their unbelief and impenitence! While the violated law continues in all its binding force against them, their condemnation will be inconceivably more dreadful than if they had never heard the gracious offers of the gospel. "This is the condemnation, that light is come into the world, and men loved darkness rather than light, because their deeds were evil" (John 3:19). "Whosoever shall fall upon that stone shall be broken; but on whomsoever it shall fall, it will grind him to powder" (Luke 20:18). Impenitent sinners under the gospel shall be punished not only for their innumerable transgressions of the law but for hating and stifling their convictions of sin and misery by it; and their punishment for contemning and rejecting the great Redeemer offered to them in the gospel will be far more tremendous and intolerable than if they had never heard of His name.

The punishment of no sinners will be so dreadful as that of them who hear of an only Savior and yet refuse to believe in Him. Suppose that He is offered and that sinners reject the gracious offer a thousand times; they are a thousand times greater sinners than they were when He began to be offered to them, and according to the greatness of their sin will their punishment be. Oh, that the secure sinner under the gospel would now begin to consider the heinousness of his sin and the horrible depth of the misery that awaits him in the place of torment! You are under the law as a broken covenant and obnoxious to its dreadful curse. You believe not on the Son of God for His salvation, and therefore the wrath of God abides on you.

Can you imagine that the omniscient and righteous Judge of all the earth will take no notice of you or that He who is "of purer eyes than to behold evil, and canst not look on iniquity" (Hab. 1:13) but with infinite abhorrence will suffer you to sin against Him with impunity? Oh, how inexpressibly dreadful will your condition be if you remain asleep in your sinfulness and misery till everlasting fire, prepared for the devil and his angels, awakens you! Alarmed by the terrors of the fiery law, let your heart be won to the compassionate Savior by the mild accents of the blessed gospel. In the glorious gospel, Jesus, with His meritorious righteousness and His great salvation, is freely and wholly and particularly offered to you as a lost sinner of mankind; and the unlimited and authentic offer affords you a right to receive and trust in Him for complete salvation. Oh, do not any longer despise this unspeakable, this inestimably precious gift! Come to the Lord Jesus, and He will in no wise cast you out. Believe in the dear Redeemer, and you shall never perish but have eternal life.

CHAPTER 7

The Difference between the Law and the Gospel

By *the law* here is meant the moral law as a covenant of works, and by *the gospel* is meant the gospel in its strict and proper sense. To know the difference so as to be able to distinguish aright between the law and the gospel is of the utmost importance to the faith, holiness, and comfort of every true Christian. It will be impossible otherwise for a man so to believe as to be filled "with all joy and peace in believing" (Rom. 15:13). If he knows not the difference between the law and the gospel, he will be apt, especially in the affair of justification, to confound the one with the other. The consequence will be that in his painful experience, bondage will be mixed with liberty of spirit, fear with hope, sorrow with joy, and death with life. If he cannot so distinguish the gospel from the law as to expect all his salvation from the grace of the gospel and nothing of it from the works of the law, he will easily be induced to connect his own works with the righteousness of Jesus Christ in the affair of his justification.

This was the great error of the Judaizing teachers in the churches of Galatia. They mingled the law with the gospel in the business of justification, and thereby they so corrupted the gospel as to alter the very nature of it and make it another gospel. They taught that except men were circumcised and kept the law of Moses, they could not be justified or saved (Acts 15:1–5). They informed the people that while the righteousness of Christ received by faith was necessary, their own works of obedience were also requisite in connection with it to entitle them to justification before God. This is a fundamental error and such a one that, if even an angel from heaven would publish it, he should be accursed. Accordingly, the apostle boldly affirmed to the Galatians, and he deliberately and earnestly repeated his declaration that though he himself or even an angel from heaven were to preach any other gospel to them than that which he had preached unto them, he should be accursed (Gal. 1:8–9). To mingle, then, the law with the gospel or to teach men to join the works of the law to the perfect righteousness of Jesus Christ as the ground of a sinner's title to justification in the sight of God is, according to our apostle, to preach "another gospel" (Gal. 1:6).

As this is a great error, so it is a very dangerous error. If a man attempts to add any works of his own to the consummate righteousness of Jesus Christ as the ground of his justification before God, Christ profits him nothing. The obedience and death of Christ have "become of no effect" to him. "Behold, I Paul say unto you, that if ye be circumcised, Christ shall profit you nothing. For I testify again to every man that is circumcised, that he is a debtor to do the whole law. Christ is become of no effect unto you, whosoever of you are justified by the law; ye are fallen from grace" (Gal. 5:2–4). If a man tries to connect his own performances with the righteousness of Jesus Christ for the pardon of his sins and the acceptance of his person as righteous in the sight of God, he deprives himself of all benefit from that perfect righteousness. If he relies on his own works of obedience for even the smallest part of his title to eternal life, "he is a debtor to do the whole law" in its covenant form, and he fixes himself under the dreadful curse of it. Christ will profit him nothing unless he relies on His infinitely glorious righteousness only for all his title to justification and eternal life. A sinner depends on the righteousness of Christ for justification to no good purpose if he does not rely on it only, and neither in whole nor in part on his own obedience.

If an exercised and disquieted Christian does not distinctly know the difference between the law and the gospel, he cannot attain to solid tranquility or established comfort of soul. He will always be in danger of building his hope and comfort partly, if not wholly, on his own graces and performances instead of grounding them wholly on the surety-righteousness of Jesus Christ; and so he shall be perpetually disquieted by anxious and desponding fear. For since the law knows nothing of pardon of sin, the transgressions that he is daily committing will be greater grounds of fear to him than his graces and performances can be of hope. The spirit of a depressed Christian cannot be raised to solid consolation but by being able so to distinguish between the law and the gospel as to rely only, and with settled confidence, on the spotless righteousness of the second Adam, presented to him in the gospel, for all his title "unto justification of life" (Rom. 5:18).

Ignorance of the difference between the law and the gospel promotes also, in a great degree, the strength and influence of a self-righteous temper. When a man is driven to acts of obedience by the dread of God's wrath revealed in the law and not drawn to them by the belief of His love revealed in the gospel; when he fears God because of His power and justice and not because of His goodness; when he regards God more as an avenging judge than as a compassionate friend and father; and when he contemplates God rather as terrible in majesty than as infinite in grace and mercy, he shows that he is under the dominion, or at least under the prevalence, of a legal spirit. If he builds his faith of the pardon of sin, of the favor of God, and of eternal life on any graces that he supposes are implanted in him or on any duties that are performed by him, he is evidently under the power of a self-righteous temper. He shows that he is under the influence of this hateful temper by grounding his hope and his comfort on conditions performed by himself and not on the gracious and absolute promises of the gospel. In a word, when his hope of divine mercy is raised by the liveliness of his frame in duties and not by discoveries of the freeness and riches of redeeming grace offered to him in the gospel; or when he expects eternal life not as the gift of God through Jesus Christ but as a recompense from God for his own obedience and suffering, he plainly shows that he is under the power of a legal spirit. Now, if he is ignorant of the leading distinctions between the law and the gospel, this ignorance will strengthen his legal propensity and confirm him in his resolution to seek justification partly, if not wholly, by the works of the law.

If awakened sinners are ignorant of the leading points of difference between the law and the gospel, this will discourage them much from attempting to come to Christ for salvation. If they cannot distinguish aright between the law and the gospel, they will mingle the works of the one with the grace of the other, and the consequence will be that they will form confused, false, and discouraging notions of the compassionate Savior. And so instead of being drawn to Him, they will be deterred from trusting in Him for salvation. They will allow themselves to apprehend that they must have something to bring with them to the Savior in order to recommend them to Him, some good qualifications to entitle them to His favor. Although it is declared in the gospel that all things are already given to Christ by the Father, yet when the thoughts of convinced sinners about the law and the gospel are indistinct, they imagine that they must still have something of their own to bring and present to Him. They conceive that they must, in some measure, have that which is commanded in the law before they can have a right to receive that which is offered in the gospel or that they must have those holy dispositions to bring to Christ which He only can bestow and for which they ought as sinners to come to Him. Thus, having the righteousness required of them in the law, and not the infinitely perfect righteousness freely offered to them in the gospel, before their eyes, their consciences are brought into trouble and perplexity; and instead of coming as sinners to Christ for righteousness and strength, they are ready to harden themselves in despair of His mercy and in aversion from Him.

As a man's ignorance of the difference between the law and the gospel is inexpressibly hurtful to him, so his being able to distinguish aright between them must be of unspeakable advantage to him. It is an attainment in which the present and future welfare of his soul is deeply concerned. If a good man understands well the leading points of distinction between them, it will, under the illuminating influence of the Holy Spirit, enable him to understand the Scriptures clearly and to reconcile all such passages as seem to contradict one another. It will also help him to determine rightly in difficult cases of conscience and so to try all doctrines by the touchstone of the Word as easily to distinguish truth from error. And if he is at any time in distress of mind, it will, in the hand of the Holy Comforter, be a special means of recovering for him that peace of conscience and joy of faith that will enable him to "serve the LORD with gladness" (Ps. 100:2). In few words, it will enable him to show such regard to the gospel as to receive, by the daily exercise of faith, the person, righteousness, and fullness of Christ therein offered to him and such respect to the law in its covenant form as to present in the hand of faith to it the consummate righteousness of Jesus Christ as the only ground of his right to justification and eternal life. It will also qualify him for honoring the law as a rule of duty by advancing in the love and practice of that universal holiness which it requires.

As it is, then, of unspeakable importance both to sinners and to saints to distinguish aright between the law and the gospel, especially in the affair of justification, I shall, in dependence on the Spirit of truth, endeavor to point out the difference between them.

The law, especially in its covenant form, and the gospel, in its strict and proper sense, may be distinguished from each other in the following respects:

1. The law, in all that is essential to it, proceeds necessarily from the very nature of God; but the gospel, in all its doctrines, offers, and promises, flows from His love, grace, and mercy, or from His goodwill to men. The manifestation of God's love, grace, and mercy in redeeming sinners to Himself was no more necessary than the display of

His wisdom, power, and goodness in creating them (Lev. 19:2; Eph. 1:4–7; 2:4–8).

2. The law is known partly by the light of nature (Rom. 2:14–15), but the gospel is known only by a revelation from heaven (Matt. 11:27). Man, though he is a fallen creature, has in some degree a natural knowledge of the law, but he has no natural knowledge of the gospel. The gospel was wrapped up in profound secrecy till it was revealed from heaven by the Son of God immediately after the fall, and therefore it is called "the mystery," and "the mystery of Christ" (Rom. 16:25; Eph. 3:4). Hence, unregenerate sinners are commonly not so averse from hearing the doctrine of the law as they are from hearing that of the gospel. Legal doctrine they can naturally understand, for it has a testimony in their consciences; but evangelical doctrine is a strange, unaccountable, and incredible doctrine to them (1 Cor. 1:23).

3. The law regards us as creatures originally formed with sufficient ability to yield perfect obedience to it; and accordingly, it requires us to retain and exert that ability in performing perfectly all the duties that we owe to God, ourselves, and our neighbors. Whereas the gospel considers us as sinners, condemned to death in all its extent and totally destitute of strength to perform the smallest degree even of sincere obedience; and it declares to us what God, as a God of infinite grace and mercy, has done and what He offers and promises still to be and do for us (Isa. 42:6–7; Matt. 18:11; Rom. 5:6–10). It declares that in the Lord Jesus believing sinners have righteousness and strength and that in Him they are justified and have life eternal. Accordingly, the doctrines, offers, and promises of it continue to be dispensed to them as long as sin remains in them, but no longer.

4. The law shows us "what manner of persons [we ought] to be in all holy conversation and godliness" (2 Peter 3:11), but it does not inform us by what means we may become such (Luke 10:27–28). Whereas, the gospel teaches us how we may be made such — namely, by union

and communion with Christ in His righteousness and fullness, or by the imputation of His righteousness to us and the sanctification of His Spirit in us (Acts 16:31; 1 Cor. 1:30; 2 Cor. 5:21; Gal. 2:16).

5. The law in its commanding power differs much from the gospel. The law says, "Do and you shall live; you shall, by performing personal and perfect obedience, entitle yourselves to eternal life" (see Matt. 19:17). Whereas the gospel says, "Live, for all is already done; all the righteousness, meritorious of eternal life for believers, is already fulfilled by the second Adam, their adorable surety. First, live in union and communion with Him, and then do—not for—but *from* life already received." The law proceeds on the supposition that we still have all that we originally had and requires perfect obedience; the gospel supposes that we have nothing and furnishes us with all that the law demands. The former requires perfection from us but offers us no supply of strength to attain to it, whereas the latter teaches us that we have it in Christ and offers it to us as an inestimable gift of grace (Rom. 5:17).

When, therefore, the law as a covenant of works comes to us with its requirements of perfect obedience as the condition of life and of complete satisfaction for sin, we ought to refer it to our divine Surety for an answer to both its demands. The law requires obedience on pain of death; the gospel attracts and encourages to obedience by the promise of life as "the gift of God…through Jesus Christ our Lord" (Rom. 6:23). The former exhibits the charge of paying what we owe for a title to life; the latter, the discharge, in consequence of its having been already paid by the Surety in our stead. The law commands faith and repentance; the gospel strictly taken does not command them, but it teaches them. It teaches every duty but commands none. The former accepts no obedience but that which is perfect and perpetual; the grace of the latter accepts, though not in a justifying righteousness, sincere obedience from persons already justified, though it is far from being perfect.

In a word, the law says, "Do this and you shall live"; but the gospel, in the dispensation of it, says, "Believe this, and you shall be saved." The law is God in a command; but the gospel is God in Christ, God in a promise. The law gives men more to do for eternal life than they are able to do; the gospel gives them less to do than they are willing to do. The law gives man all the work; the gospel gives grace all the work and all the glory.

6. The law, as it has a promise of life, is very unlike the gospel. The former promises eternal life to a man on condition of his own perfect obedience and of the obedience of no other, whereas the latter promises it on condition of the perfect obedience of Christ received by faith, and of that of no other. The promise of the law as a covenant is the promise of God as an absolute God, but the promise of the gospel is the promise of God as a God of grace in Christ. The promise of the former was to have been performed after obedience, whereas the promise of the latter begins to be performed to the true believer before, and in order to, his obedience. In the law of works the promise of privilege is grounded on the performance of duty, but in the gospel the performance of duty is founded on the promise, and even on the enjoyment, of privilege. The promise of the law is strictly conditional, but the leading promises of the gospel are, to us, entirely absolute.

7. In its condemning power, the law is very different from the gospel. The law condemns and cannot justify a sinner; the gospel justifies and cannot condemn the sinner who believes in Jesus. In the law, God appears in terrible threatenings of eternal death; in the gospel, He manifests Himself in gracious promises of life eternal. In the former, He curses as on Mount Ebal; in the latter, He blesses as on Mount Gerizim (Deut. 27:11–13). In the one, He speaks in thunder and with terrible majesty; in the other, with soft whispers or a still small voice (1 Kings 19:12). By the trumpet of the law, He proclaims war with sinners; by the jubilee-trumpet of the gospel, He publishes peace, peace on earth and goodwill toward men (Luke 2:14). The law is a sound

of terror to convinced sinners; the gospel is a joyful sound, "good tidings of great joy" (Luke 2:10). The former represents God as a God of wrath and vengeance; the latter as a God of love, grace, and mercy. The one presents Him to sinners as "a consuming fire" (Deut. 4:24); the other exhibits the precious blood of the Lamb, which quenches the fire of His righteous indignation so that it may not consume such sinners as believe. That presents to the view of the sinner a "throne for judgment" (Ps. 9:7; see Rev. 20:11–13); this a "throne of grace" (Heb. 4:16). Every sentence of condemnation in Scripture belongs to the law; every sentence of justification forms a part of the gospel. The law condemns a sinner for his first offense, but the gospel offers him the forgiveness of all his offenses.

8. The law, as it convinces sinners of sin and misery, is to be distinguished from the gospel. While the law, in the hand of the Holy Spirit, serves to convince the sinner of his sin and of his want of righteousness, the gospel presents him with a perfect righteousness for his justification before God. The law wounds and terrifies the guilty sinner; the gospel heals and comforts the guilty sinner who believes in Jesus. The one shows him that his debt is infinitely great and that he has nothing to clear it; the other informs him that by the obedience and death of Jesus, his divine surety, it is paid to the utmost farthing. The spirit of the law is a "spirit of bondage…to fear" (Rom. 8:15), but the spirit of the gospel is an ingenuous, free Spirit. The law is a house of bondage. It "gendereth to bondage" (Gal. 4:24), whereas the gospel proclaims "the opening of the prison to them that are bound" (Isa. 61:1). "By the law is the knowledge of sin" (Rom. 3:20); by the gospel is the knowledge of a Savior and remission of sin, as well as of salvation from the love, power, and practice of sin. The law says to every man, "You are a sinner." The gospel says, "The blood of Jesus Christ…cleanseth us from all sin" (1 John 1:7). The law shows the sinner his disease; the gospel presents him with healing balm, the "balm in Gilead" and the "physician there" (Jer. 8:22). The former presents grounds of fear; the latter, a foundation of hope. That reveals

God as displeased; this shows that His wrath has been endured and appeased. In the law Christ is concealed; in the gospel He, with His righteousness and salvation, is revealed and presented to sinners. The law is a killing letter, a "ministration of death"; the gospel is the "ministration of the spirit" as a spirit of life (2 Cor. 3:6–8). The former is the law of sin and death, the law that connects sin and death together; the latter is "the law of the Spirit of life in Christ Jesus" (Rom. 8:2), "the doctrine which is according to godliness" (1 Tim. 6:3). The one is "the ministration of condemnation"; the other is "the ministration of righteousness" (2 Cor. 3:9).

9. When the law is viewed in its irritating power, it differs much from the gospel. The law as a covenant, by forbidding all manner of sin and that under the most dreadful penalty, irritates the reigning depravity of the sinner; and so it is the innocent occasion of his hardening his heart the more in committing sin (Rom. 4:15), whereas the gospel and the grace revealed in it renew and melt the obdurate heart. The law, by affording sin in the depraved heart an occasion of exerting itself the more, is "the strength of sin" (1 Cor. 15:56); the grace of the gospel, on the contrary, subdues the iniquity, slays the enmity, and, in the hand of the Holy Spirit, sanctifies the heart of the believing sinner. When the love of God revealed in the gospel is known and believed with application, it melts down the obdurate heart into penitential sorrow for sin, whereas the terrors of the law increase the power of indwelling sin and harden the heart against godly sorrow.

10. Last, the law, as it admits of boasting, is very different from the gospel. "Where is boasting then?" asks the apostle Paul. "It is excluded. By what law? Of works? Nay: but by the law of faith" (Rom. 3:27). By "the law of faith" here is meant the doctrine of faith—the doctrine of a sinner's justification only on the ground of the righteousness of Jesus Christ received by faith alone. This doctrine of faith leaves the sinner no room to boast, as if he had, by his own good qualities or works, entitled himself, either in whole or in part, to justification

before God. But the law, or covenant of works, does not exclude but, when obedience is performed, admits of boasting in the creature. The gospel, or doctrine of faith, on the other hand, admits of no boasting of one's own obedience. "He that glorieth, let him glory in the Lord" (1 Cor. 1:31). "My soul," says the psalmist, "shall make her boast in the LORD" (Ps. 34:2). The apostle Paul says to the saints at Ephesus, "By grace are ye saved through faith; and that not of yourselves; it is the gift of God: not of works, lest any man should boast" (Eph. 2:8–9). The man who is under the dominion of the law of works and of a legal spirit boasts of his own works, and he hopes that they will, in a greater or lesser degree, procure justification and eternal life for him; whereas he who is under the sanctifying influence of the grace of the gospel boasts only of the righteousness of his incarnate Redeemer (Isa. 45:25; Gal. 6:14). According to the law of works, justification can only be by works of perfect and personal obedience, which admit of boasting; whereas, according to the gospel, justification can be only by faith, the only instrument of receiving Christ and His righteousness, which excludes boasting.

It may be proper here to remark that although the law and the gospel comprehend the whole doctrine of Scripture, yet they are not to be distinguished by the books of Scripture or by the Old Testament and the New. All that is contained in the books of the Old Testament is not to be considered as the doctrine of the law; neither is all that is found in the books of the New Testament to be viewed as the doctrine of the gospel. The law and the gospel are declared in each of them. In the Old Testament we find much of the gospel, and in the New we find much of the law. In many places, Moses and the Prophets publish the gospel, so that Jerome questioned whether he should call Isaiah a prophet or an evangelist. In many passages again, Christ and His apostles promulgate the law. For instance, Christ says, "He that doeth the will of my Father which is in heaven" shall enter into the kingdom of heaven (Matt. 7:21). "He that denieth me before men shall be denied before the angels of God" (Luke 12:9). "He that believeth not the Son shall not see life; but the wrath of God abideth on him" (John 3:36). His apostles also say, "The law is not of faith: but, The man who doeth them shall live in them" (Gal. 3:12). "Whosoever shall keep the whole law, and yet offend in one point, he is guilty of all" (James 2:10). "The wrath of God is revealed from heaven against all ungodliness and unrighteousness of men" (Rom. 1:18). These, and many other passages in the New Testament similar to them, contain the doctrine of the law. When a man is commanded, either in the Old Testament or in the New, to perform any work in order to secure him from temporal or eternal punishment or to entitle him to a temporal or eternal reward, it is to be accounted the doctrine of the law. On the other hand, where the blessings of salvation are declared, offered, and promised freely, without any work to be performed by sinners as the proper condition of them, all such passages, whether in the Old Testament or in the New, contain the doctrine of the gospel.

While we thus distinguish aright between the law as a covenant and the gospel strictly taken, we should always take heed that we do not apply to ourselves the gospel where the law should be applied, nor the law where the gospel ought to be applied. If we are impenitent and secure and need to be convinced of our guiltiness and misery, we ought, for this purpose, to apply the law immediately to our consciences, and not the gospel. If, on the contrary, we are truly convinced of our sinfulness and misery and are deeply sensible that we have no righteousness nor strength of our own, we should, for our relief and comfort, apply the offers and promises of the gospel to our consciences, and not the curses of the law. In the former case, we ought to apply the law as a covenant to our consciences in order to apply the gospel; in the latter, we should apply the gospel in order to be enabled to keep the law as a rule. When any question or doubt arises respecting our justification before God, the law (and works of the law) must be excluded and stand at a distance in order that grace, reigning through the righteousness of Jesus Christ to eternal life, may appear sovereign and free and that the offer and promise of the gospel, as well as the faith of the believer, may, in that momentous affair, stand alone. For although the believing sinner is not justified by a faith which is alone, yet he is justified by the instrumentality of faith alone, and that "without the deeds of the law" (Rom. 3:28; Gal. 2:16). Faith justifies not, as it is an act or work, for as such it is a work of the law, an act or work commanded in the law; but it justifies as it is the instrument or means of justification. In this instrumentality, no other grace of the Spirit and no work of the law are to be associated with it. Nor is it for its own intrinsic worth that a man is justified by the instrumentality of it, for he is nowhere said in Scripture to be justified *for* faith, but only to be justified *by* it.

⁕ REFLECTIONS ⁕

From the preceding particulars, the following reflections will be obvious to the devout and intelligent reader.

Although the covenant of works revealed in the law and the covenant of grace exhibited in the gospel are different from one another, yet they are not contrary to each other. The one is not, strictly speaking, contrary to the other but is only dissimilar to it or different from it. Whatever is required in the covenant of works as the condition of eternal life is, according to the covenant of grace, provided and given gratuitously to believing sinners. They who believe "receive abundance of grace and of the gift of righteousness [and so] reign in life by one, Jesus Christ" (Rom. 5:17). If "by one man's disobedience many were made sinners" according to the first covenant, "by the obedience of one shall many be made righteous" according to the second (v. 19). In the former, eternal life is promised to a man on condition of a perfect righteousness to be fulfilled by himself; in the latter, it is promised to a believer on condition of the infinitely perfect righteousness of Jesus Christ, received by faith and imputed by God (Rom. 8:3).

In the affair of justification, the law as a covenant of works is not only to be distinguished but to be separated from the gospel. When a true believer is at any time in doubt of his justification and title to eternal life, he ought to set the law as a covenant and the works of that law entirely aside and to rely anew, for all his title to life eternal, on the spotless righteousness of the second Adam offered to him in the gospel. He ought in that case to contemplate only the free and superabounding grace of the gospel and to embrace, by the renewed exercise of an appropriating faith, the gracious offers and promises of it. He should exclude from his view the law and all legal righteousness, and relying only on the righteousness of Christ revealed in the gospel, he should trust that this glorious, this consummate righteousness alone gives him a complete title to justification and eternal life. As it is not by the law nor the works of the law, but by means of faith only, applying the righteousness brought near in the gospel, that a man is justified before God; so in the business of his justification he must set aside all works of the law and depend wholly on the righteousness and grace of the great Redeemer. While in the business of sanctification the law as a rule is to be connected with the gospel, in that of justification the law as a covenant is always to be separated from it.

None can successfully minister true consolation to a discouraged and disconsolate believer without teaching him to distinguish, in his own case, between the law and the gospel. If the exercised Christian cannot distinguish aright between them, the consequence will be that he will often hang in anxious suspense between hope and fear. The legal temper that remains in him, availing itself of his indistinct views, will frequently prompt him to ground his hope and comfort not on the righteousness of Christ and the promises of God only, but partly on these and partly on his own endeavors to keep the law. Hence, it cannot but follow that the sins of his nature and life will often afford him greater cause to fear than his attainments and duties will to hope. Every fresh discovery of the evils of his heart and of the sin which cleaves to that obedience, on which his hope and comfort in a great measure are founded, will disquiet and perplex his soul. Thus, he will remain a stranger to settled comfort and to habitual cheerfulness of spirit in the performance of his duty. But if he is taught to distinguish aright between the law and the gospel, he will, on almost every occasion, flee from the law of works to the righteousness of Christ granted to him in the gospel and make this the sole ground of all his hope. He will rely, with settled and strong confidence, on the Lord Jesus for righteousness to justify and for grace to sanctify him.

Hence, we may also be enabled to discern when we are self-righteous and servile in the performance of our duties. We evidently are so when, instead of being constrained to obedience by the astonishing love of Christ manifested in the gospel, we are either driven to it by the slavish fear of hell or dragged to it by the mercenary hope of heaven; when we obey God not with filial affection and fear of dishonoring Him but with slavish dread of His vindictive justice and wrath; and when we labor to obey in order that our obedience may afford us a right either to salvation itself or to the Savior, either to the favor of God or to the promises of the gospel. Our manner of performing our duties is legal when we ground our comfort on anything wrought in us or done by us and when our hope of salvation rises by the liveliness of our frame in performing duties, and not by the righteousness of Christ in the offers nor by the grace and faithfulness of God in the promises of the gospel.

What has been advanced may serve likewise to show us the exceeding sinfulness, the horrible malignity, of a self-righteous temper. It strives to thwart the infinitely great and gracious design of God in giving His only begotten Son for us. The grand design of God in the inestimable gift of His dear Son to obey and suffer for us is to display in our redemption the transcendent glory of all His perfections and especially of the exceeding riches of His grace (Eph. 2:4–9). Hence, the glorious gospel is styled "the word of his grace" (Acts 20:32).

Now the legalist presumes to cross or counteract that glorious design of God as a God of grace. He would have the glory of self displayed, and not the glory of God in the person and work of

Jesus Christ; the honor of his own righteousness manifested instead of the glory of the divine Redeemer's righteousness; and the luster of his own good qualities discovered in opposition to the glory of redeeming grace. The gracious intention of the Son of God in assuming the human nature was that He might fulfill all righteousness for the elect of God, in order that grace—free, sovereign, distinguishing grace—might reign through His righteousness unto eternal life for them (Rom. 5:21). On the contrary, the intention of the legalist is to establish his own righteousness in the affair of justification and so to frustrate the design of Christ, for "if righteousness come by the law, then Christ is dead in vain" (Gal. 2:21). Thus, the self-righteous formalist resolutely sets himself in hostile opposition to the glory of redeeming grace, and so he attempts to rob the Most High of His transcendent glory as a God of grace. No man exercises evangelical repentance even in the smallest degree but he who repents of this diabolical enmity and opposition of his heart to "the glory of God in the face of Jesus Christ" (2 Cor. 4:6). And none has ever begun to mortify the members of the body of sin in his heart except he who is mortifying this self-righteous temper. Unbelief and a legal spirit are the very soul or life of the body of sin.[1] Unless the mortification of sin, therefore, begins in them, it cannot penetrate the whole body of sin.

---

1. From 1 Corinthians 15:56. Mr. Ralph Erskine infers, "The dangerous and damnable influence of legal doctrine…tends to keep sinners under the law; for thus they are under the power of sin. The legal strain, under covert of zeal for the law, has a native tendency to mar true holiness and all acceptable obedience to the law; insomuch that the greatest legalist is the greatest antinomian, or enemy to the law." [Ralph Erskine, *The Strength of Sin* (Edinburgh: Thomas Beveridge, 1729), 113.]

The Agreement between the Law and the Gospel

As the law in its covenant form and the gospel in its proper and strict sense are not contrary to one another but only different from each other, so while they differ in some respects they agree in others. As the infinitely glorious attributes of Jehovah harmonize and mingle their refulgent beams in the redemption of sinners by Jesus Christ, so His holy law and His glorious gospel agree and subserve the honor of each other in the accomplishment of that redemption.

By the harmony of the law and the gospel is meant their mutual subservience to one another, or their admirable fitness for securing and advancing the honor of each other in subordination to the glory of God—Father, Son, and Holy Spirit—as displayed in the person and work of the great Redeemer. They are admirably adapted to reflect mutual honor on one another and so to afford the most illustrious displays of the glory of their divine author. The law, as a covenant of works and a rule of life, demands nothing of sinners but what is offered and promised in the gospel; and in the gospel everything is freely promised and offered to them which the law, in any of its forms, requires of them.

The gospel presents to them for their acceptance the consummate righteousness of Jesus Christ, the surety of such sinners as believe, which fully answers every demand of the law in its covenant form and so magnifies it in that form and makes it honorable. It also exhibits to them, in its offers and promises, the infinite fullness of Christ from which they may be regenerated and sanctified and so be enabled to yield such obedience to the law as a rule of life as will in due time become perfect. While it reveals and offers righteousness to satisfy the law as a covenant, it promises and offers strength to obey the law as a rule. It promises all the supplies of grace and strength that are necessary for the acceptable performance of every duty that the law as a rule of life requires of believers. The righteousness, too, that the law as a covenant demands and the gospel affords, being imputed to believers, merits for them that holiness of heart and life that the law as a rule requires, that the gospel promises, and that is perfect in parts here and will be perfect in degrees hereafter. Thus, in general, the law and the gospel agree together or mutually subserve each other.

But more particularly, the law as a covenant of works agrees with the gospel in the following ways:

1. In its commanding power. Though it is altogether distinct from the gospel strictly taken, yet it is in concord with it. When a man cordially believes the gospel, he, in effect, presents perfect obedience to the commands of the law as a covenant. When he so believes as to "receive…the gift of righteousness" (Rom. 5:17), that perfect, that divinely excellent righteousness of the last Adam, he presents it in the hand of faith as his only righteousness for justification to the law and the justice of God; and so he cannot believe with the heart without believing unto righteousness. He cannot cordially believe the gospel without presenting, at the same time, perfect obedience to the law. Neither is it possible for him to yield perfect obedience to the law otherwise than by believing the gospel. Thus, the law and the gospel unite in serving the interests of each other. Although they are entirely distinct from each other, yet they have no separate, no interfering interest to serve. "Do we then make void the law through faith?" says the apostle Paul. "God forbid: yea, we establish the law" (Rom. 3:31).

The precepts of the law and the promises of the gospel harmoniously accord to reflect the highest honor on each other. "Is the law then," says our apostle, "against the promises of God? God forbid;

for if there had been a law given which could have given life, verily righteousness should have been by the law" (Gal. 3:21). Does the law require from the sinner a perfect human righteousness (Rom. 10:5)? The gospel affords this to it, yea, much more than this—a righteousness that is not only perfect but divine (Rom. 3:21). Are the commandments of the law "exceeding broad" (Ps. 119:96)? So is the righteousness of God our Savior revealed in the gospel. Whatever the law requires, the gospel, in the most abundant measure, supplies. Moreover, does the law command the sinner to believe in the great Redeemer (Ex. 20:3)? From the promise of the gospel, he may be amply supplied with faith (Matt. 12:21). Does it enjoin him to repent of all his sins? The grace revealed and offered in the gospel can afford him not only an occasion and a powerful motive but a disposition to "remember and turn unto the LORD" (Ps. 22:27). While the law commands the tears of penitential sorrow to flow, the gospel, and the astonishing grace promised and offered in it, *cause* them to flow (Zech. 12:10).

The authority of the law reaches to every article of the glad tidings of the gospel and obliges the sinner to believe these joyful tidings cordially and with application to himself (1 John 3:23). The law seals all the grace offered in the gospel, and the gospel, in its turn, seals, with the infinitely precious blood of Christ, all the requirements of the law. In a word, if the law requires perfect and perpetual obedience as the condition of eternal life, the gospel admits and asserts the necessity of such obedience by affording it to the believing sinner (Dan. 9:24).

2. The law in its condemning power is also in concord with the gospel. The terrors of the violated law serve, under the illuminating grace of the Holy Spirit, to show a convinced sinner his extreme need of the salvation that is presented to him in the gospel (Gal. 3:10). The tremendous curses of the righteous law pursue him closely, whatever path he chooses to take, until he begins to run upon gospel ground,

and then they drop the pursuit. If the law as a covenant is a fiery law, the blood of Jesus Christ presented in the gospel, in one view, is fuel for that flame; and in another, it serves to extinguish it. The payment of the sinner's debt of punishment by his divine Surety, offered to him in the gospel, is so complete as abundantly to answer the high demand made by the broken law (Gal. 3:13). The law's demand of satisfaction for sin is such that none but God Himself could, in a limited time, answer it; and the infinite grace of the gospel has provided that God Himself in human nature should satisfy it. "Awake, O sword, against my shepherd, and against the man that is my fellow, saith the LORD of hosts: smite the shepherd" (Zech. 13:7). The law, on the one hand, condemns all who reject the gospel (John 3:18); and the gospel, on the other, disfavors all who finally transgress the law. The terrors of the law frighten and impel convinced sinners to Jesus Christ, and the redeeming love manifested in the gospel constrains and draws them to Him (Hos. 11:4). The former lay open the wound, and the latter applies a sovereign cure. Those plow up the fallow ground, and this sows the good seed in it.

3. The law, in its commanding and condemning power considered jointly, is in harmony with the gospel. The law leads the sinner indirectly to Christ, and the gospel conducts him directly to Him. While the law is "our schoolmaster to bring us unto Christ" to teach us our absolute need of Him and, if necessary, to drive us as with a scourge to Him (Gal. 3:24), the gospel presents Christ as "the end of the law for righteousness to every one that believeth" (Rom. 10:4). The law in the hand of the Holy Spirit serves to make the awakened sinner long for and relish the grace of the gospel, and the gospel dignifies the law and renders it illustrious in his view. The law magnifies the grace of the gospel by showing the sinner his need of justification and salvation by that grace, and the grace of the gospel establishes and magnifies the law (Isa. 42:21). That the law is holy in its precepts, just

in its threatenings, and good in its promises (Rom. 7:12) the gospel not only declares but seals with the blood of the incarnate Redeemer.

While the precepts and penalties of the law serve as a guard to the gospel, the doctrines, promises, and offers of the gospel serve to support the authority and honor of the law (Matt. 5:17).

In Christ Jesus, the precepts and threatenings of the law have, to everyone who believes, their end and the promises of the gospel their establishment in order to be completely performed (2 Cor. 1:20). The truth or faithfulness pledged in the threatenings of the law and the mercy revealed in the promises of the gospel meet together in Him. The righteousness manifested in the law and the peace proclaimed in the gospel in Him embrace each other (Ps. 85:10). The law in the hand of the Spirit renders the grace of the gospel precious and desirable in the eyes of convinced sinners, and this grace, when it is received, makes the law salutary and pleasing to them (Rom. 7:22).

The law is an awful commentary on the doctrines of the gospel, especially on these: the astonishing love of God manifested in our redemption, the infinite value of the ransom paid for us, the inexpressible felicity of them who are redeemed from the curse of the law, and their infinite obligations to their God and Savior. And the gospel is a delightful commentary on the high demands and sanctions of the law. While the law is an infallible witness that sinners of mankind have those disgraceful characters under which the offers and calls of the gospel are addressed to them, the gospel exhibits in the wonderful person and work of Christ the highest proofs of the infinite authority and perpetual stability of the law. In few words, though the law does not reveal a Savior and a justifying righteousness, yet these having been revealed by the gospel, the law charges, and that on pain of the greatest condemnation, every hearer of the gospel to receive them (Mark 16:15–16). To such an infinite degree is the consummate righteousness of Jesus Christ the fulfillment of the law and the glory of the gospel that sinners of mankind are peremptorily commanded in the law and earnestly invited in the gospel to accept the gift of it and to present it in the hand of faith to the law in answer to its high demand of infinite satisfaction for sin and of perfect obedience as the condition of eternal life. Thus, the law, as it is the covenant of works, is in harmony with the gospel.

The law likewise, as a rule of life to believers, agrees with the gospel. When the law as a covenant presses a man forward or shuts him up to the faith of the gospel, the gospel urges and draws him back to the law as a rule (Lev. 11:44). The law is his schoolmaster to teach him his need of the grace of the gospel, and this grace will have his heart and his life regulated by no rule but the law (1 Peter 1:15–16). Nothing is gospel obedience but obedience to the law in the hand of Christ as a rule of duty.

The gospel is no sooner believed than obedience is yielded both to the law as a covenant and to the law as a rule. The righteousness of Christ in the hand of faith is obedience to it in the former view, and personal holiness of heart and life to it in the latter. If the law commands believers, the grace of the gospel teaches them to love and to practice universal holiness (Titus 2:11–12). What the law as a rule of life binds them to perform, the grace of the gospel constrains and enables them to do (Lev. 20:8; 2 Cor. 5:14–15). That which the precept of the law requires as a duty, the promise of the gospel affords and effects as a privilege (Ezek. 18:31; 36:26–27).

Whatever holds the place of duty in the law occupies the place of privilege in the gospel. Duties required in the law are graces, or exercises of grace, in the language of the gospel. The commands of the law reprove believers for going wrong, and the promises of the gospel, as far as they are embraced, secure their walking in the right way (Jer. 32:40). The former show them the extreme folly of backsliding; the latter are means of healing their backslidings and restoring their souls (Ps. 23:3).

The gospel, or word of Christ, dwells richly in none but in such as have the law of Christ put into their minds and written on their hearts. The law cannot be inscribed on the heart without the gospel nor the gospel without the law. As they are found together in the same divine revelation, so they dwell together harmoniously in the same believing soul. So great is the harmony between them that they can reside nowhere separate from each other. While the precepts of the law show the redeemed how very grateful and thankful they should be for redeeming grace, the grace of Christ in the gospel produces and excites that adoring gratitude. The law enjoins and excites believers to receive daily by faith more and more of the grace of the gospel to qualify them for more spiritual and lively obedience to its precepts, and the gospel supplies them with every motive, preparative, assistance, and encouragement requisite for such obedience.

The law requires true holiness of heart and of life, and the gospel promises and conveys this holiness. The former shows the nature and the properties of it; the latter, the place of it in the covenant of grace. It is by the almighty influence of the gospel in the hand of the Holy Spirit that the law is inscribed on the hearts of believers, and it is in consequence of having the law written on their hearts that they desire, trust in Christ for, and relish the blessings promised in the gospel. The law discovers to believers their duty, and the gospel the object of duty. The law enjoins the habit and exercise of faith; the gospel presents Christ, the glorious object of faith. The law requires believers to love God with all their heart, but it is the gospel only that presents God in such a view as to become an object of love to a sinner—namely, as He is in Christ reconciling the world unto Himself. The law enjoins mourning for sin; the gospel presents Christ as wounded for our transgressions—whom when believers view with the eye of faith, they mourn for Him as for an only son and are in bitterness for Him as for a firstborn. In a word, the law commands them to worship God as their God; the gospel discloses to them both the object and the way of acceptable worship.

Here it will be proper to remark that these words, "I am the LORD thy God, which have brought thee out of the land of Egypt, out of the house of bondage" (Ex. 20:2), are the preface to the Ten

Commandments as a rule of life to the true Israel of God. According to these words, all the obedience of the redeemed of the Lord to the precepts of His law is founded on His being Jehovah, their God and Redeemer. And it is remarkable that in the giving of the law at Sinai this offer or grant of Himself as Jehovah, our God and Redeemer, is five times repeated. But in these words of our redeeming God, it is the doctrine and offer of His gospel that are expressed and repeated, and that in order to enforce our obedience to every commandment of His law. The gospel, then, is that which enforces and also insures the sincere obedience of believers to the law as a rule of life. It is because God is the Lord and their God and Redeemer not only in offer but in possession that they are enabled and constrained as well as bound to keep all His commandments (Luke 1:74–75; 1 Peter 1:15–19).

So much for the agreement between the law and the gospel, or the mutual subservience of the one to the other.

✦ REFLECTIONS ✦

From the foregoing particulars, it may be inferred that a man cannot be an enemy to the gospel without being, at the same time, an enemy to the law. Every enemy to the gospel is, in the same degree, an enemy to the perfection, spirituality, and honor of the law. The law and the gospel are in such harmony with each other as to have no divided interests. The man, then, who is destitute of unfeigned love to the doctrines, offers, and promises of the gospel, however strict his profession of religion may be, is really an antinomian, an enemy to the honor of the holy law. He is an adversary to the honor of the law as a covenant of works, for by rejecting the spotless righteousness of Jesus Christ tendered to him in the gospel, he refuses to present to the law in that form the only righteousness by which it can be magnified and made honorable. He is an enemy likewise to the authority and honor of the law as a rule of duty, for by his disbelief of the offers and promises of the blessed gospel, he refuses to receive from the fullness of Christ that grace without which he cannot honor the law with so much as a single act of acceptable obedience.

Hence, also, we may learn that as the law is a transcript of all the moral perfections of God, so likewise is the gospel. The law is the image of the holiness, justice, and goodness of Jehovah, and therefore it is "holy, and just, and good" (Rom. 7:12); but so also is the gospel. Accordingly, the gospel is styled "the glorious gospel of the blessed God" (1 Tim. 1:11). The glory of the holiness, justice, and goodness of God, as well as of His wisdom and faithfulness, shines brightly in the law, but it is displayed still more illustriously in the gospel. These glorious attributes are delineated in the law, but in the gospel they are painted in the most glowing colors. Much of God is to be seen in the law, but in the gospel His infinitely glorious image is exhibited more to the life and is more eminently conspicuous (2 Cor. 3:18). The honor of His holy law, therefore, and also of His glorious gospel is infinitely dear to Him. He takes infinite complacency in beholding His righteous law magnified and made honorable by the surety-righteousness of His dear Son and in seeing a multitude that no man can number justified and sanctified according to His gospel. And all who are renewed after His image in knowledge, righteousness, and true holiness do evidence this renovation of heart by delighting in His law and by loving and admiring His gospel; by rejoicing greatly in imputed righteousness by which the demands of His law as a covenant are all answered and in salvation by sovereign grace in which the promises of His gospel are all performed.

If a man has attained a saving and experimental knowledge of the gospel, he will undoubtedly evidence it by obedience of heart and life to the law in the hand of Christ as a rule of duty. A man can never perform holy obedience to the law as long as he remains ignorant of the gospel; but when he begins spiritually to discern the truth, suitableness, and glory of the doctrine of redeeming grace, he will then begin to perform spiritual and sincere obedience to the law of Christ as a rule. Christ "died for all" who were given Him by the Father, "that they which live should not henceforth live unto themselves, but unto him which died for them, and rose again" (2 Cor. 5:15). When a man spiritually discerns and sincerely loves the grace of the gospel, he at the same time sees and loves the holiness of the law. The consequence will be that he will sincerely and cheerfully obey the law. He will yield this obedience not only because the authority of God obliges him and the love of Christ constrains him but because he discerns the beauty of the holiness that is in the law itself and loves it. While the law as a covenant is the appointed means of convincing the secure sinner of his need of that justifying righteousness which is offered to him in the gospel, the gospel, bringing righteousness and salvation to him, is the instituted means of conciliating his affection to the law as a rule of duty. Everyone, then, who knows by experience the boundless grace of the gospel will perform sincere, cheerful, and constant obedience to the law as a rule.

Is everything that is required in the law provided and promised in the gospel? Then every duty is, at the same time, a privilege or advantage to a real Christian. "Godliness with contentment is great gain" (1 Tim. 6:6). Practical godliness is the most profitable, pleasant, satisfying, and permanent gain, both for this world and that which is to come. A true believer is, in proportion as he is sanctified, rich in faith and in good works. Although the exercise of graces and the performance of duties gain nothing at the hand of God for the believer, yet they themselves are unspeakably great gain to him. He accounts it a privilege and a pleasure to have duties to perform and to have a disposition given him to perform them to the glory of his God and Savior. For as there can be no happiness without holiness, so the believer is comfortable and happy in proportion as he is holy. The more he believes the gospel with application and trusts cordially in the Lord Jesus for salvation to himself in particular and the more his "faith…worketh by love" (Gal. 5:6), so much the more communion with Christ and enjoyment of God as his infinite portion does he attain. The legalist expects happiness for his duties, but the true believer enjoys it in them; and the less he expects for them, the more he enjoys in them.

Finally, do the law and the gospel harmoniously agree and subserve the honor of each other? Then let believers always take heed that they do not set them in opposition to one another. Beware, O believer, of ever setting the law in hostile opposition to the gospel or the gospel in opposition to the law. Never, in your exercise of graces or performance of duties, set them at variance one against the other. Study to understand clearly, on the one hand, the difference; and on the other, the agreement between them, that knowing distinctly in what respects they differ and in what they agree, you may, in your exercise, make the one subservient to the honor of the other and both subservient to the glory of God in your sanctification and consolation. Clear and just views, especially of the agreement between the law and the gospel, tend exceedingly, under the influences of the Spirit of truth, to promote an evangelical, holy, and cheerful frame of spirit. Under such views, you will be able to guard more effectually against setting the law in opposition to the gospel by relying on your own graces and duties for a right to the favor and enjoyment of God and against setting the gospel at variance with the law by taking the smallest encouragement from the gospel to neglect the performance of any of the duties required in the law.

CHAPTER 9

The Establishment of the Law by the Gospel

Although in the immediately preceding chapter I have anticipated some of the thoughts that will be expressed here, yet the subject of this chapter is of such inexpressible importance that I cannot forbear considering it by itself. After the apostle Paul had, in the third chapter of his epistle to the Romans, asserted and proved that all mankind are sinners and that the justification of believing sinners in the sight of God is utterly unattainable by their own righteousness and is entirely founded on the surety-righteousness of Jesus Christ, imputed by grace and received by faith, he has in the following words obviated an objection which he foresaw would be made to that fundamental doctrine: "Do we then make void the law through faith? God forbid; yea, we establish the law" (Rom. 3:31). One of the objections then made, and still urged by the enemies of the gospel, against the doctrine of a sinner's free justification for the righteousness of Christ received by faith is that it derogates from the honor and obligation of the law—nay, that it annuls or abrogates the law. "Do we then," says he, by asserting that a man is justified by faith only and not by the works of the law, "make void," or nullify, the obligation of the moral law? With deep abhorrence of such an insinuation, he replies, "God forbid"—far be it from us; on the contrary, we, by that doctrine, do "establish the law."

It is as if he had said, "We are so far from making void or annulling the law through faith that we thereby establish and make it stand in all its force." By "the law" here, the apostle cannot mean the ceremonial law, for by the word of faith as preached by the apostles of Christ this was made void, but the moral law, and that both as a covenant of works and as a rule of life. By "faith," in this place, the apostle seems to mean both the doctrine of faith and the grace of faith. The doctrine of faith is the gospel strictly taken as distinguished from the law. The grace of faith is that grace of the Holy Spirit in the hearts of regenerate persons by the exercise of which they receive that doctrine and the righteousness and salvation exhibited in it.

It will be proper here, in order to prevent mistakes concerning what is afterward to be advanced, to remark that to make the law void is so to abrogate, abolish, or set it aside as to prevent it from being any longer binding on the conscience. It is to annul the divine authority and obligation of its precepts and penalties. The moral law, as the law of the infinitely glorious Jehovah, is enforced by all His sovereign and immutable authority. His infinite authority enforces every precept of it and lays every rational creature under the firmest obligations possible to yield perfect obedience to it. Now, to make this law void is to set aside its high authority and obligation, or to decline the authority and dissolve the obligation of its righteous precepts. Not that any man can do this effectually, but his attempting either directly or indirectly to do it is as criminal as if he could accomplish his design. To make it void is also to attempt setting aside the perfection, spirituality, and great extent of it. A man may be said to make void the law when he practically declares that the perfection, spirituality, and vast extent of it are not to be regarded, or when he puts it off as a covenant with imperfect and even with carnal, selfish, superficial, and partial obedience. Every sinner is guilty of this who goes about to establish his own righteousness in order to his justification, or endeavors to satisfy the law with imperfect instead of perfect obedience, with carnal instead of spiritual performances, and with partial instead of universal obedience.

To make the law void is likewise to invalidate the perpetuity of it. Not that any sinner has it in his power effectually to do this—for the moral law continues to be of immutable and eternal obligation on all who are under it—but he attempts to abolish the perpetuity of it with respect to himself by persuading himself that although it originally obliged him to perform perfect obedience, yet now, in consequence of the mediation of Christ, it obliges him to yield such obedience no longer (Jude 4) and by presuming to satisfy the requirements of it as a covenant with sincere instead of perfect obedience, as if it ceased to require perfection of obedience any longer.

Moreover, when sinners under the curse of it labor to persuade themselves that it cannot now exact from them perfect and perpetual obedience on pain of its tremendous curse or when they stifle their convictions and try to keep their consciences easy under the condemning sentence of it, they do what they can to make it void. In few words, they may be said to make the law void when they deliberately set aside any of the uses of it. Though it cannot, since the entrance of sin into the world, justify sinners on the ground of their own obedience to it, yet, as was observed above, it is of standing use to sinners as well as to saints. Now if sinners set aside any of its uses, or refuse to "use it lawfully" (1 Tim. 1:8), they thereby treat it with contempt, as if it was useless and insignificant. It is in these ways especially that self-righteous men attempt to make void the law of God.

I shall now endeavor to show that all true believers do, through faith, not only not make void the moral law but, on the contrary, establish it or make it stand in all its force. To establish the law is, as was hinted above, to make all the infinite authority and obligation of it stand firm, or to place them on their original and immovable basis and instead of invalidating to confirm or strengthen them. Believers, then, do by faith—that is, by the doctrine and the grace of faith—establish the law.

In the first place, by the doctrine of faith, they do not make the law void but establish it, and that both as a covenant of works and as a rule of life.

1. By the doctrine of faith, or the gospel strictly taken, all true believers and faithful ministers of the word do establish the law as it is a covenant of works. For in the first place, it is the doctrine of faith that shows men how firm and irreversible the law as a covenant is and how infinitely concerned the glorious Majesty of heaven is for the stability and honor of that holy law. According to that doctrine, He will save no transgressors of it but on condition of His only begotten Son's being made under it as their surety and of His answering completely all the demands of it in their stead. He will not save them from the full execution of its righteous and awful penalty but upon Christ's enduring it for them, nor account them righteous and entitled to eternal life but upon His performing as their substitute the perfect obedience which it requires as the condition of life. Thus, by the doctrine of faith, the sovereign authority of the law in its covenant form is acknowledged and declared, its infinite obligation on sinners of mankind is confirmed, and its honor is completely secured.

Second, according to the doctrines of grace in general and to the doctrine of a sinner's justification by faith without the works of the law in particular, the law in that form is, as has been already said, of standing use to convince sinners of their sin and misery, to discover to them their need of a better righteousness than their own, and so to render Christ and His perfect righteousness precious to such of them as believe. A sinner must be convinced by the law that justification on the footing of his own obedience is absolutely impossible before he will listen to what the gospel says of Christ and His righteousness (Rom. 7:9). Accordingly, the Spirit of God does not lead a man to Christ by the gospel without first convincing him of sin and of his want of righteousness by the law.

Third, by that doctrine we are informed that the law received a complete answer to all its high demands by the unsinning obedience and satisfactory death of the Lord Jesus, the surety of elect sinners. We are thereby instructed that He came into the world not to destroy but to fulfill the law (Matt. 5:17) and that He "is the end of the law for righteousness to every one that believeth" (Rom. 10:4). According to the doctrine of faith, the law as a covenant receives from our divine Surety all the obedience and satisfaction which it can demand. He, in the room and as the representative of an elect world, fulfilled all the righteousness of it (Matt. 3:15). He yielded to it perfect holiness of human nature, perfect obedience of life, and complete satisfaction for sin; and from His divine nature, united to the human in His infinitely glorious person, His whole righteousness has derived such infinite value as to be strictly meritorious of eternal life for His spiritual seed.

According to that doctrine, the law in its federal form is far more honored by the righteousness of the second Adam than it was dishonored by the disobedience of the first. It is represented as honored not only by a perfect righteousness but by the righteousness of God, the righteousness of Him who is God as well as man. In proportion to the stupendous humiliation of the Son of God, who stooped so low as to become subject to a law that was adapted only to creatures who as such are infinitely beneath Him, is the honor done to the precept and penalty of that law by His obeying the one and His enduring the other. It required only a human righteousness, but it is infinitely honored with one that is divine (Isa. 42:21; 2 Cor. 5:21). Now by this consummate, transcendently glorious righteousness that is revealed in the gospel, the sovereign authority and high obligation of the law are most illustriously displayed and most firmly established.

2. By the doctrine of faith, the law is also established as rule of life to believers. According to this doctrine, it is established in the hand of the Son of God, the glorious Mediator, whom the eternal Father has given for a "commander to the people" (Isa. 55:4) and has set as His king and lawgiver "upon [His] holy hill of Zion" (Ps. 2:6). In the hand of the adorable Mediator, the sovereign authority of the law, as the instrument of government in His spiritual kingdom and as the rule of duty in His holy covenant, is confirmed; and the high obligation of it is not only confirmed but increased.

Although believers are, in their justification, delivered from the law as a covenant of works (Rom. 7:4–6), yet according to the gospel they are represented as "being not without law to God, but under the law to Christ" (1 Cor. 9:21; see also Gal. 6:2). In the doctrine of faith, the eternal obligation of the law on them is declared; obedience to it is enforced by the strongest motives and represented as performed under the best influences, from the best principles, and for the best ends. According to that doctrine, all believers are bound by infinite authority to obey; they are enabled sincerely to obey; they are constrained by redeeming love to obey; they resolve and delight in dependence on promised grace to obey; and they cannot but obey the law as a rule of duty. The love of Christ, as revealed in the gospel, urges them; the blood of Christ redeems them; the Spirit of Christ enables them; and the exceeding great and precious promises of Christ encourage them to obey and yield spiritual and acceptable obedience. The holy law as a rule is written on their hearts, and therefore they "consent unto the law that it is good" (Rom. 7:16) and "delight in the law of God after the inward man" (v. 22). While they do not obey it for life, but from life, they account obedience to it not only their duty but their privilege and their pleasure. Thus, according to the doctrine of faith, they present, in the hand of faith, perfect righteousness to the law as a covenant of works; and they perform, as the fruit of faith, sincere obedience to it as a rule of duty. And so effectually do they, by the doctrine of faith, establish the law as a rule of duty that they never account their obedience to any of the precepts of it sincere and acceptable but in proportion as their performance of it flows from the unfeigned faith of that doctrine. In their view, nothing is obedience to it but what proceeds from evangelical principles and is excited by evangelical motives.

In the last place, by the grace of faith also, believers do establish the law, and that both as a covenant of works and as a rule of life.

1. By the grace of faith, they do not make void the law but, on the contrary, they establish it as it is a covenant of works. Sinners who are destitute of the grace of faith have such mean, disparaging notions of the holy law as to offer to it, in answer to its demand of perfect obedience as the condition of life, their own partial, superficial, and polluted works instead of the perfect righteousness of Jesus Christ. But true believers have such high and honorable sentiments of the authority and obligation, as well as of the perfection, spirituality, and vast extent of the divine law in its federal form, as to receive and present to it, in the hand of faith, the consummate and glorious righteousness of their adorable Surety.

Instead of making void the law, they, by the habit and exercise of their holy faith, consult in the most effectual manner the stability and honor of its precepts and penalties. Instead of presuming to put it off as a covenant with their own mean and imperfect performances, they, by the exercise of their faith, appropriate and present to it the infinitely perfect and meritorious righteousness of their divine Redeemer as the only ground of their security from eternal death and of their title to eternal life. By faith they receive and exhibit to it Christ's holiness of human nature and obedience of life in answer to its demand of perfect obedience as the condition of life and His suffering of death in answer to its demand of infinite satisfaction for sin. Thus, by the habit and exercise of their faith, they recognize and assert the sovereign authority and high obligation of it as a covenant, and so they establish and make it honorable in that form. By presenting to it the only righteousness that can fully satisfy its just demands, they practically assert the divine and immutable authority of it as well as the equity and reasonableness of its demands. "Surely, shall one say, in the LORD have I righteousness and strength: even to him shall men come; and all that are incensed against him shall be ashamed. In the LORD shall all the seed of Israel be justified, and shall glory'" (Isa. 45:24–25). "I will make mention of thy righteousness, even of thine only" (Ps. 71:16). "Yea doubtless, and I count all things but loss for the excellency of the knowledge of Christ Jesus my Lord…that I may win Christ, and be found in him, not having mine own righteousness, which is of the law, but that which is through the faith of Christ, the righteousness which is of God by faith" (Phil. 3:8–9). "The LORD is well pleased for his righteousness' sake; he will magnify the law, and make it honorable" (Isa. 42:21).

2. By the grace of faith, believers do not make void the law but establish it likewise as a rule of life. Instead of setting it aside as the rule of duty, faith makes it stand in all its binding force. By the habit and exercise of their faith, the saints not only believe that the authority of the law in the hand of the glorious Mediator is infinite, immutable, and eternal and that the obligation which it lays on them even to perfect obedience is firm and unalterable, but they derive from the fullness of Christ continual supplies of grace to enable them to perform sincere and increasing obedience to all the commands of it. By the exercise of faith, they receive from His fullness that conformity of heart to the holy law which is perfect in parts and that conformity both of heart and of life to it which will afterward be perfect in degrees. And when they shall attain perfect conformity, or ability to yield perfect obedience to it in the mansions of glory, this they shall attain as the end of their faith, as the completion of that eternal salvation which they receive by faith. All acceptable obedience to the law in the hand of Christ must be "the obedience of faith" (Rom. 16:26), obedience springing from vital union with Him by faith as the principle of it and performed in consequence of grace derived by faith from His overflowing fullness. As it is believers, and they only, who are under the law as a rule in the hand of the Mediator, so it is they, and they only, who are enabled to perform that sincere, holy obedience which flows from faith working by love. That faith is neither a true nor a living faith which is not accompanied with sincere and universal obedience to the law of Christ; and that obedience is neither sincere nor

universal nor acceptable to God which does not proceed from the habit and exercise of a living faith (Heb. 11:6).

Till a man has saving faith implanted in his heart by the omnipotent agency of the Holy Spirit, he can do nothing but transgress the commandments of God's holy law (Prov. 21:4). He can trample on the authority and despise the obligation of it, but he cannot, either in principle or in practice, establish it. It is only they who are justified and sanctified by the instrumentality of faith who begin and advance in such holy obedience as honors and establish the law as a rule of duty. We may as soon suppose that a living man can be without vital acts as that a man who is by faith vitally united to Christ can live without yielding such obedience to His law. When that living faith which works by love is implanted and increased in his heart, vital motions and acts of spiritual obedience cannot but follow. Such a man will not only account it a privilege and a pleasure to yield sincere obedience to the law as the rule of his duty in time but will rejoice in the cheering prospect of being able to honor it with perfect obedience through eternity. He delights in it after the inward man (Rom. 7:22), and therefore he rejoices in the hope that, by the grace of his adorable Redeemer, he shall be eternally bound *by* it and eternally conformed *to* it.

Thus, it is evident that true believers and faithful ministers of the gospel do not, either by the doctrine or the grace of faith, make void the law of God; but on the contrary, they establish it, and that both as a covenant of works and as a rule of life.

✦REFLECTIONS✦

From what has been said, we may learn what reason we have to highly esteem the divine law. The establishment of this holy law, by both the doctrine and the grace of faith, has entered deeply into the wonderful plan of our redemption by Jesus Christ. That amazing scheme has been so devised as to secure, in the most effectual and astonishing manner, the stability and honor of the law as well as the manifested glory of the sovereign Lawgiver. As the ultimate end that God has proposed to Himself in our redemption is the glory of His infinite perfections, so His chief subordinate end, as the righteous governor of the universe, is the honor of His holy law.

Such is the inestimable value that Jehovah the Father sets on His righteous law that, rather than suffer the honor of it to be in the least obscured, He would expose His only begotten, His infinitely dear Son to the deepest abasement, the most direful anguish, and the most ignominious and tormenting death. He would have His only Son, in the human nature, to live a holy and righteous life under the curse of His law. This was in order to answer its demand of perfect obedience as the condition of life and to endure the infinite execution of that curse due to His elect for sin, so as to be brought to the dust of death in order to answer its demand of infinite satisfaction for sin. The Lord Jesus, according to the everlasting covenant made with Him, must submit to all this humiliation, service, and suffering so that the honor of the divine law might be vindicated and the sovereign authority of it established. Ought not we, then, to regard the law of God with the highest esteem and veneration and to tremble at the most distant thought of ever disobeying any of its holy commands?

Is the law established by the gospel? Surely the gospel, then, cannot have the smallest tendency to licentiousness, either in principle or in practice. If it tends to establish the sovereign authority of the divine law, it cannot, surely at the same time, tend to weaken or set aside that authority. The gospel, when it is accompanied with the demonstration of the Spirit of God and is received in the love of it, does not only excite the believer to obey the law as a rule of duty, but it is the only doctrine that can excite and dispose him to yield to it voluntary and sincere obedience. It does not only establish the law, but it is the only doctrine that infinite wisdom employs to establish it, the only "doctrine which is according to godliness" (1 Tim. 6:3).

It is true that this heavenly doctrine which God has made the city of refuge for guilty sinners is by many, alas, made a sanctuary for sin, and so is wickedly abused to licentiousness. But it is one thing to view the gospel in itself and in its genuine tendency, and another to consider it as it is perversely abused by wicked men (Rom. 3:8). The immediate principle of all acceptable obedience to the law as a rule of life is supreme love to God, but we cannot love God supremely except we first know and believe His love to us as it is exhibited in the blessed gospel. "We love him," says the apostle John, "because he first loved us" (1 John 4:19). As the sun cannot be without light and heat, so the faith of Christ and of redeeming love as offered to us in the gospel cannot be without that love to Christ and to God in Him which "is the fulfilling of the law" (Rom. 13:10).

The second Adam's perfect holiness of human nature and obedience of life to the precept of the law as a covenant are as necessary to the justification of sinners as His suffering of its penalty is. The doctrine of justification by faith establishes the law, the whole law, the honor of the precept as well as that of the penal sanction. But this it could not do if it did not represent the righteousness of Jesus Christ as consisting in His active obedience as well as in His passive. Active obedience, strictly speaking, cannot be said to satisfy vindictive justice for sin. And, on the other hand, "suffering for punishment gives right and title unto nothing, only satisfies for something; nor does it deserve any reward."[1]

Christ's satisfaction for sin could not render His perfect obedience to the precept unnecessary, nor could His perfect obedience make His satisfaction for sin by suffering the penalty unnecessary because it was not of the same kind. The one is that which answers the law's demand of perfect obedience as the ground of title to eternal life; the other is that which answers its demand of complete satisfaction to divine justice for sin. The meritorious obedience of Christ to the precept could not satisfy the penal sanction, and the sufferings and death of Christ could not satisfy the precept of the law. The

---

1. Owen on justification. [John Owen, *The Doctrine of Justification by Faith*, in *The Works of John Owen*, ed. William H. Goold (1850–1853; repr., Edinburgh: Banner of Truth, 1965), 5:266.]

commandment of the law as a covenant requires doing for life; the curse of that law demands dying as the punishment of sin. These, though they are never to be separated as grounds of justification, yet are carefully to be distinguished. The perfect obedience of Christ is as necessary to entitle believers to eternal life as His suffering of death is to secure them from eternal death. His satisfaction for sin, applied by faith, renders them innocent or guiltless of death; and His obedience makes them righteous or worthy of life (Rom. 5:19). As the latter, then, is as necessary to complete their justification, according to the gospel, as the former, so it is as requisite as the former to establish the honor of the law.

It is evident also from the foregoing particulars that the righteousness of Christ which is revealed in the gospel and which is presented in the hand of faith to the law as a covenant is not only the meritorious cause but the matter of our justification before God and in the eye of the law. It is right, indeed, to style it the meritorious cause of justification, but this is not sufficient; it is, besides, the matter of it. Many pharisaic professors of religion have admitted that the righteousness of Christ is the meritorious cause of justification; that is, as they understand the phrase, that Christ, by His righteousness, has merited that our own obedience should justify us. It is not enough, then, to say that His consummate righteousness is the meritorious cause but beside, that it is the matter of our justification; the very righteousness for which, or on account of which, we are justified. The righteousness of our divine Surety, received by faith and according to the doctrine of faith, imputed to us is that which justifies, that which is the immediate and the only ground of justification, and that only in which it can be safe, consistently with the authority and honor of the law, to stand before the dreadful tribunal of the omniscient and righteous Judge of the world.

The divine law is established and honored more in the salvation of one sinner than in the damnation of all the sons of men. In the justification and salvation of a believing sinner, both the precept and the penalty of the law are established and honored; but in the damnation of unbelievers, it is the penal sanction only that is honored. The holy precept will never, in their case, be honored with obedience, far less with perfect obedience. The convinced and alarmed sinner who wishes to believe in the Lord Jesus may, for his encouragement, warrantably and successfully plead that at the throne of grace.

Is the holy law as a rule of life put into the reader's mind and written on his heart? Then it rejoices his heart. "The statutes of the LORD are right, rejoicing the heart" (Ps. 19:8). The apostle Paul accordingly says, "I delight in the law of God after the inward man" (Rom. 7:22). When a man is justified and, as an evidence of that, is sanctified, he rejoices to think that the law as a covenant is honored and established by the righteousness which his faith receives for his justification and that the law as a rule is established by the grace which his faith derives from Christ for his sanctification. He rejoices to reflect that as the law is established forever, so it is "holy, and just, and good" (Rom. 7:12). Instead of wishing that it were less extensive or spiritual or strict, he rejoices that every command and even every threatening are what they are. He meditates on the holy commandments of God with delight and takes pleasure in hearing them explained to him and enforced on him. Nothing, perhaps, is a surer symptom of reigning hypocrisy in a man than to take pleasure in hearing the promises and blessings of the gospel preached to him but to disrelish all such discourses as, even by evangelical motives, enforce the duties of the law on him. It is only the man who is secretly resolved not to perform all his duties who commonly is unwilling to hear of them.

What has been said may serve to suggest to us how deep and inveterate the depravity of human nature is. Unregenerate men either suspect that the law is made void if it is asserted that a man is justified by faith without the works of it, or they suppose that good works are unnecessary. The spirit which is in them is either that of the Pharisee or that of the libertine. They are ready to conclude that if they are not to be justified on the ground of their own obedience to the law, the authority of the law is annulled (Gal. 3:19) or that if their works are to form no part of their righteousness for justification, they need not perform good works at all. They choose to be at liberty either to establish their own righteousness in the affair of justification or to continue secure in the love and practice of sin; either to expect justification by the law as a covenant or to trample on the authority of the law as a rule. They either quarrel with the gospel, as if it made void the law, or dishonor the law, as if it was an enemy to the gospel. To leave the self-righteous man no works of his own to boast of is too humbling to be endured. It appears strange to him that he himself should do nothing in order to merit his justification. Whenever he reads or hears that justification is by faith only, "without the deeds of the law" (Rom. 3:28), he is disposed to count it a licentious doctrine. He can see no necessity for his obedience but to merit divine favor and eternal life by it. And no sooner does a man under the dominion of enmity to God and His law pretend to be justified without his own works than he neglects good works, as if they were wholly unnecessary. Thus, do unregenerate men discover their inveterate enmity both against the law and the gospel of God.

Was it requisite that the Lord Jesus, in order to repair the honor of the law, should, as the surety of elect sinners, endure the full execution of its condemning sentence due to them for sin? We may hence see what a malignant, detestable, and horrible thing sin is. How exceeding sinful, how infinitely displeasing to the Lord, and how injurious to the honor of His righteous law must it be when even His own dear Son must suffer infinite punishment, and that without the smallest abatement, in order to satisfy His justice and vindicate the honor of His law! How inconceivably detestable must it be to the holy Lord God, seeing He chose rather that His only begotten Son should endure all the tremendous punishment of it than that it should pass unpunished! Should not we, then, learn to abhor, to repent of, and to forsake all manner of sin?

Is it by the doctrine and the grace of faith that we establish the law? Then it is plain that they who transform the gospel or doctrine of faith into a new law requiring faith, repentance, and sincere obedience as the proper conditions of salvation thereby make void the law. By substituting sincere faith and sincere obedience in place of perfect obedience as grounds of title to justification, they make void the law as a covenant; and by inventing what they call "gospel precepts," requiring sincerity only in place of those old and immutable precepts that require of believers perfect obedience, they invalidate the authority of the law as a rule. By asserting that "Christ, having satisfied for the breach of the old law of works, has procured and given a new law, a remedial law, or a law of milder terms than the old, suited to our fallen state and accepting of sincere obedience instead of that perfect obedience which the old law required"; that "Christ has, by His death, obtained that our sincere obedience to this remedial law should be accepted for a gospel righteousness and that we are truly justified before God by gospel works"; that "the act of faith as the principle of all sincere obedience is our righteousness, which entitles us to justification and eternal life"; and that "the act of faith is our justifying righteousness, not as it receives the righteousness of Jesus Christ, but as it is our obedience to that new law."

By these assertions, I say, they set aside the obligation of the moral law and so make it void. Though such men have usually been called legalists, yet perhaps they may, with more propriety, be termed antinomians, or enemies to the authority and honor of the divine law.[2] They undermine, as was already hinted, the whole authority and honor of it both as a covenant of works and as a rule of life. Reader, the moment you rely on your faith and obedience for a title to justification before God, you thereby rob the law as a covenant both of its commanding and condemning power; and no sooner do you satisfy yourself with yielding merely sincere obedience instead of

---

2. See Simeon's *Helps to Composition*, skeleton 71. [Charles Simeon, *Helps to Composition; or, Six Hundred Skeletons of Sermons*, 3rd ed. (London: Luke Hanserd and Sons, for T. Cadell and W. Davies, 1815), 1:454–57.]

pressing on to perfection than you invalidate the high obligation of the law as a rule of duty.

Finally, it may hence also be inferred that it is the first duty of every unregenerate sinner to come to Jesus Christ and to trust cordially in Him for deliverance from the law as a covenant and for ability to perform acceptable obedience to the law as a rule. Be assured, O secure sinner, that you cannot otherwise be delivered from the law as a covenant of works than by union with the second Adam and communion with Him in His righteousness, and that without deliverance from the dominion of the law as a covenant, you cannot be saved from the guilt and dominion of sin. "The strength of sin is the law" (1 Cor. 15:56). Now, it is absolutely impossible for you ever to attain union with Christ and communion with Him in His righteousness otherwise than by a true and living faith. "The righteousness of God," of Him who is God in our nature, "is by faith of Jesus Christ unto all and upon all them that believe" (Rom. 3:22). Believe then in the Lord Jesus, that by means of faith you may be found in Him and be justified in Him. Trust in Him who is Jehovah Our Righteousness (Jer. 23:6) for justification and complete salvation. Receive the gift of His glorious righteousness and, as a guilty sinner, rely on it for all your title to justification before God. Present it in the hand of faith as your justifying righteousness, to the law as a covenant of works in answer to its just demands of perfect obedience and of complete satisfaction for sin. So shall you, by faith, establish the law as it is a covenant of works.

Trust in Christ also for grace and strength to perform sincere obedience to the law as a rule of life. Rely on His consummate righteousness for all your title to sanctification and glorification; trust in Him with all your heart for sufficient supplies of sanctifying and comforting grace to enable you to yield acceptable obedience to the law as a rule and to press on toward perfection of obedience. And by this obedience of faith, you will establish His law as a rule of duty. By well doing, you will put to silence the ignorance of such foolish men as presume to say that the doctrine and faith of the gospel are unfriendly to the interests of true morality.[3]

Indeed, both the doctrine and the grace of faith are evidently, yea, and designedly injurious to heathen morality as well as pharisaic righteousness. But with regard to true morality, which forms a necessary part of godliness or evangelical holiness instead of being, in the smallest degree, injurious to this, they directly tend to it; yea, and they are the necessary, the fundamental principles of it. Sooner might fire be without heat and a solid body be without weight than a true faith of the gospel be without evangelical holiness.

---

3. This reminds me of what Theodorus long ago replied to Philocles, who was often hinting that he preached doctrines which tended to licentiousness because he enlarged diligently and frequently upon faith in Jesus Christ:

> "I preach salvation by Jesus Christ," said Theodorus, "and give me leave to ask, whether you know what salvation by Christ means?" Philocles began to blush, and would have declined an answer. "No," said Theodorus, "you must permit me to insist upon a reply. Because if it is a right one, it will justify me and my conduct. If it is a wrong one, it will prove that you blame you know not what, and that you have more reason to inform yourself than to censure others." This disconcerted him still more, upon which Theodorus proceeded. "Salvation by Jesus Christ means not only a deliverance from the guilt, but also from the power of sin. 'He gave Himself for us, that He might redeem us from all iniquity' (Titus 2:14) and 'redeem us from our vain conversation' (cf. 1 Peter 1:18) as well as deliver us from the wrath to come. Go now, Philocles, and tell the world that, by teaching these doctrines, I promote the cause of licentiousness. And you will be just as rational, just as candid, just as true, as if you should affirm that the firemen, by running the engine and pouring in water, burnt your house to the ground, and laid your furniture in ashes."

[James Hervey, *Theron and Aspasio* (London: John and James Rivington, 1755), 2:66–67n. Hervey may have created a fictional dialogue here, similar to the conversation between Theodorus and Philonous in David Fordyce, *Theodorus: A Dialogue concerning the Art of Preaching* (London: R. Dodsley, 1752).]

CHAPTER 10

The Believer's Privilege of Being Dead to the Law as a Covenant of Works, with a Highly Important Consequence of It

The apostle Paul, when speaking in his epistle to the Romans of this important privilege, expresses himself thus: "Wherefore, my brethren, ye also are become dead to the law by the body of Christ.... But now we are delivered from the law, that being dead wherein we were held" (Rom. 7:4, 6). By "the law" in these passages, our apostle evidently means not so much the ceremonial as the moral law under the form of a covenant of works. For it is the same law that says that "a man should not steal" and "should not commit adultery" (2:21–22). It is also the law which, "what things soever the law saith, it saith to them who are under the law: that every mouth may be stopped, and all the world may become guilty before God" (3:19). It is also the law by which "is the knowledge of sin" and which is not "made void… through faith" but on the contrary is established (vv. 20, 31). It is the law, likewise, which "entered, that the offence might abound" (5:20) and of which the apostle speaks thus:

> When we were in the flesh, the motions of sins, which were by the law, did work in our members to bring forth fruit unto death.... I had not known sin, but by the law: for I had not known lust, except the law had said, Thou shalt not covet.... I was alive without the law once: but when the commandment came, sin revived, and I died.... The commandment, which was ordained to life, I found to be unto death.... The law is holy, and the commandment holy, and just, and good.... Sin by the commandment [became] exceeding sinful.... We know that the law is spiritual.... I consent unto the law that it is good.... I delight in the law of God after the

inward man.... With the mind I myself serve the law of God" (7:5, 7, 9–10, 12, 13, 14, 16, 22, 25).

The law in question is that law, the work of which the Gentiles show to be "written in their hearts" (Rom. 2:15); that law by the transgression of which "Jews and Gentiles...are all under sin" (3:9); that law against which "all have sinned, and come short of the glory of God" (v. 23); and that law without which "there is no transgression" (4:15). It is also the law to which, as their first husband, the believers in Rome were, in their unregenerate state, espoused and by which they were held (7:4–6). But most, if not all, of those believers were Gentiles (1:13; 11:13), who were never held by the ceremonial law of the Jews and therefore could not be said to have been delivered from it. In a word, it is that law the righteousness of which was fulfilled in those believers (8:4).

Now in most, if not all, of those passages the things asserted by our apostle are peculiar to the moral law. This, then, is the law that he had in view when he affirmed to those believers that they had become dead to, or were delivered from, the law and that the law in which they had been held was dead to them. But lest they should imagine that it was the law of creation and the law as a rule of life to which they were dead, he compared the law of which he was speaking to the law of a husband (Rom. 7:2–3), which is a covenant or contract between him and his spouse and which establishes her relation to him as long as they both live. By this comparison he plainly hinted to them that it was the moral law not as a rule of life but as a covenant of works, only to which they were dead. The believers at Rome, then, were dead to the law in its covenant form, or were delivered from it, and it was dead to them, so that it could no longer hold them in subjection to its precept of perfect obedience as the condition of life nor to its sentence of condemnation for sin (v. 6).

As it was the privilege of the Christians in Rome, so it is the privilege of all true Christians in every place and in every age, that they are dead to the law as a covenant of works and that the law in that form is dead to them. They are dead to it—that is, they are delivered from the dominion or obligation of it in that form and also from a prevailing desire to be under it. The righteousness of the second Adam, by which He fully answered in their stead all the requirements of it as a covenant, is graciously imputed to them; and therefore, in that form, it has nothing more to demand from them. Its demands of perfect obedience as the condition of eternal life and of complete satisfaction for sin have, by their divine Surety, been fully answered for them. His surety-righteousness, received by faith and imputed by God to them, is their righteousness for the "justification of life" (Rom. 5:18), their complete answer to all the demands of the law as a covenant of works.

The consequence is that though the law in that form is not, with regard to them, abrogated, yet it is fulfilled and satisfied; and being fully satisfied by them in their Surety and representative, it will not, it cannot, oblige them in their own persons to answer the same demands a second time. The holy and just law of God will never exact from them a double payment of the same debt. Thus, true believers are, in their justification, "delivered" from the dominion and obligation of the law, as it is a covenant of works. And, as they are delivered from it, or dead to it, in that form, so it is dead to them. For the apostle not only compares it to a dead husband, to whom the surviving spouse is, by the law of marriage, no longer bound, but he says plainly "that being dead wherein we were held" (Rom. 7:6; see also v. 2). The law as a covenant is dead to believers since it will not and cannot exercise any commanding or condemning power over them. It can neither justify them for their personal obedience nor condemn them for their disobedience (8:1–3). "True believers," as our excellent confession of faith expresses it, are "not under the law as a covenant of works, to be thereby justified or condemned."[1] On the ground of Christ's fulfilling it in their stead, they are delivered from all its demands of personal

---

1. Westminster Confession of Faith 19.6.

and perfect obedience and of punishment for sin in order to justification before God.

In order to explain the meaning of what has now been said, as well as to pave the way for what is afterward to be advanced on this fundamental and important subject, it will be proper to remark that since Christ, the second Adam, performed perfectly all that, according to the covenant of works, was to have been done by man himself to entitle him to life, and that seeing all that He did and suffered is imputed to sinners who believe, believers therefore are justified in the sight of God. They are in the very same state, with respect to righteousness entitling them to life, in which they would have been had the first Adam fulfilled for himself and his posterity the condition of life in the covenant of works. Accordingly, we read that the just by faith are entitled to the same life to which man, by his fulfillment of that condition, would have been entitled (Hab. 2:4; Rom. 10:5).

If Adam had continued to yield perfect obedience until the time appointed for his trial had elapsed, he, as the representative of his descendants, would have entered on a state of confirmation in holiness and happiness or in the begun possession of eternal life; and the covenant of works, as a contract fulfilled on his part, would henceforth have continued to be an everlasting security to him for his own and his posterity's enjoyment of the eternal life promised him for himself and them. But in this state of confirmation, the law as a covenant could not have continued to be the rule of his obedience because to subject him still to the law in its federal form as the rule of his duty would have been to reduce him again to a state of trial and to require him to work over again for that life to which he was already entitled by his having performed the condition of the covenant.

At the same time, as man could in no state whatever be released from his obligation to obey his Creator, he must have had a rule of obedience. And as the law as a covenant could not, for the reason now mentioned, have been a rule to him, it follows that in his state of confirmation the law of nature, divested of its covenant form or of its promise of life and threatening of death, would have been the immutable rule of his obedience, both in time and in eternity. As the first Adam, then, upon his having fulfilled the condition of the covenant of works for himself and his posterity, would have been released from the obligation of the law in that form, so they to whom the righteousness of the second Adam is imputed for the justification of life are delivered from the law in its federal form and, at the same time, they continue under it as the law of Christ and as divested of that form.

The Lord Jesus, as the representative and surety of elect sinners, condescended to subject Himself, in their stead, to the moral law as a covenant of works in order to redeem them from it in its covenant form. The apostle Paul informs us that "God sent forth his Son, made of a woman, made under the law, to redeem them that were under the law" (Gal. 4:4–5). From this passage it is plain that Christ was made under the law in that form in which they whom He came to redeem were under it. Now as they were under it as a covenant of works, it was requisite that He also should be made under it as a covenant of works in order to answer for them all its demands in that form and so to redeem them from the bondage of it. Were any man to suppose or affirm that Christ was made under the law not as a covenant but merely as a rule, according to such a supposition the meaning of the passage cited above would be this: "God sent forth his Son, made under the law as a rule, to redeem them who were under the law as a rule from the authority and obligation of it and consequently from all obedience to it." Now would not this be the very soul of antinomianism? Would it not be to make the Holy One of God the minister of sin? Far be it from us to suppose it possible for the holy, inspired apostle to teach such doctrine as that!

As it is chiefly the moral law of which our apostle is there speaking, his meaning then must be that the Son of God became subject to that law not as a rule of life to believers but only as a covenant of works in order to redeem sinners from it in its covenant form.

By the covenant of works, a twofold connection is established between sin and eternal death—one between a state of sin and eternal death, and another between thoughts, words, and acts of sin and eternal death. The former is indissoluble and cannot but remain firm. A sinner cannot be in a state of unbelief and sin without being, at the same time, under the dominion of spiritual death and bound over by the curse of the violated law to death eternal. Accordingly, such threatenings as these, "He that believeth not the Son shall not see life; but the wrath of God abideth on him" (John 3:36); and "If ye live after the flesh, ye shall die" (Rom. 8:13) do bind over all unbelieving and impenitent sinners, continuing in their state of sin under the law as a covenant, to eternal death. The latter is dissolvable and, to all true believers, is actually dissolved. In the satisfaction given by Christ and imputed to believers, the penalty of eternal death with regard to them is already satisfied; and therefore, the execution of it can never be renewed on them. Their debt of satisfaction for sin, being already discharged, cannot be charged a second time (John 5:24). The covenant form of the law, or "the law of sin and death" (Rom. 8:2), is so dissolved to believers that it can no longer promise eternal life to them for their personal obedience nor threaten them with eternal death for their disobedience. And indeed, how can it either threaten eternal death or promise eternal life to believers who, in their justification on the ground of the infinitely perfect righteousness of Jesus Christ imputed to them, have already escaped eternal death and have already not only a complete title to life eternal but a begun possession of it (John 3:16; Acts 13:39; Rom. 6:14). In the Oracles of Truth, we are informed that saints on earth are, upon their vital union with the second Adam, as really possessed of eternal life as the saints in heaven are and that sinners who have no such union with Him are as really under the begun execution of the sentence of eternal death as the damned in hell are, though in a far lower degree (John 3:36; 5:24).

Believers are dead to the law as a covenant, relatively and really. They are dead to it relatively, or with respect to their state before the

Lord. This is the happy, inestimable privilege of all who are instated in the covenant of grace and justified before God. As the relation between husband and spouse is dissolved by death (Rom. 7:2), so the relation between the law as a covenant and believers is, in the moment of their justification, dissolved (v. 4). The moment they become alive in the eye of the law, they become dead to the law. And as their justification is at once perfect, so is their deliverance from the law as a covenant. As the former admits of no higher and lower degrees, neither does the latter. It is the peculiar privilege of them who are in a state of union with Christ and of justification in Him to be wholly delivered from the covenant of works. They "are not under the law, but under grace" (6:14)—not under the law or covenant of works, but under the covenant of grace. Believers are also dead to the law as a covenant really, or in respect of their inclination and practice. Though a legal temper remains in them, yet the dominion of it is taken away; and therefore, they no longer desire to be under the law as a covenant or to go about as formerly "to establish their own righteousness" in the affair of justification (10:3). But they rely only on the righteousness of God their Savior for all their title to life eternal.

At the same time, seeing that some degree of a legal spirit, or of an inclination of heart to the way of the covenant of works, still remains in them and often prevails against them, they sometimes find it extremely difficult to resist that inclination to rely on their own attainments and performances for some part of their title to the favor and enjoyment of God. If at any season they are uncommonly frequent and lively in their exercise of graces and performance of duties, they then especially find it inexpressibly difficult to refrain from flattering themselves that such exercises and duties entitle them, in some degree, either to the Savior Himself or to the joy of His salvation. Indeed, they find nothing in their spiritual exercise more difficult than so to mortify their legal temper as to die to all hope from the law as a covenant. This death to the law, then, admits of degrees in believers, and it will not be perfect in any of them as long as sin remains in them. They cannot, in their practice, become perfectly dead to the law till they are perfectly dead to sin. Their relative death to the law of works is perfect, but their real death to it is imperfect. The former is the dissolution of a relation; the latter is the gradual extinction of a disposition. The one refers to their justification; the other to their sanctification.

There are two errors respecting the deliverance of believers from the law that are equally contrary to the Oracles of Truth. The one is that of the legalist who maintains that believers are still under the moral law as a covenant of works; the other is that of the antinomian who affirms that believers are not under it even as a rule of life. These errors are as contrary to the Scriptures of truth as they are to each other, and they are equally subversive to that evangelical holiness which is a principal part of eternal life and which is so requisite that without it no man shall see the Lord (Heb. 12:14). The plain doctrine of Scripture is this: that while true believers are dead to or delivered from the law as a law or covenant of works, they are under it and account it their high privilege to be under the infinite obligation of it as a rule of life. Indeed, to be freed from the law in its federal form is nothing more than to be delivered from the covenant of works and from an inclination to cleave to that covenant; and our affirming according to the Scriptures that believers are delivered from the law as a covenant of works necessarily implies that they are under the law in some other respect. Accordingly, the apostle Paul informs us that they are "not without law to God, but under the law to Christ" (1 Cor. 9:21); that is, they are under the law of the Ten Commandments as the law of Christ, or as the law in the hand of Christ the Mediator. No man can live to God, in point of sanctification, till after he becomes dead to the law as a covenant in justification; neither can he otherwise live to God than by holy conformity of heart and life to the law as a rule of duty (Gal. 2:19). The death of legal hope in him is necessary to a life of evangelical obedience.

Having premised these observations in order to prevent mistakes and to enable the candid reader to understand with more ease that which is to follow, I shall now take a more particular view of the important subject and consider, first, what it is in the law as a covenant of works to which believers are dead; second, what is included in their being dead to the law under that form; in the third place, the means of their having become dead to the law as a covenant; fourth, the consequence of it; and last, the necessity.

⋅ SECTION 1 ⋅
What It Is in the Law as a Covenant of Works to Which Believers Are Dead

It is true believers, and they only, who are become dead to the law as a covenant. All unbelievers are alive to it. They are under the dominion of it, and indeed they so cleave to it as to desire to be under its dominion. They resolutely persist in relying on their own obedience to that law for a title to justification and eternal life. On the contrary, all true believers, having been convinced of their utter inability both to yield perfect obedience to the precept as the condition of life and to suffer the dreadful penalty of it so as to give full satisfaction to divine justice for their innumerable transgressions, receive the perfect righteousness of Jesus Christ, which not only satisfies but magnifies the law; and so they "become dead to the law by the body of Christ" (Rom. 7:4). Upon their union with the second Adam and communion with Him in His righteousness, they are delivered, as has been observed above, both from the obligation of the law in its federal form and from a reigning inclination of heart to be under it in that form. Being already justified and, in their justification, wholly delivered from condemnation (8:1), they are no longer "under the law as a covenant of works, to be thereby justified or condemned."[2] They are set free from the dominion, or power, of it. There are four sorts of power belonging to the law as a covenant from which believers are delivered—namely,

---

2. Westminster Confession of Faith 19.6.

the commanding power, the promising or justifying power, the condemning power, and the irritating power of it.

1. Believers are, in the act of justification, set free from the commanding power of the law as a covenant of works. This will be evident if we consider that in case of transgression, the commanding and condemning power of the law as a covenant are inseparable. By the condemning sentence of the law of that covenant, every transgressor of its commands is bound over to eternal death. "Cursed is every one that continueth not in all things which are written in the book of the law to do them" (Gal. 3:10). "Now we know that what things soever the law saith, it saith to them who are under the law" (Rom. 3:19); as if the apostle had said, "Whatever things the law says, especially in its condemning sentence, it says to those who are under the commanding power of it." If believers, then, are still under the commanding power of the law as a broken covenant of works, they must also be still under its condemning power and so be, every moment, bound over to eternal death since every moment they come short of perfect obedience to its commands. But they are not under the condemning power of the law as a covenant of works (Rom. 8:1; Gal. 3:13). And therefore, they are not under the commanding power of the law in its covenant form.

Our apostle does not say to the believers in Rome, "You have become dead to the curse of the law merely," but, "Ye also are become dead to the law," and, "We are delivered from the law" (Rom. 7:4, 6)—from the law itself, from that which is most essential to the law in its federal form. In another place he addresses them thus: "Ye are not under the law, but under grace" (6:14). Neither does he say here, "You are not under the condemning sentence or curse of the law," but, "Ye are not under the law."

The style of the apostle on this topic is remarkable. Of Christ he says He was "made under the law" (Gal. 4:4). To believers in union with Christ he says, "Ye are not under the law." This plainly shows that they are not under it as a covenant, in the sense in which He was under it. But He was under its commanding power as a covenant as well as under its condemning power. Considered as the surety of elect sinners, He was as much bound to perform perfect obedience to its precept as to suffer the full execution of its penalty (Matt. 3:15; Heb. 10:9). Therefore, believers are not under the commanding power of it as a covenant of works. Justified on the ground of that consummate righteousness that Christ in their stead fulfilled in answer to its demands of perfect obedience and full satisfaction for sin, they are delivered as much from the commanding as from the condemning power of it. He discharged their debt of perfect obedience to the precept for eternal life as fully as He did their debt of infinite satisfaction to the penalty of the law of works.

The precept requiring perfect obedience as the condition of life is the principal part of the law, or covenant of works. "This do, and thou shalt live" (Luke 10:28). "If thou wilt enter into life, keep the commandments" (Matt. 19:17). It is to this precept requiring perfect and personal obedience as the condition of life, and requiring it on pain of eternal death for the smallest failure, that believers are dead. The reader, I hope, will not mistake me. I do not say that believers are delivered from the precepts of the law simply, but only that they are set free from them in their federal form. The precept to perform perfect obedience simply is not the command of the covenant of works. Man was bound to perfect obedience previous to the covenant of works and would have been obliged to perform it though such a covenant had never been made with him, for it is essential to the divine law to be a rule of human obedience but not to be a covenant of works.[3] But

---

3. The reader is here requested to observe that although the law and its commands as a covenant and a rule are *formally* different, yet they are *materially* the same. Though the true believer, therefore, is in his justification delivered from them in their federal form or under the form of a covenant of works, yet he still is, and cannot but be, under the whole original authority and obligation of them as his rule of duty. He continues to be firmly bound, as will afterward be explained, by the precepts of the law as a rule of life to personal and perfect obedience not only in time but even to all eternity. His

the command to perform perfect obedience as the condition of life is the form of that covenant.

Now it is from the command only in this form that believers are set free. And the ground of their deliverance from the precept of the law in its federal form, or from the rigorous demand of perfect obedience as the condition of life, is the perfect obedience of their divine Surety to it in their stead. This is the proper condition of life to all His spiritual seed. "By the righteousness of one the free gift came upon all men unto justification of life.… By the obedience of one shall many be made righteous" (Rom. 5:18–19). The obligation to do, or to obey, the law is eternally binding on all believers; but from the obligation to do and live, to do in order to procure a title to eternal life, they are delivered. They are under immutable and eternal obligations to yield perfect obedience to the law of the Ten Commandments as a rule of life, but they are delivered from the obligation and, in a great measure, from the desire to yield in their own persons perfect obedience to it as a covenant of life. Eternal life is, by the perfect obedience of their adorable Surety, already merited for them; and therefore, though they are under every obligation to obey from life, they are under no obligation to obey for life.[4] Nay, to attempt obedience in order to procure a title to eternal life, especially after they have been already, by the consummate righteousness of Jesus Christ imputed to them, perfectly entitled to it would, instead of being their duty, be their aggravated sin (Gal. 5:4).

---

obligation to perfect and perpetual obedience, instead of being in the smallest degree relaxed by his having been delivered from them in their federal form, is thereby increased and confirmed.

4. The famous Dr. Owen was not afraid to say "that the whole power and sanction of the first covenant was conferred upon Christ, and in Him fulfilled and ended." [John Owen, "To the Reader," in Samuel Petto, *The Difference between the Old and New Covenant Stated and Explained* (London: Elizabeth Calvert, 1674), no pagination. For a modern reprint, see Samuel Petto, *The Great Mystery of the Covenant of Grace* (Port St. Lucie, Fla.: Solid Ground Christian Books, 2020).]

2. Believers are also set free from the promising or justifying power of the law as a covenant of works. The promise of the covenant of works is a promise of eternal life on condition of personal and perfect obedience to the law in its covenant form. Now, since believers are released from their obligation to yield perfect obedience for life, as required in that covenant, they are no more to expect eternal life as promised in it. They hold all their title to life eternal in the second Adam, their blessed Surety. In Him they have that perfect righteousness to which eternal life is promised and which is the only foundation of their sure title to it. Their own sincere obedience is not the legal ground of their title to life; and therefore, it has not the legal promise of life. Their evangelical obedience is an evidence of their union with the last Adam, and communion with Him in His righteousness has, indeed, a promise of the covenant of grace connecting eternal life with it (Rom. 2:7; 1 Tim. 4:8). But of the promise of eternal life in the covenant of works, which makes a man's own obedience the ground of his right to justification and eternal life, the law to believers is wholly divested. The law as a covenant makes no promise of life but to the man who performs personal and perfect obedience. But to believers, this rigor of the law in that form is relaxed; a responsible surety is admitted and allowed to take their place in law, to whose perfect and meritorious righteousness imputed to them eternal life is promised. Believing, then, in the Lord Jesus, they have eternal life not according to the promise of the first covenant but according to that of the second (Titus 1:2; Rom. 5:21, respectively).

3. Believers are, in their justification, delivered likewise from the condemning power of the law as a covenant. The law in its federal form condemns every sinner who is under it to death in all its dreadful extent. Spiritual, temporal, and eternal death is the awful penalty of the law in that form. "In the day that thou eatest thereof thou shalt surely die" (Gen. 2:17). "The wages of sin is death" (Rom. 6:23). But as the law is so divested of its promise of life to believers that it cannot

justify them for their obedience, so it is denuded of its threatening of death to them, and it cannot condemn them for their disobedience. In consequence of communion with Christ in His righteousness, by which the law's demand of infinite satisfaction for sin is completely answered, they are dead to it as a covenant of works, and it is dead to them. It has no more power to frown on them or condemn them than a dead husband has to frown on his deceased spouse.

Hence are these cheering passages of Scripture: "Christ hath redeemed us from the curse of the law, being made a curse for us" (Gal. 3:13). "He that heareth my word, and believeth on him that sent me, hath everlasting life, and shall not come into condemnation" (John 5:24). "There is therefore now no condemnation to them which are in Christ Jesus, who walk not after the flesh, but after the Spirit" (Rom. 8:1). When a man is justified in the sight of God, all his past, present, and future sins are together and at once pardoned. The guilt of eternal wrath for his past and present iniquities is actually and formally removed. The obligation under which he was lying to suffer eternal punishment for those transgressions is completely dissolved. And the guilt of eternal wrath for sins to come is, in the act of his justification, effectually prevented from recurring on him. For although this pardon of sins yet to come is not a formal remission of these sins but merely a nonimputation of them, yet it effectually secures the believer from ever coming into or falling under condemnation (John 5:24). This distinction between the formal remission of sins past and present and the not imputing of sins to come is clearly marked in the Oracles of Truth (Ps. 32:1–2; Rom. 4:7–8). Thus, in their justification, true believers are fully and forever set free from the condemning sentence or curse of the law as a broken covenant.[5] For as in legal estimation they sinned and fell under the condemning sentence of the law as a covenant in the first Adam, so they endured the execution of

---

5. Westminster Confession of Faith 20.1.

that sentence and thereby satisfied divine justice in the second Adam (Gal. 2:20; Eph. 2:6).

4. Last, believers are, in consequence of their justification, set free from the irritating power of the law as a covenant. While the commanding, promising, and condemning powers of the law in its federal form are essential to it in that form, the irritating power of it is only accidental. It is occasional or accidental merely that motions of sin are by the law. When a man under the covenant of works and the dominion of sin obtains a transient view of the purity, spirituality, and strictness of the law and at the same time of his innumerable and aggravated transgressions of it, with the tremendous wrath to which they have exposed him, this not only fills his mind with a disquieting dread of hell but inflames the corruptions of his heart and makes them rage vehemently against the holy law. The evil passions of his depraved nature, irritated by the purity of the precepts and the severity of the curses of the law as a covenant, urge him more violently to the commission of that which it prohibits. The law, strictly forbidding all motions of sin in his heart, and that without affording him the smallest degree of strength to resist them, irritates, provokes, and so renders them fiercer and more intractable.

Accordingly, the apostle Paul says of himself and of the believers in Rome in their unregenerate state, "When we were in the flesh, the motions of sins, which were by the law, did work in our members to bring forth fruit unto death" (Rom. 7:5). And of himself in particular he says, "Sin, taking occasion by the commandment, wrought in me all manner of concupiscence" (v. 8). This is not to be imputed as a fault to the holy law but is wholly to be charged to the reigning depravity of the sinner's nature; for although the law never gives the sinner any just occasion of committing sin, yet the inveterate corruption of his nature takes occasion from the holy strictness of its precepts and the awful severity of its threatenings to rise in violent opposition to it and to work in him all manner of sinful desire to that which is forbidden in it and because it is forbidden. Like a mighty torrent that rises, rages, and overflows, the more that means are employed to stop its current, the reigning depravity of the heart, rising in rebellion against the holy commandment, bursts forth with the greater impetuosity and irresistibly employs all the faculties of the soul and all the members of the body "as instruments of unrighteousness unto sin" (6:13). Now believers are graciously delivered from this irritating power of the law as a broken covenant. Trusting in the Lord Jesus for complete salvation, relying on His meritorious righteousness for all their title to life eternal, constrained by His redeeming love, and enabled by His sanctifying Spirit to mortify their depravity and perform spiritual obedience, they delight in the law as a rule of duty and serve God in newness of Spirit (7:6).[6]

Thus, it is plain that true believers are dead to the commanding, promising, condemning, and irritating power of the law as a covenant of works.

✦ SECTION 2 ✦

*What the Believer's Being Dead to the Law
as a Covenant Includes*

It is the inestimable privilege as well as the indispensable duty of all who have believed through grace to be "dead to the law" as a covenant of works (Rom. 7:4). To be dead to it relatively, or with respect to their state, is their exalted privilege; and to become dead to it really, in the disposition of their minds, is their bound duty. The latter is both a consequence and an evidence of the former. Now to be dead to the law in its federal form comprises especially the following particulars:

---

6. It is not here insinuated that believers are, in this world, *perfectly* set free from the irritating power of the law. As, in their practice, they are dying to it only as a covenant, so in proportion to the degree of the legal temper that remains in them they may on many occasions be exposed to its irritating power.

1. Their despairing of salvation by the works of the law. In death there is no hope, but "to him that is joined to all the living there is hope" (Eccl. 9:4). They who are alive to the law as a covenant have hope from the law and from their own works of obedience to the law. They presume to hope that God will justify and save them because they intend well and do well, because they are just in their dealings and diligent in their duties, or because they wrong no man and endeavor to perform as many good works as, consistently with human infirmity, they can. Thus, they are "going about to establish their own righteousness" as the foundation of their hope (Rom. 10:3); and "touching the righteousness which is in the law," they fancy that they are "blameless" (Phil. 3:6). And though they say that without Christ they cannot be saved, yet their hope of salvation is founded on their own obedience to the law. On the contrary, they who are justified by the faith of Christ and are dead to the law have no expectation from the law, no hope of justification or title to life by the works of the law. They see plainly that no righteousness can secure them from eternal death and entitle them to eternal life but one that is in all respects perfect.

2. Believers being dead to the law includes an entire dissolution of the relation between them and the law as a covenant. In death the relations between husband and wife, master and servant are dissolved. "The servant is free from his master" (Job 3:19). In like manner, when they who are justified by faith are dead to the law, the former relation between them and it is dissolved. As long as they were alive to the law as a covenant, that relation stood firm. They were "debtor[s] to do the whole law" (Gal. 5:3). They were bound to give infinite satisfaction for their sins and to yield perfect and perpetual obedience as the condition of life.

But now that they have, in the hand of faith, presented to the law the perfect and infinitely meritorious righteousness of their divine Surety, which answers fully all its demands on them, they are honorably as well as legally acquitted from their obligation to suffer for satisfaction to divine justice and to yield perfect obedience for a right to eternal life. They are, indeed, obliged still to obey the holy law of God, but not to obey it as a covenant of works, not to obey it in order to procure a title to justification and eternal life. They are now divorced from the law as a covenant, their first husband, and are "married to another, even to him who is raised from the dead" (Rom. 7:4). They are dead to the law in that form and the law is dead to them, so that their relation to it as a covenant is entirely dissolved. The redeemed of the Lord, therefore, should no more expect eternal life for their own works than a widow would hope for favors and comforts from a dead husband. They are no more exposed to the curses of the broken law than a widow is to the threats of a husband who is lying in the grave. For inasmuch as deliverance from a covenant is the dissolution of a relation that does not admit of degrees, they, in respect of their state before the Lord, are perfectly or wholly set free from the covenant of works.

3. The death of believers to the law comprises also their deliverance from anxious concern or care about the works of the law in the affair of justification. "There is no work," says Solomon, "nor device, nor knowledge, nor wisdom, in the grave, whither thou goest" (Eccl. 9:10). In death there is no concern or solicitude about performing any work. A dead body in the grave is nowise careful to do any of the works in which it was employed when alive. So they who are dead to the law as a covenant of works, though they are careful to maintain good works, yet have no care about the works of the law in the affair of justification. They work, but they do not, as formerly, work for life. While they were alive to the law, all their concern was "to establish their own righteousness" and to rely on it for the justification of life (Rom. 10:3); but now that they are dead to the law, they no longer have any allowed solicitude of that kind.

4. Last, in their becoming dead to the law as a covenant, believers enter into rest. When a man dies, he rests from his labors. There is no labor, no wearisome toil, in the grave. "There the weary be at rest"

(Job 3:17). They who are alive to the law are wearied in the greatness of their way (Isa. 57:10). The law, as a covenant, appoints them a wearisome task. It requires from them perfect and continual obedience as the condition of life, and that without affording them the smallest degree of strength to perform it; and it loads them with direful and overwhelming curses if the task is not performed. The consequence is that in going about to establish their own righteousness, they are weary and heavy laden. But when a sinner, in compliance with the call of the gospel, comes wearied and heavy laden as he is to the Lord Jesus, He gives him rest (Matt. 11:28). Having thus "become dead to the law by the body of Christ" (Rom. 7:4), the weary is at rest. He attains rest to his conscience in the righteousness of Christ, for He "is the end of the law for righteousness to every one that believeth" (Rom. 10:4). He also obtains rest to his affections in the fullness of Christ and in God as his God and portion. In proportion as his legal spirit is mortified, he rests from his legal and slavish fear of that wrath which is threatened in the law. He is at rest also from those legal cares and sorrows which attended his self-righteous and laborious efforts. He rests from his legal desires and delights.

Formerly, he desired to be under the law as a covenant, and he sought righteousness "as it were by the works of the law" (Rom. 9:32). He delighted, too, in his own righteousness and in the hope of justification on the ground of it. But now that he has become dead to the law, he ceases from these desires and delights. He no more delights in himself nor in his legal performances, for he now sees that all such "righteousnesses are as filthy rags" (Isa. 64:6). Nay, though, instead of being so polluted and defective as they are, they were even perfect, yet he now takes no pleasure in justification by the works of the law as a covenant (Job 9:15, 21). On the contrary, beholding the incomparable excellence of the way of justification and salvation in the covenant of grace, he desires above all things to be found in Christ Jesus, not having his own righteousness that is of the law, but "that which is through the faith of Christ," that he "may know him, and the power of his resurrection, and the fellowship of his sufferings" (Phil. 3:9–10).

✦ SECTION 3 ✦

The Means of Becoming Dead to the Law as a Covenant of Works

The apostle Paul, in his epistle to the Galatians, says of himself, "I through the law am dead to the law" (2:19). The means, then, of becoming dead to the law as a covenant is the law itself. This, at first view, may seem a very strange and unlikely means of attaining such a purpose; but on due attention to the subject, it will be found that no means are, in the hand of the Holy Spirit, so well adapted to divorce a sinner from the law in its federal form as the law itself. The law indeed is not the cause, but it is the occasion of a man's becoming dead to it as a covenant; for it accuses, condemns, and terrifies the awakened sinner, and so it urges him to flee speedily for refuge to Jesus Christ, who is the real cause of one's becoming dead to the law. "The law was our schoolmaster," says the apostle, "to bring us unto Christ, that we might be justified by faith" (Gal. 3:24). To bring a sinner to Christ is no proper effect of the law, but yet it is occasioned by the law inasmuch as the law forces him away from itself and leaves him no ground of hope that he shall ever be justified by his own obedience to it. The law, by the strictness of its precepts and the severity and terror of its threatenings, is an occasion to him of seeking righteousness and eternal life where they are to be found. To be dead, then, to the law through the law is, by means of the strictness and rigor of the law, or of a work of legal conviction and humiliation, to be driven to Christ for justification by faith "without the deeds of the law" (Rom. 3:28).

When the Holy Spirit sets the law home to the conscience of a sinner, the following effects of the work of the law are means of his becoming dead to it as a covenant of works:

1. Through the law as a covenant, an awakened sinner attains discoveries of the infinite holiness, justice, and majesty of the Lord. Since the law is not only a declaration of the will of God but a transcript of His moral image, no sooner is the understanding of a sinner enlightened than, in the glass of the law and by the light of the Spirit, he begins to discern the spotless holiness of God. He perceives in God's forbidding the smallest degree of sin and requiring the highest degree of every duty, and that on pain of the most tremendous punishment, that He hates sin and loves holiness in an infinite degree and, therefore, His nature and will are infinitely and immutably holy. In the glass of the law, the sinner also discerns the inflexible justice of the divine nature. He sees that, in requiring perfect conformity of heart and life to His righteous law, the Lord requires nothing but what every rational creature owes Him, and that in threatening death in all its dreadful extent and duration for the very smallest sin, He threatens nothing but what is justly due to the sinner.

Perceiving that God requires nothing but what is just and reasonable and that He prohibits nothing but what is unjust and unreasonable, the sinner now sees that the strictest equity is displayed in all the precepts of the law. Discerning at the same time that every sin committed against the infinite Majesty of heaven justly deserves infinite punishment, he sees that the highest justice appears also in the penalty of the law. Through the law, he discerns, likewise, the glorious majesty of the Lord. The law of the King eternal, immortal, and invisible is a royal law. The greatness and dignity of it deserve that it should be honored with perfect and perpetual obedience. It is clothed with majesty, it binds the conscience, it demands the obedience of the heart as well as of the life, and it must be universally as well as perfectly obeyed. Through the law, then, the awakened sinner discerns not only the holiness and righteousness but the majesty of the sovereign Lawgiver, "who is able to save and to destroy" (James 4:12). When therefore the commandment, clothed especially with the majesty of the Lord, comes into his conscience, sin will revive, and self-confidence and legal hope will die (Rom. 7:9). When he hears the great and terrible God Himself speaking to him in His law, he will be constrained to cry, "Enter not into judgment with thy servant: for in thy sight shall no man living be justified" (Ps. 143:2).

2. By means of the law in the hand of the Spirit, a sinner is made to discern the divine authority and majesty of the law itself. Under a convincing work of the Holy Spirit, he begins to consider the law in its federal form as the law of Jehovah, as the ordinance of the one Lawgiver who is the uncreated fountain of authority and the sovereign Judge of angels and of men. Regarding it as the law of the infinite Majesty of heaven, he, in the light of the Spirit, begins to see that it bears immutable impressions not only of truth and rectitude but of divine authority and supreme majesty. Beholding the face of Jehovah in His righteous law and conscious that his provocations of Him are innumerable, the sinner cannot but be struck with remorse and dread. When he hears the Most High God speaking to him in His fiery law, he will be ready to exclaim, "If thou, LORD, shouldest mark iniquities, O Lord, who shall stand?" (Ps. 130:3). Thus, the divine authority and majesty of the law, coming into the conscience, destroy all expectation of life by the works of the law.

3. Through the law, an awakened sinner also discerns the holiness, spirituality, vast extent, and perfection of the law itself in its covenant form. The Holy Spirit opens the eyes of his understanding to see the strict conformity of the commandment to the holy nature and will of God. The apostle Paul, speaking of himself as unregenerate, says in a passage quoted above, "I was alive without the law once: but when the commandment came, sin revived, and I died" (Rom. 7:9), as if he had said, "Touching the righteousness which is in the law, I was blameless. I imagined that I was sufficiently holy and righteous. But when I began to discern the spotless holiness of the divine law, sin revived and I died. I then was convinced that I was a sinner indeed, and so I

died to all hope of justification and of eternal life by my own obedience to the law."

By the same means the sinner discerns not only the holiness but the spirituality of the law. "We know," says the apostle, "that the law is spiritual" (Rom. 7:14). No sooner are the eyes of a man's understanding opened than he sees that the law is the authoritative and binding rule of all the dispositions, thoughts, and motions of his heart, as well as of all the words and actions of his life. When he begins, under the convincing influences of the Holy Spirit, to understand the meaning and to feel the power especially of this command, "Thou shalt not covet" (v. 7), his hope of life by his own righteousness perishes. He now sees that every divine precept requires spiritual obedience, the service of the whole heart as well as of the whole life. He also discerns the great extent of the holy law. "Thy commandment," says the psalmist, "is exceeding broad" (Ps. 119:96).

When he sees that the commandment extends to all his inclinations, affections, and designs and to all his thoughts, words, and actions, he begins to be convinced that he has no righteousness answerable to the requirements of the holy law. No sooner is his awakened conscience informed of the breadth and length of the righteousness required in the law than he is convinced that his own righteousness is a bed "shorter than that a man can stretch himself on it: and the covering narrower than that he can wrap himself in it" (Isa. 28:20). Thus, through his discovery of the vast extent of the law as a covenant, sin revives in his conscience, and he dies to all hope of justification by his own righteousness.

Moreover, "the law of the LORD is perfect" (Ps. 19:7). It requires, on pain of eternal death, perfect and unceasing obedience as the condition of eternal life. So absolutely perfect, indeed, is this holy law that the man who "yet offend[s] in one point, he is guilty of all" (James 2:10). To disobey any one command, though in a single instance, is an insult offered to the divine authority of the whole law. When a man, then, is convinced that he has, in innumerable instances, presumed to transgress this righteous and perfect law, he cannot but acknowledge himself to be so guilty before God as to be justly condemned by the violated law to eternal death. And when that conviction is not counterfeit but true, he cannot but renounce all confidence in his own righteousness for a right to eternal life and so "become dead to the law" (Rom. 7:4).

4. By means of the law as a covenant, a sinner attains the knowledge of sin. "By the law is the knowledge of sin" (Rom. 3:20). In proportion as a man is truly convinced of sin or is conscious of his having transgressed the divine law, he discerns not only the reality but the malignancy and hatefulness of his sin. He sees that while it is a transgression of the law of God, it is directly opposite to the holy nature and will of God. Sin now appears sin and, by the commandment, becomes in his view exceeding sinful (7:13). By the commandment, the Holy Spirit convinces him that his nature is not only destitute of original righteousness but is wholly corrupted; that this corruption of his whole nature is not merely the consequence and evidence of his having been guilty of Adam's first sin, but is the source of all the innumerable transgressions of his life; that he is under the dominion, or power, of sin; and that the law, instead of having the smallest tendency to rescue him from the power of sin, is itself "the strength of sin" (1 Cor. 15:56). Now, when he is enabled thus to discern the nature and dominion of the sin that dwells in him, he becomes dead to all hope of eternal life by the works of the law.

5. Through the law, he likewise attains alarming discoveries of that tremendous wrath which is revealed from heaven against him for his innumerable transgressions. Convinced of sin by the law, the sinner is made to see that by the curse of the broken law he is bound over to suffer eternal punishment. As by the precept of the law in its federal form he is convinced of the evil nature of sin and of its desert of punishment, so by the penalty of the law he attains the knowledge of the dreadful consequences of sin. The law, under the convincing

influences of the Holy Spirit, shows him plainly that the fiery indignation, the intolerable, overwhelming, and endless wrath of the great and terrible God, is the sure, the direful consequence of his transgression. This "wrath of God is revealed from heaven" to him not in groundless alarms of approaching danger but in threatenings as certain as they are terrible (Rom. 1:18).

Now when the convinced sinner thus begins to see that "the wages of sin is death" (Rom. 6:23) and that he in particular is justly condemned to endure the fierceness of Jehovah's wrath, the fury of His almighty indignation not for an age or millions of ages but forever and ever, his hope of salvation by the works of the law will perish. He now sees clearly that the penalty of the violated law is not to be satisfied by doing, but by suffering. Thus, his conviction of guilt and wrath by the threatenings of the law tends to destroy his confidence in his own righteousness, and so to render him dead to the law. For he cannot now but see and feel that he is imprisoned or "concluded all under sin" (Gal. 3:22) and that none can say to such a prisoner, "Go forth," but He whom God has given "for a covenant of the people" (Isa. 49:9, 8, respectively). "Knowing therefore the terror of the Lord" (2 Cor. 5:11), he is now convinced that his own righteousness is but a refuge of lies which the hail shall sweep away.

6. By the instrumentality of the law as a covenant, a man is at the same time convinced that it would be just in God to punish him for the very least of his transgressions with everlasting destruction. He is made to know that sin, as it is committed against the infinitely great Jehovah, deserves an infinite punishment, even the everlasting perdition of the sinner. Convinced of the malignity and demerit of sin by the law, he is satisfied that God could do him no manner of injury though He should consign him to the place of torment and there punish him with all the severity of almighty vengeance. He sees that infinite justice could not be glorified nor the credit of it maintained unless infinite punishment were inflicted either on himself or on a responsible surety in his stead for the infinite offense given to it by his

transgression. He is persuaded that the Lord is righteous in executing vengeance, adequate to the infinite evil of presuming to sin against His infinitely glorious majesty.

Accordingly, the apostle Paul says, "Is God unrighteous who taketh vengeance?… God forbid: for then how shall God judge the world?" (Rom. 3:5–6). The sinner now sees, in the glass of the law, that it is highly proper and even necessary that divine justice should be honored by a complete satisfaction. And indeed, if he did not see damnation to be just, he could not discern salvation to be free. But discerning as he now does the equity and righteousness of God in the infliction even of eternal punishment on him for sin, he is well pleased with the doctrine and the offer of a free salvation through the infinite satisfaction given to divine justice by Jesus Christ and is content that the justice of God should receive a satisfaction far more complete than he himself could give, though he should suffer in the place of torment through all eternity. And so he becomes "dead to the law" as a covenant "by the body of Christ" (Rom. 7:4).

7. Finally, by means of the law, a man is convinced of his great need of the righteousness of Jesus Christ offered to him in the gospel. Contemplating in the glass of the law and by the light of the Spirit his sinfulness and his misery; dreading the wrath of God, which he has provoked by his great transgressions; convinced of the equity of God, though He should punish him with everlasting destruction; and despairing of deliverance by his own "righteousness and strength" (Isa. 45:24), he perceives his extreme need of the righteousness of Jesus Christ to answer for him the high demands of the law as a covenant. While he discerns by the gospel the suitableness and sufficiency of that consummate righteousness for his justification, he discovers by the law his absolute need of it for that purpose. He sees plainly in the glass of the law that he must inevitably and eternally perish without communion with Christ in His righteousness. The consequence is that, under the renovating influences of the Holy Spirit, he is disposed to be an eternal debtor to the glorious righteousness of the

last Adam for all his security from eternal death and all his right to eternal life. The righteousness that the law as a covenant demanded from Christ, the representative and surety of elect sinners, is not only a glass in which the sinner sees that righteousness which he must fulfill if he would enter into life on the ground of his own obedience; but in the gospel it is offered to him as a lost sinner, that by receiving the gift of it "the righteousness of the law might be fulfilled in" him (Rom. 8:4). And no sooner does he receive the gift of that spotless righteousness than it is imputed to him for justification, and so he who is unrighteous in himself becomes "the righteousness of God in [Christ]" (2 Cor. 5:21). Thus, he becomes dead to the law of works not only in point of legal hope but in respect to his state before God.

✦ SECTION 4 ✦

The Important Consequence of a Believer's Being Dead to the Law as a Covenant of Works

The consequence, or fruit, of a believer's having become dead to the law as a covenant is, by the apostle Paul, expressed thus: "Wherefore, my brethren, ye also are become dead to the law by the body of Christ; that ye should be married to another, even to him who is raised from the dead, that we should bring forth fruit unto God" (Rom. 7:4). Here our apostle informs the believers in Rome, and all believers to the end of time, that they have become dead to the law as a covenant of works so that it can neither justify them nor condemn them and that they are dead to it by the body of Christ—that is, by the service and suffering of the body or human nature of Christ (Heb. 10:5). As the obedience and suffering of Christ in human nature, which have answered all the demands of the law as a covenant, are imputed to them for their justification, so the law in that form, being thereby satisfied with respect to them, has nothing more to demand of them for a title to life. They have become dead to the law, and so, in its federal form, it has no more dominion over them than the civil law has over a man after he is dead.

The design, according to our apostle, of believers being "dead to the law" is that they "should be married to another, even to him who is raised from the dead" (Rom. 7:4). As long as the law, their first husband, continued to have dominion over them, they could not justly or honorably be married to another; but when that husband is dead to them, or when they are set free from the dominion of the law as a covenant, they are at liberty to be honorably espoused to another, even to Him who is raised from the dead. The Lord Jesus, having been "raised from the dead dieth no more" (6:9). He continues always to be a living husband to His saints. And therefore, as they can never be loosed from the bond of their union with Christ, so they shall never be released from the law of this husband. Although, then, they are set free from the obligation of the law as a covenant of works, yet they are "under the law to Christ" (1 Cor. 9:21), under the law as a rule of duty in the hand of Christ, under obligation to yield even perfect obedience to it and they shall never be released from that obligation.

Now the main design of their deliverance from their first husband and of their conjugal relation to Christ is, as our apostle expresses it, that they may "bring forth fruit unto God" (Rom. 7:4). It is not that they may be left at liberty to live as they please "without law to God" (1 Cor. 9:21), but that by union and communion with Christ, their head of spiritual influences, they may bring forth "fruits of righteousness, which are by Jesus Christ, unto the glory and praise of God" (Phil. 1:11). As children begotten and born in marriage are legitimate and all before marriage are illegitimate, so those works only that are the fruits of union with Christ, that are performed in faith and to the glory of God, are genuine fruits of righteousness; whereas all that are done before union with Christ are spurious. According to our apostle, then, the certain consequence of believers' being dead to the law as a covenant and of their being united to Christ is that they "bring forth fruit unto God." As long as sinners are alive to the law as a covenant, which is the ministration of death, they "bring forth fruit unto death"

(Rom. 7:5), but no sooner are they dead to the law than they have their "fruit unto holiness, and the end everlasting life" (6:22).

In another passage, our apostle expresses the consequence of being dead to the law thus: "But now we are delivered from the law, that being dead wherein we were held; that we should serve in newness of spirit, and not in the oldness of the letter" (Rom. 7:6). Here the apostle affirms that believers are delivered from the law not indeed as a rule of duty but only as a covenant of works; that they who hitherto were held fast under subjection to it as their first husband are delivered from it because it is dead to them: "that being dead wherein we were held." Although in their unregenerate state they were held fast under the dominion and obligation of it as a woman who has a husband is held "by the law to her husband" (v. 2), yet now that is dead to them; they are delivered or discharged from it as a widow is from the bond of marriage to her dead husband. They are delivered from the rigorous exaction, the dreadful curse, and the irritating power of it.

But for what purpose are believers delivered from the law as a covenant? They are delivered, says our apostle, not in order that they may live a loose or licentious life but that they may "serve in newness of spirit, and not in the oldness of the letter" (Rom. 7:6). To serve in newness of spirit is, in consequence of their standing in a conjugal relation to Jesus Christ and under a new and better covenant, to serve the Lord their God, "without [slavish] fear, in holiness and righteousness before him" (Luke 1:74–75); to serve Him under the renewing influences of His Holy Spirit, the former of the new creature in their souls; and to serve Him from a new heart and a new spirit from new principles and motives to new ends and by walking in newness of life. It is to serve Him in a new manner, with filial confidence in Him, with reverence and godly fear, with freedom and delight as persons renewed in the spirit of their minds and with their minds to serve His law by yielding unfeigned and unreserved obedience to it as the only rule of their duty. Believers are also delivered from the law as a covenant that they may serve "not in the oldness of the letter"

(Rom. 7:6)—not with an old covenant spirit or in a mere outward observance of the law as a rule of life and not in a bare external compliance with some to the neglect of others of its injunctions. "The letter killeth" by its bondage and terror (2 Cor. 3:6), but they are set free from it in order that they may serve the Lord not only without servile fear but "in spirit and in truth" (John 4:23). The consequence, or fruit, then, of being delivered from the law as a covenant of works is that believers become capable of serving God "in newness of spirit, and not in the oldness of the letter" (Rom. 7:6).

Our apostle in another place expresses the consequence and fruit of having become dead to the law in its federal form in these very remarkable words: "I through the law am dead to the law, that I might live unto God" (Gal. 2:19). According to these words of the inspired apostle, a believer's living unto God is the native consequence and fruit of his being dead to the law as a covenant of works. As long as a man continues alive to the law, he is dead to God; but when he becomes dead to the law in point of justification, he begins to live unto God in respect of sanctification. The death of his legal hope is in order to his life of evangelical obedience. His becoming dead to the law issues in his living unto God; in his living a new, spiritual, holy life, and that "unto the glory and praise of God" (Phil. 1:11). If he did not become dead to the law as a covenant, he could not live to God in conformity to the law as a rule. His living unto God, then, is the necessary fruit, the sure consequence of his having become dead to the law in its covenant form.

The life that the true Christian lives, in consequence of his having become dead to the law, is not a life either of perfect or of imperfect conformity to the law as a covenant of works (Rom. 5:6; 9:31–32); but it is a spiritual life, the life of a spiritual man in conformity to the law as a rule. It is the result of the inhabitation and gracious operation of the Holy Spirit in his soul (Ezek. 36:27). It is called in Scripture "the life of God" (Eph. 4:18), for it "is hid with Christ in God" (Col. 3:3). God lives in Himself, and the believer lives in union and communion with Him. It is wholly in and of God and is a living in favor and fellowship with Him. Our apostle styles it a living "by the faith of the Son of God," and he says of himself, "I live; yet not I, but Christ liveth in me" (Gal. 2:20). Christ is the purchaser, the bestower, the restorer, and the preserver of the believer's life. Christ is the principle of his life from whom, the pattern of his life according to whom, and the end of it to whom he lives. Indeed, Christ the living Redeemer, the resurrection and the life, is *all* in his spiritual life. "To me to live," says the apostle, "is Christ" (Phil. 1:21). It is also styled a living and walking in the Spirit (Gal. 5:25), a living in the strength of the Spirit as a Spirit of life under the guidance of the Spirit (Rom. 8:2, 14), in the liberty of the Spirit (2 Cor. 3:17), in the comforts of the Spirit (Acts 9:31), and in the fruits of the Spirit (Gal. 5:22–23).

Living unto God, as the consequence of being dead to the law in its covenant form, is moreover styled a holy, humble, and heavenly life. It is called a "conversation" such as "becometh the gospel of Christ" (Phil. 1:27), a walking "circumspectly" (Eph. 5:15), and a living "soberly, righteously, and godly" (Titus 2:12). It includes the love and practice of all those duties of piety toward God, of sobriety with respect to himself, and of righteousness toward his neighbor, which the believer is commanded in the law as his rule of duty to perform and which he is bound to perform under the influences of the Spirit of grace from the principles and motives, according to the rules and patterns, and to the ends exhibited in the word of grace.

To live unto God, that unspeakably important consequence of having become dead to the law of works, comprises more particularly:

1. The believer's living suitably to the endearing relations in which God in Christ as his covenant God stands to him. It is his living to God as his Father, his Redeemer, his head and husband, as his judge, lawgiver, and sovereign, as his portion, and as the object of his supreme love, of his high admiration, and of his holy adoration.

2. It includes his living suitably to the inestimable blessings of salvation that he has received from God. Has God enlightened the minds of His people in the saving knowledge of Himself and of Christ? Then to live to Him is to "walk as children of light" (Eph. 5:8). Has He called them with a holy calling? To live to Him is to walk worthy of the vocation wherewith they are called. He has brought them into a state of grace and of reconciliation to Himself; they therefore live to Him when they live not as persons in a state of nature but in a state of grace, or as persons "not under the law, but under grace" (Rom. 6:14). Has He graciously forgiven their iniquities and justified their persons? To live to Him is to "stand fast therefore in the liberty wherewith Christ hath made us free" (Gal. 5:1). Has He renewed and sanctified them according to His own image? They live to Him when they are "holy in all manner of conversation" (1 Peter 1:15). Has He given them "exceeding great and precious promises" and faith to rely on them (2 Peter 1:4)? They live to Him when, having such promises, they cleanse themselves "from all filthiness of the flesh and spirit, perfecting holiness in the fear of God" (2 Cor. 7:1). Has He made them heirs of a glorious inheritance in heaven? Then to live to Him is as "strangers and pilgrims on the earth" (Heb. 11:13), to "set your affection on" and to "seek those things which are above, where Christ sitteth on the right hand of God" (Col. 3:2, 1, respectively). In a word, has He graciously advanced them to joy and peace in believing? They live to Him when they "live in peace" and "serve the LORD with gladness" (2 Cor. 13:11; Ps. 100:2, respectively).

3. It also comprises his living in comfortable communion with God in Christ as his God. To live in the style of the Holy Spirit is to live comfortably. To live to God, then, is to live in delightful fellowship with Him. Believers live in such communion with God when they daily contemplate His glory in the face of Jesus Christ and sanctify Him in their hearts; when they trust in Him at all times, receiving all communications of grace from Him by the exercise of faith and returning all to Him in grateful obedience; and when they have His love so

shed abroad in their hearts as to be constrained by it, constantly to love and delight in Him. They also live to God when they live in the comfortable enjoyment of Him as all their portion and felicity, all their salvation and desire, renouncing all in heaven and on earth as a portion but Him alone (Ps. 73:25–26).

4. Last, it includes his living in conformity to God as his covenant God. To live unto God is to live in conformity to His holy and perfect nature, to be holy as He is holy, and to be pressing on toward perfection of holiness. It is to live in conformity to His manner of living. God's way of living is a holy, just, good, merciful, gracious, and faithful way. His way is to have a general goodwill to all men and a special goodwill to some, and so will that of His people be in proportion to the degrees of their sanctification. It is a living also in conformity to His ends. The chief end that the Lord proposes to Himself in all His works is the glory of His infinite name, the honor of His beloved Son and His blessed Spirit, the advancement of the Redeemer's kingdom, the overthrow of Satan's kingdom, and in all "the praise of the glory of his grace" (Eph. 1:6). To live unto God, then, is to make these the chief end of all our thoughts, words, and works. In a word, to live unto God is to live in conformity to that law of God as the rule of life which is a transcript of His holy nature and a revelation of His holy will. They who live to Him from love as well as from conscience study to keep all His holy commandments. They not only account it their duty but their privilege and their pleasure to yield spiritual obedience to His holy law.

✦ SECTION 5 ✦

*The Necessity of a Believer's Being Dead to the Law
as a Covenant in Order to His Living unto God*

As the believer living unto God according to the law as a rule of life in the hand of the Mediator is, as I showed above, the necessary consequence, or fruit, of his having become dead to the law as a covenant of works, so his being dead to the law is necessary to his living unto God—so absolutely necessary that were he not dead to the law as a covenant, it would be utterly impossible for him to live unto God in conformity to the law as a rule. This will be evident to the devout reader if he considers the following particulars:

1. The man who is under the power of the law as a broken covenant is under the power of sin, for the law under that form is "the strength of sin" (1 Cor. 15:56). Hence, our apostle, as was noticed above, said to the saints in Rome, "Sin shall not have dominion over you: for ye are not under the law, but under grace" (Rom. 6:14), intimating to them that if they had been still under the law as a covenant, sin would have had dominion over them. The believer's deliverance, then, from the dominion of sin, so as to be rendered capable of living to God, necessarily depends on his having "become dead to the law" in its covenant form (7:4).

2. The sinner who is under the law as a covenant is without strength; and therefore, he cannot serve God in a holy and acceptable manner (Rom. 5:6). And the law, being "weak through the flesh," is as unable to sanctify him as it is to justify him (8:3).

The works of the law cannot sanctify him, seeing they are evil and not good works. They can render him more and more unholy, but they cannot make him holy. He must be "created…unto good works" before he can perform them (Eph. 2:10). But the new as well as the old creation is the work of God alone. While, therefore, a man is under the law as a covenant of works and is unregenerate, he cannot perform a single holy or good work. He may do many things that are materially good, but he can do nothing that is formally good. All his works are "dead works" (Heb. 6:1), the works of a man who is "dead in sins" and dead to God (Eph. 2:5); and therefore, it is as impossible for them to make him alive to God as it is to merit for him eternal life.

3. He who is under the law as a covenant is without Christ, in whom only quickening and sanctifying grace is to be found. They who live unto God "are sanctified in Christ Jesus" (1 Cor. 1:2) and are saints in Him (Phil. 1:1). Their implantation in Christ, instead of being from the law or works of the law, is wholly from grace; and their sanctification, while it is wholly from grace, is only in Christ, who "loved the church, and gave himself for it; that he might sanctify and cleanse it with the washing of water by the word" (Eph. 5:25–26).

4. The man who is under the law as a covenant of works has no principle of holiness in him. The grand principle of evangelical holiness, or of living unto God, is the holy, sanctifying Spirit of Christ dwelling in the heart. Now a man receives the Spirit of sanctification not "by the works of the law, [but] by the hearing of faith" (Gal. 3:2). He becomes a partaker of the Holy Spirit not by obedience to the law of works but by means of hearing and embracing the doctrine of faith. It is the "new testament," or covenant, and not the law or legal covenant that is "the ministration of the spirit" (2 Cor. 3:6, 8). It is the glorious gospel in which the new covenant is offered and the Spirit promised that, through grace, calls a sinner effectually to a life of sanctification (2 Thess. 2:13–14). When the sinner is effectually called, he "receive[s] the promise of the Spirit through faith" (Gal. 3:14), the faith of the gospel, "not by the works of the law" (2:16). As long, then, as a man is under the law of works and is of the works of the law, he is destitute of the Spirit of Christ, the main principle of living to God.

5. Once more, the sinner who is under the law as a covenant has no promise of sanctification by that law. The law in its federal form promises life to him only on condition of perfect obedience to be performed by himself, and performed in that strength which was given him in the first Adam; but it promises him no quickening or sanctifying influences to enable him to obey. On the contrary, by its awful curse, it bars effectually all sanctifying influence from his soul and shuts it up under the dominion of sin. Indeed, if true holiness or

ability to live unto God were to be found in the man under the covenant of works, the promises of the covenant of grace, with reverence it is said, might be altered, and that of sanctification be expunged from it. We might erase from that well-ordered covenant especially these promises: I "shall put my spirit in you, and ye shall live" (Ezek. 37:14). "A new heart also will I give you, and a new spirit will I put within you.... And I will put my spirit within you, and cause you to walk in my statutes, and ye shall keep my judgments, and do them" (36:26–27). Were it possible for a sinner, while he continues under the law as a covenant and, consequently, under the dominion and strength of sin to possess, notwithstanding, true holiness or ability to live unto God, there would, I repeat it, be no need of these and similar promises. But suppose we had no other proof of it; the very existence of those absolute promises in the covenant of grace proves, with the highest degree of certainty, that no man, while he continues under the law as a covenant of works, is capable of living to God.

Thus, it is evident that a man must be dead to the law as a covenant in point of justification and must be dying daily to it in point of temper and practice in order to his living unto God in reference to sanctification. The former is indispensably requisite to the latter, and the latter is not only the consequence, but the necessary consequence, of the former. It is absolutely necessary that a sinner be dead to the law in its federal form with respect to his state before God, and also that he be dying to it in respect of his inclination and practice in order to his being capable of living a holy life. But to evince still more dearly the necessity of a man's becoming dead to the law in order to his living unto God, I shall take a different view of this fundamental subject and inquire what causality or influence his having become dead to the law as a covenant has on his living unto God.

In the first place, a man's being dead to the law has a physical, or rather a spiritual influence on his sanctification, or his living unto God. They who are become dead to the law are "married to another, even to him who is raised from the dead"; and so they cannot but live, or "bring forth fruit unto God" (Rom. 7:4).

In union and communion with Christ Jesus, they have life, spiritual and eternal life. While they were under the law as a covenant, they were spiritually as well as legally dead, "dead in trespasses and sins" (Eph. 2:1); but now in Christ, their head of righteousness and life, they "have life, and…have it more abundantly" (John 10:10). Because He lives, they shall live also (14:19). "He that hath the Son hath life" (1 John 5:12). Now that they have been divorced from the law of works, their first husband, and are united to Christ, they live and act spiritually.

In Christ, their head of influences, they have light as well as life. As long as a man is under the law as a covenant, he dwells in darkness and cannot see to work the works of holiness or be spiritually active in living unto God. He is blinded with ignorance, prejudice, and self-conceit; and as he cannot see the vanity of his legal works, so neither can he discern the way of evangelical holiness. But no sooner is he united to Christ, who is "a light to lighten the Gentiles" (Luke 2:32), than he receives "the spirit of wisdom and revelation in the knowledge of [Christ]" (Eph. 1:17); and by this spiritual light, shining on the word of Christ, he sees distinctly how to live to God. He discerns the beauty and amiableness as well as the manner of true holiness.

In the Lord Jesus, they who are dead to the law have strength likewise. Sinners who are joined to the law as their husband cannot live to God, for they have no strength for acceptable obedience, and the law cannot afford them any. But believers have in Christ, their spiritual husband, strength to enable them to perform spiritual obedience. He affords them, from His overflowing fullness, sufficient and continual supplies of grace and strength. His "grace is sufficient" for them, for His "strength is made perfect in weakness" (2 Cor. 12:9). The consequence is that "all things are possible to him that believeth" (Mark 9:23). When, by trusting in Him at all times, they are "strong in the Lord, and in the power of his might" (Eph. 6:10), they "can do all things through Christ which strengtheneth" them (Phil. 4:13).

In union with Christ, their covenant head, they also have liberty, the glorious liberty of the children of God. While they were under the law as a covenant that "gendereth to bondage" (Gal. 4:24), they were in bondage, severe bondage to the command of perfect obedience on pain of eternal death, and were also in bondage to the curse of the law and the fear of eternal wrath. In this miserable condition it was impossible for them to live unto God; they could not have either a heart or a hand to serve Him. But in union and communion with the Lord Jesus, believers have liberty. "If the Son therefore shall make you free, ye shall be free indeed" (John 8:36), free to serve God in a spiritual and acceptable manner. "Where the Spirit of the Lord is, there is liberty" (2 Cor. 3:17). Partaking of the Spirit of the Lord Jesus, they "walk at liberty"; yea, they "run the way of [God's] commandments," for He enlarges their hearts (Ps. 119:45, 32, respectively). Now that they are "delivered out of the hand" of their enemies, they serve the Lord "without fear, in holiness and righteousness before him, all the days of" their life (Luke 1:74–75). They serve Him willingly, affectionately, and cheerfully. They are now at liberty to serve Him in hope, knowing that their labor shall not be in vain (1 Cor. 15:58). They are now at liberty to serve Him spiritually and acceptably, for as they are so joined to the Lord Jesus, as to be one spirit, so they are made "accepted in the beloved" (Eph. 1:6). Christ, their representative and surety, satisfied all the demands of the law as a covenant for them; they are therefore accounted in law as having answered them all in Him and so are accepted in Him. In union with Him, their persons are accepted as righteous and their performances as sincere. Oh, how grateful, how cheering is this liberty to the exercised believer! And what a delightful and powerful inducement is it to that holy and acceptable obedience, which is a living unto God!

In the last place, a man's being dead to the law as a covenant has not only a physical but a moral influence on his sanctification, or living unto God. The love of Christ, manifested in delivering believers from the law as a covenant of works, "constraineth" them to live not "unto themselves, but unto him which died for them, and rose again" (2 Cor. 5:14–15). Men's natural way of thinking and speaking is, "We should serve God that He may save us"; but the evangelical way is, "He saves us that we may serve Him. He redeems us from the law as a covenant that we may serve Him and so live to Him in obedience to the law as a rule." When our apostle said, "I…am dead to the law, that I might live unto God," in the next verse he enlarges in these words: "The life which I now live in the flesh I live by the faith of the Son of God, who loved me, and gave himself for me" (Gal. 2:19–20).

It is true believers only who are dead to the law of works and are united to the Son of God, who have a true faith and sense of His immense love to them, and who are powerfully constrained by it to love and live to God. And while redeeming love to them constrains them to love God as their covenant God, they see that they have every encouragement to live to Him. They see that their adorable Surety has, in wonderful condescension, fulfilled all that righteousness of the law as a covenant for them which they could never have fulfilled for themselves; and when by the eye of faith they perceive this, they are sweetly impelled and encouraged by it to holiness of heart and of life.

If a man has no faith in the love of God in Christ, no hope of His favor as a God of grace, how can that man be "pure in heart" (Matt. 5:8) and "holy in all manner of conversation" (1 Peter 1:15)? Nay, he cannot; it is only the "man that hath this hope in him [who] purifieth himself, even as [Christ] is pure" (1 John 3:3). All exercised Christians know by experience that when their souls are most comforted and their hearts most enlarged with the faith of God's favor in Christ and with the hope of His salvation, then it is that they are most disposed and encouraged to live to His glory. And on the contrary, when through the prevalence of unbelief they are most suspicious of God and His love to them, they then find themselves most averse from the exercise of graces and performance of duties.

But that the moral influence which dying to the law as a covenant of works has on living unto God may be more evident, it will be proper to show how every part of the law itself—having been changed to believers from the form of a covenant of works into that of a rule of life in the hand of the Mediator—constrains them to evangelical obedience. The law in the hand of Christ as a rule of duty, in all the commands, promises, and threats of it, is, as it were, a chariot paved with love for believers (Song 3:9–10). It wears a smiling, inviting, encouraging aspect to them.

1. The commandments of the law in the hand of Christ, having been divested of their old covenant form, discover to believers much of the love and grace of God. The command of the law as a covenant, as was observed above, is "Do and live"; but that of the law as a rule is "Live and do." The precept of the law of works is "Do or you shall die," but that of the law of Christ is "You are redeemed from eternal death; therefore do." The command of the law in its federal form is "Do perfectly that you may be entitled to eternal life," but that of the law in the hand of Christ is "He has merited for you and given you eternal life; therefore do, by His grace, as perfectly as you can until you attain absolute perfection."

The command of the law as a rule is materially the same as that of the law as a covenant; and therefore, though as much obedience is required in it as in that of the law of works, yet less is accepted from those who have the perfect obedience of their divine Redeemer imputed to them. And as the command is materially the same, so the authority which enjoins obedience is originally the same and yet vastly distinct, for the commandment of the law as a covenant is the command of God out of Christ; but the command of the law as a rule is the precept of God in Christ, of God as a God of grace and love in Him. The sovereign authority of God in commanding obedience is not in the smallest degree lessened in that His law is in the hand of Christ; for He, as the eternal Son of God, is the Most High God and coessential with the Father and the Holy Spirit. But while it is not and cannot be in the least degree lessened, it is, notwithstanding, rendered so mild, so amiable, and so desirable to believers as powerfully to constrain them to spiritual obedience. For His design in commanding their obedience is not to require from them a righteousness for their justification but to show them the holiness of His nature, to beautify them with His holy image, to afford them illustrious displays of His glorious grace, to do their soul good in the most effectual manner, and to favor them with daily opportunities to glorify Him, to edify their neighbor, and so to manifest their love and gratitude to Him for having redeemed them from the law as a covenant.

2. The promises of the law in the hand of Christ, having dropped their old covenant form, display to believers much of the love of God and so constrain them to live to Him. The law in its federal form promises eternal life as a reward of debt for perfect obedience, but the law as a rule in the hand of Christ promises rewards of grace in and after evangelical obedience, especially as this obedience is an evidence of union with Him in whom believers are justified and in whom all the promises of God are yea and amen (2 Cor. 1:20). The consideration that "in keeping" His commandments "there is great reward" (Ps. 19:11), that in the way of evangelical obedience there is a gracious promise of delightful communion with God and Jesus Christ (John 14:21, 23), and that after the course of such obedience in this world is ended, there will be an eternal reward powerfully constrains and greatly encourages believers to live unto God.

3. Finally, the threatenings of the law as a rule of life are also divested of their old covenant form and are changed into paternal threats issuing from redeeming love, which powerfully incite true Christians to live unto God. There is now no such threatening to the believer as this: "If you do not, you shall die." Now that he is dead to the law of works and delivered from condemnation, he has no more cause to fear its threatening of eternal death than a woman has to fear the threats of a dead husband (Rom. 8:1; 7:1–2). Believers, because they are "not

under the law" as a covenant "but under grace" (6:14), are under no threatening of eternal wrath, no sentence of condemnation to eternal punishment. The law in the hand of Christ has indeed threats of chastisement, but they are fatherly and all from love.

> If his children forsake my law, and walk not in my judgments; if they break my statutes, and keep not my commandments; then will I visit their transgression with the rod, and their iniquity with stripes. Nevertheless my lovingkindness will I not utterly take from him, nor suffer my faithfulness to fail. My covenant will I not break, nor alter the thing that is gone out of my lips. Once have I sworn by my holiness that I will not lie unto David. (Ps. 89:30–35)

It is as if Jehovah had said, "Although I will not send them to hell nor deprive them of heaven any more than I will break My covenant or violate My oath to My eternal Son, yet, as a father, I will chasten them. I will not only visit them with the rod of external affliction, but I will hide My face from their souls. I will deny them that sensible communion with Me which they have sometime enjoyed, and I will fill them with trouble instead of comfort, with bitterness instead of sweetness, and with terror instead of hope." A filial fear of these paternal chastisements will do far more to influence the believer to holy obedience than all the despondent fears of eternal punishment can do. Accordingly, when he has gone aside, it is commonly such a reflection as this that through grace makes him return to the Lord: "Oh! How am I now deprived of those delightful interviews with my gracious God and Savior, which I formerly enjoyed! Therefore, 'I will go and return to my first husband; for then it was better with me than now'" (Hos. 2:7). And when he is enabled to see that he is delivered from the threatenings of eternal wrath and that he is only under threats of fatherly correction, this breaks and melts his heart more than all the fire of hell could do. The slavish dread of avenging wrath disquiets and discourages him, weakens his hands in spiritual obedience, and disposes him to flee from God; whereas the filial fear of God's fatherly anger, which is kindly, is a motive of love that excites and urges him to holy living. The former works on his remaining enmity and rouses it, but the latter acts on his love and enflames it.

But here the attentive reader may be ready to ask, "Ought not the believer to live unto God without respect to the threats of paternal chastisement?" I answer that as long as he is in this world a body of sin dwells in him; and therefore, he needs to be incited to his duty by threats of fatherly correction. He ought indeed to serve the Lord, as the redeemed in heaven do, merely from love to the command itself and because it is his God and Savior who commands him. Still, however, as on the one hand he is perfect in Christ, his federal head and representative, he needs not have respect to what the law in its covenant form either promises or threatens;[7] so, on the other, as he is imperfect in himself while here, it is his duty to have, in his obedience, regard to what the law as a rule in the hand of Christ promises and threatens, which indeed is a holy and affectionate regard tending to promote holiness in his heart and life.

Thus, it is manifest that the whole form of the law as a covenant of works, having been dissolved to believers, the law as a rule of life in the hand of Christ, is all love, all grace; and so it influences and constrains them to advance, with increasing ardor, in evangelical holiness. Instead of affording them the smallest encouragement to commit sin, it not only requires but, like a cord of love, it draws them to the love and practice of universal holiness.[8]

---

7. It is not here meant that believers need not regard with holy admiration and gratitude the grace manifested in the promise of the covenant of works nor that they need not regard with holy awe the terrible wrath revealed in the threatening of that broken covenant, but *only* that they need not, and should not, have respect to them or take them into their view as motives to live unto God or to obey the law as a rule of life.

8. For the greater part of what has been advanced in the last two sections, I have been indebted to the substance of four excellent sermons by Mr. Ralph Erskine. If the reader chooses to receive further information respecting the highly important subject of the whole chapter, he may peruse Mr. Booth's treatise entitled *The Death of Legal Hope, the Life of Evangelical Obedience*; Mr. Hall's sermon on Galatians 2:19; and Mr. Boston's sermon on Romans 6:14. [See Ralph Erskine, "Law-Death, Gospel-Life: or, the Death of Legal Righteousness, the Life of Gospel Holiness," in *The Works of Ralph Erskine*

So much for the influence that a believer's being dead to the law as a covenant has on his living unto God.

✦ REFLECTIONS ✦

A few reflections from what has been said will conclude this chapter.

Is it the privilege of true believers only to be dead to the law as a covenant of works? Then the law in its covenant form is, to every unregenerate sinner, as much in force as ever it was. It retains all the authority and dominion over unconverted sinners that ever it had. As it is dead to believers and they dead to it, so sinners in their unregenerate state are alive to it, and it is alive to them. Retaining all its original authority over them, it continues to demand from them perfect obedience as the condition of life and complete satisfaction for sin. This is clearly taught us not only by the Lord Jesus but also by the apostle Paul (Luke 10:25–28; Gal. 3:10), and all who continue to reject the second Adam and His consummate righteousness shall, to their everlasting confusion, find it so. Oh, that secure sinners would believe this and flee for refuge to the great Redeemer before it is too late!

Does the law as a covenant require of every descendant of Adam personal as well as perfect obedience? Then it inevitably follows that the obedience of two or more cannot form a justifying righteousness. Righteousness for justification must be the obedience of one only. It must be the obedience either of the sinner himself alone or Christ alone. The Lord Jesus will either save sinners Himself alone or not save them at all (Acts 4:12). If a man would be justified before God,

---

(1865; repr., Glasgow: Free Presbyterian Publications, 1991), 2:9–101; Abraham Booth, *The Death of Legal Hope, the Life of Evangelical Obedience. An Essay on Galatians ii. 19* (London: E. and C. Dilly, 1770); and Archibald Hall, "Believers' Death to the Law, a Doctrine according to Godliness," in *Two Discourses* (London: G. Keith, J. Mathews, W. Watts, and D. Murray, 1777); also in *The Evangelical Preacher* (Edinburgh: J. Pillans and Sons, 1802), 1:284–314; Thomas Boston, "Believers Not under the Law, but under Grace; or, the Difference between the Covenant of Works, and the Covenant of Grace," in *Scattered and Kept: Twenty-Eight Lost Sermons of Rev. Thomas Boston* (Brighton, UK: Ettrick Press, 2022), 299–314.]

he must exhibit to the law either a perfect righteousness of his own, and have no dependence on that of Christ; or the perfect righteousness of Christ, in the hand of faith, and place no reliance on his own (Phil. 3:9). The righteousness of Jesus Christ, imputed to believers for their justification, is a righteousness without works—a righteousness wholly unconnected with works of any kind performed by themselves. These two cannot stand together in the affair of justification. "I will make mention of thy righteousness," says the holy psalmist, "even of thine only" (Ps. 71:16). Oh, let my reader take heed that in the affair of justification he does not connect his own obedience with that of Christ nor Christ's obedience with his own; that he never presumes to make up a justifying righteousness for himself, partly of his own works and partly of those of Christ. Let him be zealous for good works and perform them as fruits and evidences of justification, but never as grounds of right to it. For it will be impossible for him to live unto God till he begins to die to all hope of justification and salvation, either in whole or in part, by his own performances.

Is it through the law that a man becomes dead to the law? It is obvious, then, that ignorance in unregenerate sinners is a principal cause of their self-righteous temper (Rom. 10:3). Their ignorance of the infinite holiness, justice, and faithfulness of God; of the precept and penalty of His righteous law; of the covenant, promise, and design of His gospel; of the person, righteousness, fullness, and glory of Christ; and of their own extreme need of Christ—this willful, pharisaic ignorance is a special cause of their desire to be under the law of works (John 3:19; Gal. 3:1). Oh, that they would no longer condemn the counsel that the exalted Redeemer offers to each of them! "I counsel thee to buy of me gold tried in the fire, that thou mayest be rich; and white raiment, that thou mayest be clothed, and that the shame of thy nakedness do not appear; and anoint thine eyes with eyesalve, that thou mayest see" (Rev. 3:18).

Ah, secure sinner, how gross, how reproachful is your ignorance when you expect to become righteous in the sight of an omniscient and holy God by your own partial and polluted obedience! How blind are the eyes of your understanding when you can presume to hope that the holy and righteous law will accept your amendment and sincere obedience, your penitence and tears, instead of perfect obedience and perfect satisfaction for your innumerable sins! Alas! You do not know that the violated law demands, and cannot but demand from you, perfect obedience and, at the same time, complete satisfaction for all your aggravated crimes; and that it will not absolve you till all its high demands are fully satisfied. Oh, continue no longer ignorant of the exceeding sinfulness of sin of your inexpressible misery and danger under the law as a covenant and of your extreme need of the righteousness and grace of the second Adam.

Is a man's being dead to the law as a covenant the reason why he lives unto God? Then it must be admitted that the reason, or at least one reason, why unbelievers and formalists live not to God but to sin and self and the world is that they are not dead to the law in that form. The very reason why sin reigns in the sinner is because he is under the dominion of the law, which stands as a bar to prevent sanctifying influences from flowing into his heart. The law, especially in its condemning and irritating power, is "the strength of sin" (1 Cor. 15:56). Every man, therefore, who is under the dominion of the law as a covenant is, and cannot but be, under the dominion and strength of sin (Rom. 6:14). It is impossible for that man who continues alive to the law to be a holy or a godly man. He may have the form, but he cannot experience the power of godliness. He may take his encouragement from the law as a covenant and delight in the works of it, but he cannot delight in the holiness and spirituality of the law as a rule. He may advance to a high degree of counterfeit virtue, but he remains an entire stranger to true holiness.

Reader, the only way in which it is possible for you to attain true or evangelical holiness is to be so convinced of sin and righteousness as to part with your legal righteousness. You cannot trust cordially in the Lord Jesus for righteousness and strength till you begin utterly to despair of being able to work out for yourself such a righteousness as the law requires. You cannot desire the great salvation offered to you in the gospel until you despair utterly of salvation by the works of the law. Nor is it possible for you to live unto God till you die to all hope of redemption from the curse of the broken law and from the justice of an offended God by any righteousness of your own. Be assured that you must be dead to the law as a covenant in order to be either able or willing to yield the smallest degree of acceptable obedience to the law as a rule.

How inexpressibly miserable are they who are alive to the law as a covenant of works! They may have a name to live, but they are dead (Rev. 3:1). They are dead to God—to the favor, the image, the service, and the enjoyment of God. They are legally dead, for they are under the tremendous curse of the violated law and are liable every moment to the intolerable and eternal wrath of Almighty God. They are morally dead, likewise, for they are destitute of spiritual life, and they have no inclination or ability to live unto God. Such persons know not what it is to live a life either of justification or sanctification or consolation. The righteous law condemns them because they have transgressed it, and its awful sentence not only shuts them up under the dominion of spiritual death but binds them over to all the horrors of death eternal. Oh, secure sinner, the state in which you are is that of a criminal condemned to death—temporal, spiritual, and eternal! Do not say, "I hope that is not my state," for you "are of the works of the law"; you are depending on your own works for a title to the favor of God and the happiness of heaven. And this renders it certain that you are under the curse or condemning sentence of the law, for thus said the Spirit of inspiration, "As many as are of the works of the law are under the curse" (Gal. 3:10). Oh, renounce, and that without delay, all dependence on your own works. Believe that the Lord Jesus, with His righteousness and salvation, is freely, wholly, and particularly offered to you. And relying on His consummate righteousness alone for all your right to justification and salvation, trust in Him not only for deliverance from the curse of the law but for complete salvation. So shall you become dead to the law of works and, in union with the second Adam, be instated into the covenant of grace.

All believers have, in the eye of the law as a covenant of works, obeyed, suffered, and satisfied fully in Jesus Christ, their federal representative and surety. As all mankind has sinned and become subject to death in the first Adam, so all true believers have obeyed, died, and so satisfied the law and justice of God in the second Adam. Thus, they have answered and completely satisfied all the demands of the law as a covenant. The consequence is that the law in that form, having received all that it had to demand from them, absolves them from guilt and declares them righteous. Hence, they become dead to the law, and the law to them. The Representative and the represented, the Surety and the principal debtor are, in legal estimation, but one person. They therefore are accounted in law to have done and suffered all that Christ, their representative and surety, did and suffered for them. Accordingly, they are said in Scripture to be "crucified with Christ" (Gal. 2:20), to be dead and buried with Him (Rom. 6:4, 8), and to be raised up together in Him (Eph. 2:6). They have obeyed and suffered and so satisfied every demand of the law as a covenant not in their own persons but in the person of Christ.

Although the sins that believers commit after the commencement of their vital union with Christ are not formally transgressions of the law as a covenant of works, yet they are all, by legal interpretation, sins against it. In the justification of believers, in which they have become dead to the law as a covenant, all their future sins, considered as transgressions of the law in that form, are forgiven. As sins against the law as a covenant, in the act of justification they are so pardoned that a nonimputation of them to believers is inviolably secured. "Blessed is the man," says the apostle Paul, "to whom the Lord will not impute sin" (Rom. 4:8). All the sins of believers after as well as before their vital union with Christ were charged and punished on Him as transgressions of the law in its federal form and as such are, in their justification, freely and wholly pardoned. The Lord Jesus, their divine surety, has satisfied the justice of God for all their sins committed after as well as before the act of their justification, and that by enduring in their stead the punishment threatened in the covenant of works. Though, therefore, their sins after union with Christ are directly and formally committed against the law as a rule of duty, yet by legal interpretation, they are transgressions likewise of the law as a covenant of works.

Are believers wholly delivered from the condemning power of the law as a covenant? The guilt of sin, then, in reference to them is twofold: the guilt of eternal wrath and the guilt of paternal anger. The guilt of eternal wrath is a sinner's obligation or liableness to the avenging and eternal wrath of God as the just punishment of his sin. The guilt of fatherly displeasure, on the other hand, is a believer's obnoxiousness to the awful effects of God's paternal anger as chastisements for his disobedience.

Accordingly, the pardon of sin is twofold: namely, a removal of the guilt of eternal wrath from him in the act of his justification, and an absolving of him from the guilt of paternal displeasure in the progress of his sanctification. The former is called legal pardon, the latter gospel pardon. The one is the instantaneous and perfect removal of all that guilt which was contracted by transgressing the law as a covenant; the other is the gradual removal of that guilt which is contracted daily by disobeying the law as a rule. That is afforded completely and at once to a converted sinner on his first acting of faith, when he becomes dead to the law as a covenant. This is vouchsafed to a believer repeatedly on his renewed exercise of faith and repentance. When, therefore, a true Christian who is in some happy measure assured of his justification prays with understanding for the pardon of his iniquities, he prays that the Lord may preserve and increase in him his assurance of the pardon that was given him in his justification[9] and also that he may

---

9. Westminster Larger Catechism 194.

graciously remove from him the guilt of fatherly displeasure that he is daily contracting (Ps. 51:8–12). And when he asks for divine acceptance, he prays that the Lord may preserve and increase in him his assurance of the acceptance of his person in the Beloved and that He may favor him daily with the acceptance of his performances.

Are believers dead to the law as a covenant, and is it dead to them? Then it cannot either promise eternal life or threaten eternal death to them. "What things soever the law saith," either in its promise of life or its threatening of death, "it saith to them who are under the law" (Rom. 3:19). But believers "are not under the law, but under grace" (6:14); and therefore, the law in its federal form can say nothing to them. In their justification by faith, they are delivered from condemnation to eternal death and are accounted so righteous as to be fully entitled to eternal life (John 3:16). They are already redeemed from eternal death, and they have already the begun possession of life eternal. How, then, can the law either promise eternal life or threaten eternal death to those who, by their communion with Christ in His righteousness and fullness, have already attained the one and escaped the other? Though believers ought always to regard the threatenings of the law as a covenant with holy awe, like a glass in which they may contemplate the dreadful demerit of their sins and their infinite obligations to redeeming grace, yet they ought not to consider those threatenings as directed to them or as denunciations of evil against them. They should regard them at all times with filial awe but never with slavish dread.

Is every man who is justified before God, and so dead to the law as a covenant, taught to believe that his own works of obedience form no part at all of a justifying righteousness for him? It would surely be very unreasonable and unjust to infer from this that he need not perform good works. He is indeed delivered, and wholly delivered, from the law as a covenant of works; but he is still under the infinite and eternal obligation of it as a rule of duty. To infer, then, from a believer's being directed and exhorted to place no confidence in his good works for a title to justification and eternal life that it is not necessary for him to perform and maintain good works would be as absurd as if a man should conclude that because it is the ear only that hears, there is no need of the foot or the hand (Rom. 3:8; Jude 4).

Once more, are true believers delivered from the commanding, condemning, and irritating power of the law as a covenant? Let them then, amid all their trials and all their conflicts with spiritual enemies, be of good comfort. Oh, let them rejoice exceedingly in that almighty, compassionate, dear Redeemer who, in His love and pity, has redeemed them from the dominion and curse of the broken law (Gal. 3:13). You, O believer, have become dead to the law by the body of Christ and are married to another husband, even to Him who is raised from the dead, that you may bring forth fruit unto God (Rom. 7:4). You are dead to the law of works; nevertheless, you live. You live to God as your own God, your covenant God, and you serve Him in newness of spirit. In union with your living Redeemer, who loved you and gave Himself for you, you live a life of justification, and consequently, it is your privilege as well as your duty to live a life of sanctification and consolation. Being justified by faith, you have peace with God through our Lord Jesus Christ and, in some measure, peace of conscience. If then the law as a covenant of works should at any time enter your conscience again and require perfect obedience from you as the ground of your title to eternal life, saying, "This do, and thou shalt live" (Luke 10:28), present to it, in the hand of faith, the perfect obedience of your divine Surety in answer to that demand. And as often as the law in your conscience repeats the high demand, renew your application of His consummate obedience and trust firmly that it was performed for you in order to entitle you to eternal life. The righteous law, magnified and made honorable by that meritorious obedience, will, in proportion as you do so, cease to disturb the peace of your conscience. The spotless obedience of the second Adam is, as was observed above, the only obedience that you should present to the law as a covenant of works; and your own personal obedience is the only obedience that you ought to exhibit to it as a rule of life.

And should the law as a covenant ever be permitted to rise again as from the dead and to attempt exercising its condemning power over your conscience by demanding from you satisfaction for your innumerable transgressions of it, present to it, in the hand of an appropriating faith, the infinite satisfaction for sin given by your adorable Surety in answer to that demand. Trust anew that your living head, your heavenly husband, has given complete satisfaction for all your sins, and so, referring the law to Him, plead that if it has any charge to exhibit against you, the action must lie between it and Him. Never say to the law, in answer to any of its demands, "Have patience with me, and I will pay thee all" (Matt. 18:26, 29); but without delay present it with full payment. In answer to its demand of perfect obedience as the condition of life, present in the hand of faith to it the perfect obedience of the second Adam, and in answer to its demand of complete satisfaction for sin, exhibit to it His infinite atonement for the sins of all who believe in Him. That is the way to honor it and, at the same time, recover and maintain peace of conscience.

The High Obligations under Which Believers Lie to Yield Even Perfect Obedience to the Law as a Rule of Life

All who are united to Christ and justified for His righteousness imputed to them are dead to the law as a covenant not that they may be "without law to God" but that they may be "under the law to Christ" (1 Cor. 9:21); not that they may continue in disobedience but that they may be inclined and enabled to perform sincere obedience in time, and perfect obedience through eternity, to the law as a rule of life. One design of their being delivered from the obligation of the law in its federal form is that they may be brought under the eternal obligation of it as a rule of duty in the hand of the adorable Mediator. Divested of the form of a covenant of works to believers and invested with that of the covenant of grace, it stands under the covenant of grace as the law of Christ and as the instrument of government in its spiritual kingdom, enforced by all its original and immutable authority. It loses nothing of its original authority by its being conveyed to believers in such a blessed channel as the hand of Christ since He Himself is God over all and since the majesty, sovereignty, and authority of the Father, the Son, and the Holy Spirit are in Him as Mediator (Ex. 23:21).

Indeed, it behooved the law of the Ten Commandments, inasmuch as it is the substance of the law of nature, a delineation of God's moral image, and a transcript of His unspotted holiness, to be a perpetual and unalterable rule of conduct to mankind in all the possible states and circumstances in which they might be placed. Since God is unchangeable in His moral image, nothing but the entire annihilation of every human creature can divest His holy law of that office. Its being an immutable rule of duty to the human race does not in the least depend on its having become the matter of the covenant of works. Whatever form it might receive, whether that of the covenant of works or that of the covenant of grace, still it could not but continue an authoritative rule of conduct. No form, no covenant whatever, could at any time lessen its high obligation as a rule of duty on the reasonable creature. As the form of the first covenant was merely accessory to the moral law, so the law continues, and will forever continue, under that form as the rule of duty to sinners, even in the place of torment. And as the form of the second covenant is also accessory to it, so it will remain eternally under this form, the rule of life, to saints in the mansions of glory.

The sovereign authority of the divine law continues eternally the same, and it can never be in the least impaired by any of the forms under which that law is promulgated to us. And seeing that God the Father has so consulted the necessity of His redeemed, in subordination to His own glory, as to put His law into the hands of His eternal Son as Mediator, from these hands they receive it invested with all the sovereign authority that ever belonged to it, together with all that God the Son as their great Redeemer has added to it. That believers ought not to receive—nay, and cannot receive—the law otherwise than from the hand of the infinitely glorious Mediator is so far from being injurious to the infinite majesty of God, the sovereign Creator, or to the high obligation of His holy law, that the infinite honor of His glorious majesty and His holy law is thereby most illustriously displayed. As the law as a covenant of works was honored in an infinite degree by its having been obeyed and satisfied by the eternal Son of God in our nature, so, as a rule of life to believers, it is magnified in no less a degree by its being conveyed to them in His hand. Their obligation to perform not only sincere but even perfect obedience to it is on these accounts confirmed and increased. Now the obligation under which all true believers are to yield such obedience to the law as a rule of life proceeds chiefly from the following sources:

1. It arises from God being the Lord, or from His being the sovereign, supereminent, and supremely excellent Jehovah. The obligation under which believers lie to yield obedience to His law arises from His universal supremacy and sovereign authority over them as rational creatures. "Ye shall therefore keep my statutes, and my judgments.... I am the LORD" (Lev. 18:5). "And ye shall keep my statutes, and do them: I am the LORD which sanctify you" (20:8). Because God is Jehovah, "the eternal, immutable, and almighty God, having His being in and of Himself, and giving being to all His words and works,"[1] all obedience is due Him. The infinite greatness, excellence, and amiableness of the perfections of Jehovah make it the duty of all men, and especially of all believers, to love Him supremely, to obey Him in all things, and to make His glory the chief end of all their obedience to Him. The infinite supereminence and amiableness of Jehovah lay them under inconceivably high obligations to love Him above themselves and to live to Him ultimately and not to themselves. And as His greatness, excellence, and loveliness are infinite, immutable, and eternal, and as the highest possible degree of love and obedience is therefore due to Him, so the obligation under which believers lie to love and obey Him even in a perfect degree is infinite, immutable, and eternal.

They are thus bound to love and obey Him with all their hearts because He is the Lord, or because He is what He is. On this account principally, and antecedently to every other consideration of Him, He is inexpressibly amiable; and therefore, they are under the firmest obligation to love and obey Him, and that in the highest possible degree. This obligation, arising from that infinite greatness, excellence, and loveliness of God that result from His natural and moral perfections, is binding on believers previously to any consideration of

---

1. Westminster Larger Catechism 101.

rewards or punishments, or even of the revealed will of God; and it is that from which all other ties to duty derive their obligatory force. It is from the infinite excellence and amiableness of the divine nature that every additional obligation under which they lie to perfect love and perfect obedience derives its binding force.

2. The obligation under which believers are to yield perfect obedience to the law as a rule flows also from God being their Creator and they being His creatures. It is He who made them and not they themselves (Ps. 100:3). They receive life, breath, and all things from His creating hand. His right, therefore, to them and to their perfect and perpetual obedience is not only original, underived, and perfect, but infinite. The power that He employed in creating them was infinite, and therefore He has an infinite right to all that they are, have, and can perform. By right of creation, the Lord has an irreversible and perpetual claim to their supreme love and their cordial and grateful obedience.

The relation subsisting between Him as their Creator and them as His creatures lays them under the firmest bond of subjection and obedience to Him, and the grace of the gospel, instead of diminishing, increases the force of that natural obligation. The sovereign Creator is far from having resigned His right of dominion over His saints by His having afforded them, independent of their own works, a title to eternal life. For as they cease not to be creatures by being made new creatures, so they are and shall eternally continue bound, by the sovereign authority of the triune God as their Creator, to yield personal and perfect obedience to His law as a rule of life. The divine law, as I have already observed, loses nothing of its original obligation by being divested of its covenant form and conveyed to believers in the hand of Christ, for "by him were all things created, that are in heaven, and that are in earth, visible and invisible" (Col. 1:16). And the sovereignty, authority, and all other excellencies of the Father are in the Son; yea, "in him dwelleth all the fulness of the Godhead bodily" (Col. 2:9). Indeed, that high obligation cannot cease to retain its original force as long as the immutable and eternal Jehovah cannot cease to be the Creator and the saints to be His creatures.

3. Their obligation to obey the divine law as a rule of duty arises from God being their continual preserver. "In him," says the apostle Paul, "we live, and move, and have our being" (Acts 17:28). And, says the holy psalmist, "LORD, thou preservest man and beast" (Ps. 36:6). His eyes are on all His works, so that even a sparrow cannot fall to the ground without Him (Matt. 10:29). "By the word of his power," He upholds all His creatures in their being and operation (Heb. 1:3). Every living creature lives on His goodness and subsists by His bounty. His infinite power every moment upholds all, His unsearchable wisdom governs all, and His unbounded goodness cares and provides for all. He opens His "hand, and satisfieth the desire of every living thing" (Ps. 145:16). But in a special manner, "he preserveth the souls of his saints" (97:10). "The LORD preserveth all them that love him" (145:20). "The LORD shall preserve thee from all evil: he shall preserve thy soul. The LORD shall preserve thy going out and thy coming in from this time forth, and even for evermore" (121:7–8).

Since believers, then, are every moment dependent on God for the continuance and comfort both of their natural and spiritual life, they are bound, in obedience to His law as the rule of their life, to love Him supremely, to serve Him constantly, and to glorify Him in their body and spirit, which are His (1 Cor. 6:20). The necessary relation in which they stand to Him as their constant preserver obliges them to devote cheerfully all that they are, have, and do to His service and glory. Their being and their welfare are continually upheld and defended by His omnipotent arm; and therefore, these ought at all times to be employed for Him. And because His manifested glory is His chief end in preserving His saints, they are bound to make it their chief end also in all that they do (1 Cor. 10:31).

4. The obligation under which the spiritual seed of Christ lie to perform perfect and perpetual obedience to the law of God flows also from His being their God in covenant.

He is their God in Christ and in the covenant of grace, and this obliges them to perform universal obedience to His righteous law as it is in the hand of Christ and as it stands under the covenant of grace.

He is also their God in grant or offer. He offers Christ, the blessed Mediator, to them in common with all the other hearers of the gospel, and He also offers Himself to them, to be in Christ their God. In the preface to the Ten Commandments, He says to every hearer of the gospel, "I am the Lord thy God," as if He had said, "I am your God in offer." And in the first commandment, as was observed above, He requires everyone to believe the gracious offer with application to himself, saying, "Thou shalt have no other gods before me" (Ex. 20:3). He commands every man "to know and acknowledge God to be the only true God, and our God"[2] on the ground of the unlimited offer, and He enables all His own people to believe cordially that He is their God in offer.

He is also their God in choice. In the exercise of their faith, they choose the Lord Jesus to be their Savior and God in Him, to be their covenant God, saying, "What have I to do any more with idols?" (Hos. 14:8). "This God is our God for ever and ever" (Ps. 48:14). Each of them is enabled to say to the Lord, as the psalmist did, "I trusted in thee, O LORD: I said, Thou art my God" (31:14), as if he had said, "Thou art my God not only in offer but in choice (or in preference to every other god); and I, accordingly, have trusted in Thee as my God and placed all my hope and happiness in Thee."

He is their God also in possession. By believing cordially that He is theirs in offer and by choosing Him for their God and portion in preference to every other god, as well as by trusting that in Christ He will perform the part of a God to them, they take possession of

---

2. Westminster Shorter Catechism 46.

Him as their God. According to their faith in Him is their possession and enjoyment of Him; and in bestowing Himself on them as their God and portion, He makes over to them all that He is and has and does and will do to be theirs in time and through eternity (Hos. 13:4; Ps. 84:11; 1 Cor. 3:21, respectively). Seeing, then, that in amazing condescension He bestows Himself on them as their God, they are under infinite obligations to devote themselves and all that they are, have, and do to Him as His people. By His being their God, they are firmly bound as well as powerfully excited to love Him supremely and to delight in yielding spiritual and universal obedience to Him. "Because God is the Lord, and our God…we are bound to keep all his commandments."[3] And because it is of sovereign grace that He has been pleased to become their God, they are bound to obey His law as it stands in His covenant of grace—to obey it not that He may become their God but because He already is their God. The covenant right that, according to His gracious promise, they have to Him as their God gives Him an additional claim to them and to all their love and obedience.

5. Their obligation to obey His law as a rule of conduct proceeds likewise from His being their redeeming God. "In his love and in his pity he redeemed them" (Isa. 63:9). From eternity He, according to the good pleasure of His will, has chosen them to everlasting salvation and has devised the amazing scheme of their redemption. In the immensity of His redeeming love and in the exceeding riches of His glorious grace, God the Father has sent His only begotten Son to purchase redemption for them and His adorable Spirit to apply it to them. He has appointed His only Son to answer the demands of His law as a covenant for them that they might be justified, and His Holy Spirit to write His law as a rule on their hearts that they might be sanctified. As means of attaining the inestimable benefits of eternal redemption,

---

3. Westminster Shorter Catechism 44.

He has moreover favored them with the doctrines, promises, and ordinances of His blessed gospel. Thus, the Father, Son, and Holy Spirit—one Jehovah—stands in the endearing relation of a redeeming God to all true believers; Christ the glorious Mediator stands in the relation of a near kinsman, an incarnate Redeemer; and the Holy Spirit in the relation of a sanctifier and comforter to them. And while God the Father and Christ and the blessed Spirit stand in these and other endearing relations to believers, believers stand in all the correspondent relations to them. Now, from those relations an additional obligation to love and to good works arises that, instead of impairing, greatly strengthens all the other ties under which believers lie to yield evangelical and universal obedience. Because God graciously redeems them from the hand of all their enemies, and that with an infinite price and by infinite power, they are surely under the firmest possible obligations to "serve him without fear, in holiness and righteousness before him, all the days of [their] life" (Luke 1:74–75). The notion of a divine redeemer implies that of a creator: "Thus saith the LORD, thy redeemer, and he that formed thee from the womb, I am the LORD that maketh all things" (Isa. 44:24).

As God's being the Redeemer of His people, then, implies His being their Creator, in subordination to His glory in the redemption of them, so the obligation to obedience arising from His being their sovereign Creator is implied in and strengthened by the obligation flowing from His being their Redeemer. The redeeming grace of God in Christ is so far from lessening the force of the natural obligation under which believers as creatures lie to love and obey Him that it increases this obligation in the highest possible degree. The great God who is glorious in holiness has not resigned His right of sovereign authority over His saints by redeeming them from the law as a covenant and from their spiritual enemies; but on the contrary, He has hereby laid them under further and stronger obligations to universal obedience to the law as a rule. The more illustrious the displays of His glorious perfections and especially of His infinite goodness are that He has afforded in their redemption, the greater are their obligations to obedience. When they consider that they have the righteousness of the incarnate Redeemer imputed to them to entitle them to eternal life and His Spirit dwelling in them to make them meet for the perfection of it, they must surely acknowledge themselves to be under the firmest obligations possible to devote themselves entirely to the service and glory of their redeeming God.

In order to be satisfied of the truth of this, we need only to consider the new relations mentioned above, from which arises a set of new duties that no man is capable of performing or has access to perform unless he previously is a partaker of those relations. Of this class of duties are the faith, love, reverence, and worship that believers owe to Christ the adorable Mediator; to God in the relations of a friend, Father, and God in covenant; and to the Holy Spirit dwelling in them as a quickener, sanctifier, and comforter—also the duties that they owe to fellow saints as members of Christ's mystical body. From those endearing relations and the inestimable blessings issuing from them, believers cannot but be laid under new and peculiar obligations not only to perform these but all the other duties required of them in the law as a rule of life.

6. The holy will of God, revealed in His law as a rule of duty to believers, lays them under infinite obligations to obedience. The law in the hand of Christ is to His spiritual seed not only the rule but the reason of their duty. They are bound not only to do that which is required in the law and to leave undone that which is forbidden, but they must do what is commanded for the very reason that the Lord requires it and abstain from what is forbidden because He forbids it. "Thou hast commanded us," says the holy psalmist, "to keep thy precepts diligently. O that my ways were directed to keep thy statutes!" (Ps. 119:4–5). To keep His commandments is, according to the phraseology of Scripture, to do His will. "He that doeth the will of God," says the apostle John, "abideth for ever" (1 John 2:17). And,

says another apostle, "This is the will of God, even your sanctification" (1 Thess. 4:3). It is the will not only of God the Father but of God the Son: "I have…ordained you, that ye should go and bring forth fruit, and that your fruit should remain" (John 15:16). It is the will also of God the Holy Spirit, whom believers grieve and even quench when they do not study to advance daily in the love and practice of universal holiness.

The law as a rule is not only a transcript of the infinite purity of God's holy nature, but it is, at the same time, a declaration of His holy will respecting the duty that His people owe to Him. They are, then, under the firmest ties to keep His holy commandments because it is His will that they should keep them. His will declared in His law is infinitely, eternally, and immutably holy, and therefore, in connection with the other sources of obligation already mentioned, it lays believers under the highest possible obligations to perfect and perpetual obedience of heart and life to His holy law.

7. Once more, the obligation under which believers are to obey the law as a rule arises also from the inexpressible benefit or advantage of holiness to themselves. The law in the hand of Christ is not only holy and just, but it is good. It is good in itself and good for believers. It requires nothing of them but what is good for them to perform and to endure nothing but what is suitable and advantageous to them—nothing but what is agreeable and delightful to the new and holy nature imparted to them in regeneration. To be enabled, then, from principles of faith and love and for the glory of God to perform spiritual obedience to such a law is profitable, honorable, and delightful to real believers.

It is profitable for them. "Godliness is profitable unto all things" (1 Tim. 4:8). "Godliness with contentment is great gain" (6:6). "Charge them that are rich in this world, that…they do good, that they be rich in good works" (vv. 17–18). "These things are good and profitable unto men" (Titus 3:8). "To love the Lord our God with all our heart, with all our soul, with all our strength, and with all our mind; and our neighbor as ourselves" is the very perfection of our nature, the highest advantage of which it is capable.[4]

Holy obedience to the law in the hand of Christ is also honorable to believers. "If any man serve me," said our blessed Lord, "him will my Father honour" (John 12:26). And again, "If a man love me, he will keep my words: and my Father will love him, and we will come unto him, and make our abode with him" (14:23). What a high honor, what an exalted distinction is conferred on sinful worms of the dust when they are not only beautified with the holy image of God but are advanced to intimate fellowship with Him! Conformity of heart and of life to the divine law is true honor. To resemble Him who is the brightness of the Father's glory and the express image of His person is the honor and glory of a man.

To yield obedience to the law of Christ is delightful also to holy souls. As they delight in the law itself, so they take pleasure in yielding spiritual obedience to all its holy commandments. Wisdom's ways are "ways of pleasantness" to them (Prov. 3:17). Holiness is not only connected with happiness but is itself happiness. A man is miserable in proportion as he is sinful, and happy in the same degree in which he is holy. In obedience there is a present and a great reward. True holiness is the health and happiness, the peace and pleasure of the soul. It renders the external comforts of the believer doubly pleasant and his heaviest crosses light, his life valuable and his death desirable. The holy commandments are inscribed on his heart; and therefore, he is well pleased with the purity, spirituality, and goodness of them. He delights in meditating on them (Ps. 1:2) and especially on the holiness of them. He counts them an easy yoke, and he chooses and resolves to perform spiritual and perpetual obedience to them. He knows by experience that he is happy in proportion as his inclinations, thoughts, words,

---

4. Westminster Shorter Catechism 42. See also Deut. 6:5; Lev. 19:18; and Matt. 22:37–40, respectively.

and actions are holy and that he is in his proper element only when he is exercising graces and performing duties.

Now, seeing holiness is, in subordination to the glory of God, profitable, honorable, and pleasant to believers themselves and so is highly beneficial to them, they are bound to make continual progress in the love and practice of it. As they are bound to glorify God as their redeeming God and, in subordination to this, to advance in the enjoyment of Him, so they are under strong obligations, in obedience to His holy law, to advance in conformity to Him and in communion with Him. For they cannot glorify Him but in proportion as they enjoy Him, and they cannot enjoy Him but by such conformity to His image as is the fruit of communion with Him. Let every believer, then, endeavor diligently to advance in faith and holiness according to the law of Christ; for "blessed is the man that trusteth in the LORD, and whose hope the LORD is" (Jer. 17:7), and "blessed is the man that feareth the LORD, that delighteth greatly in his commandments" (Ps. 112:1).

✦ REFLECTIONS ✦

From what has now been said, we may warrantably infer that all they to whom the law of the Ten Commandments is given as the authoritative rule of their life have already received spiritual life as the beginning of life eternal. They have all been quickened by the Spirit of Christ, united to Him as their living head, instated in His covenant of grace, and justified for His righteousness imputed to them. And so they have received already the beginnings of eternal life as the gift of God through Him. "He that believeth on the Son hath everlasting life" (John 3:36). And again, "Whosoever liveth and believeth in me shall never die" (11:26). The law as a covenant of works says to the dead sinner, "Do this and live; do this for life." The law as a rule of life, on the contrary, says to the living saint, "Live and do this; do this not *for* but *from* life already received." All they, then, to whom the law as a rule of life in the hand of the Mediator is given already have, in their regeneration, received the beginning of eternal life prior to their being capable of performing the smallest degree of obedience to the law in that form. They cannot obey the law as a rule of life otherwise than by working from life, but this supposes them to have life previous to such working and as the principle of it. Christ lives in them, and they live by the faith of Him. Their spiritual and eternal life is the life of Christ, life that is wholly derived from Him; and the rule of it by which all its activity is to be regulated is the divine law as the law of Christ (Gal. 6:2). Regeneration and vital union with Christ are previously and absolutely necessary to the smallest act of acceptable obedience to the law as a rule of life.

Does the law as a rule of life oblige believers to yield even perfect obedience to its precepts? We ought not to infer from this that it can either justify them before God or condemn them. To justify or to condemn a man belongs to the law as a covenant but not to it as a rule. To be under the law as a rule of life is the privilege only of believers who are already justified freely by grace through the redemption that is in Christ Jesus and who are thereby placed forever beyond the reach of condemnation (Rom. 8:1). The law as a rule cannot justify believers for their obedience to it, for they were perfectly justified in the sight of God before they began their course of sincere obedience; and besides, their obedience is far from being perfect. Neither can it condemn them to eternal wrath for their disobedience, for in their justification they were delivered from condemnation before they began, strictly speaking, to disobey it. It can indeed adjudge them to endure the painful effects of paternal anger but not to suffer the direful effects of avenging wrath (John 5:24). The law as a rule can direct and bind believers even to perfect obedience, but it cannot either justify them to eternal life or condemn them to eternal death. Their title to eternal life and their security from eternal death have been merited for them by the obedience and death of the last Adam, and they are secured to them by His intercession. This consideration should endear exceedingly the holy law as a rule of duty to the true believer and should constrain him to rejoice in the thought that he is bound, and in the prospect that to all eternity he shall be bound, by the authority of it to perfect and perpetual obedience (Ps. 119:77; Rev. 22:3).

Hence, also it is evident that the main reason why many true believers have but little holiness of heart and life is that they have much of a legal spirit still remaining in them. It is only with their renewed nature that they obey, or are capable of obeying, the law as a rule. Their unrenewed nature still cleaves to the law as a covenant. In proportion, then, to the degree of corruption remaining in them is that of their legal or old covenant spirit, and the more this prevails in them, the less holy they are. Evangelical or true holiness is a conformity of heart and life not to the law as a covenant of works but to it as a rule of life standing in the covenant of grace. Although believers, as we said above, are wholly delivered from the dominion of the covenant of works as a rightful sovereign, yet many times it is permitted to reenter their consciences and usurp authority over them. At such times it will venture either to promise eternal life to them for their obedience or to threaten eternal death to them for their disobedience. Now in exact proportion to the degree of their legal temper they are disposed to hearken to the voice of the law in their consciences; and as far as they regard the usurped authority of the law as a covenant of works, they so far disregard the high authority and obligation of it as a rule of duty.

Believer, you cannot advance in holy conformity to the law as a rule but in proportion as you, by the Spirit, mortify your legal temper. You may be eminently strict, exact, and uniform in your external performance of every duty; but in as far as a legal spirit prevails and influences your performance of them, they are so far unholy and unacceptable to God. He will accept none of your works but those that are done from evangelical principles and in an evangelical manner. Nothing will more effectually retard your progress in true holiness than either to hope that you shall obtain heaven for your works of obedience or to fear that you shall be cast into hell for your sins. If you trust your habits of grace rather than the fullness of grace in Christ, if you derive your comfort from your lively frames and religious attainments rather than from Christ and the promises, and if you make either the good dispositions implanted in you or the good works performed by you the ground of your right to trust daily in Him for salvation instead of trusting in Him on the ample warrant afforded you by the offers and calls of the gospel, by doing so you will assuredly decline from holy and cheerful obedience to the law as a rule of life. If instead of coming always as a sinner to the compassionate Savior and placing direct confidence in Him for salvation to yourself in particular, you refuse to trust in Him except when you can bring some good qualification or work with you to recommend you to Him, you cannot advance in that holy obedience to His law which is "the obedience of faith" (Rom. 16:26).

It is no less manifest from what has been said that the state to which believers are advanced on their vital union with Christ is so far from being a state of liberty to commit sin that it is a state in which they are laid under the highest possible obligations even to perfect obedience. If all men are bound to keep the commandments of God because He is Jehovah, the redeemed are especially and still more firmly bound to yield all obedience to them because He is not only Jehovah but is besides their God and Redeemer. None are under such high and strong obligations to holiness of heart and life as the ransomed of the Lord are. He is their God in covenant, and this lays them under the firmest ties to be His obedient, holy people. He is their almighty and gracious Redeemer, and therefore they are not their own but His and are infinitely bound to glorify Him in their bodies and in their spirits, which are His (1 Cor. 6:20).

Why do the saints bitterly bewail the strength of their corruptions and the weakness of their graces, the innumerable sins of which they have been guilty, and the want of perfect conformity to the holy law of which they are sensible? Is it not because they feel their infinite obligations not to merely sincere but even to perfect obedience? And why do they, in their exercise of evangelical repentance, loathe themselves in their own sight for their iniquities and their abominations (Ezek. 36:31)? Don't they do it because they are enabled to account their want of that perfect conformity to the law to which they are bound an abominable defect? The wonderful grace of God displayed in their justification and deliverance from the law as a covenant of works, instead of leaving them at liberty to continue in sin, disposes and powerfully constrains them to depart from all iniquity and advance resolutely in universal obedience to the law as a rule of life (2 Tim. 2:19; Titus 2:14). There is not a true believer in the world who does not know this by experience.

What has been advanced may also serve to throw some light on the doctrine of vowing to the Lord and of the obligation that arises from a lawful vow. Believers are far from being left at liberty to vow or not to vow as they please. They are expressly commanded to vow to God and also to perform their vows. "Vow, and pay unto the LORD your God" (Ps. 76:11). "Pay thy vows unto the most High" (50:14). It is clear from the context that the vows mentioned in this last passage are not legal and ceremonial but spiritual or moral vows—vows that believers in all ages of the church are bound both to make and to perform. Isaiah, when predicting the conversion of multitudes in New Testament times, and especially in the millennial period of the church, says, "The Egyptians shall know the LORD in that day…; yea, they shall vow a vow unto the LORD, and perform it" (Isa. 19:21).

Accordingly, the venerable assembly at Westminster teaches that vowing to God is a duty required in the second commandment of the moral law.[5] All true converts, in every age of the church, dedicate themselves and all that they are, have, and do to the Lord; and in doing so they either expressly or implicitly vow to Him. That is to say, they solemnly purpose and promise that in dependence on

---

5. Westminster Larger Catechism 108.

promised grace—or that in as far as the Lord Jesus will, according to His promises, enable them—they shall, all the days of their life, yield sincere and increasing obedience to His holy law as the rule of their duty. They do not engage or promise to yield perfect obedience in their present state of imperfection or to perform as much as a single duty in the strength of grace already received, but to perform, in the strength of that grace which is promised and which they trust will be given them, all necessary duties. This is not a particular but a general vow. Neither is it a legal and ceremonial but a spiritual and moral vow. It is the believer's baptismal vow that, if opportunities are afforded, he will be sure willingly, explicitly, and frequently to renew at the Table of the Lord.

Now, from this vow or promissory oath arises an obligation on the believer to do as he has said. He vows to perform nothing but what he was previously under the firmest obligations possible to perform; and therefore, though his vow cannot add to the authority of God in His law nor, strictly speaking, strengthen those obligations to obedience which are already as strong as it is possible for them at the time to be, yet it is the source of a new, a distinct, and a superadded obligation. It is not, indeed, a primary source of obligation to obedience like those mentioned above, but still it lays the believer under a new and distinct obligation to fulfill his engagement. He engages or obliges himself, by his own voluntary act, to perform sincerely all those duties to which he is already bound by the law. And the more often he repeats his vow, the obligation arising from it becomes the firmer. If a lawful vow, with respect to things indifferent, founds an obligation, as generally seems to be allowed, much more, surely, must a lawful vow concerning necessary duties be binding. The new obligation to necessary duties, arising from a deliberate and solemn vow to perform them, is not in the least inconsistent with those high obligations to them which flow from the other sources already explained. It is, indeed, associated with these obligations, but it is no disparagement to them.

Should any still be disposed to question if a lawful vow respecting moral duties can found a new and distinct obligation to perform them, I would only add that it either lays the believer who makes it under a new obligation or it does not. There can be no medium here. If it lays him under an obligation, it must be an obligation posterior to those considered above, and therefore a new and distinct one. If it lays him under no obligation, it will follow that lawful vows do not bind. If they do not bind or impose an obligation, they cannot be broken; and, if so, the saints in all ages have acted an unwise, yea, and a superstitious part when they have confessed and bitterly bewailed their breach of vows. Many professors of religion in our day seem unwilling to vow to the Lord for fear that, by the breach of vows, they should increase the number of their sins. But this discovers both a want of knowledge and a want of sincerity. Matthew Henry, commenting on Isaiah 45:23, says well, "If the heart be brought into obedience to Christ, and made willing in the day of his power…the tongue will swear to him, will lay a bond upon the soul to engage it for ever to him; for he that bears an honest mind never startles at assurances."[6]

In conclusion, believers are under every obligation not only to obedience to the divine law but to free and voluntary obedience. They are bound to yield such obedience as cannot be performed under the law as a covenant of works, as cannot be performed from the principle either of slavish fear or of servile hope. They are under the strongest ties to yield voluntary obedience to the law as a rule of life. They are firmly bound, but it is to free obedience—to the obedience not of slaves or hirelings but of sons and daughters. The Lord Jesus says in His law to them, as on a particular occasion He did to His disciples, "Freely ye have received, freely give" (Matt. 10:8). With infinite willingness, He obeyed the law as a covenant for them in order that they,

---

6. [Matthew Henry, *Matthew Henry's Commentary on the Whole Bible* (Peabody, Mass.: Hendrickson, 1994), on Isa. 45:20–25 (1166).]

by His grace, might with sincere willingness and, in due time, with perfect willingness obey it as a rule.

The law as a rule of life to believers has, as was said above, no threatening of eternal death and no promise of eternal life annexed to it. No obedience, therefore, is suitable to it but that which is free and voluntary, proceeding from love to God, delight in His will, and concern for His glory. In proportion, accordingly, as the saints are enabled to believe the astonishing love of God with application to themselves and to contemplate the infinitely free grace manifested in redeeming them from the broken covenant of works and in bringing them under the law of the hand of Christ, they yield free and unconstrained obedience to this law. Made a "willing" people in the day of the Redeemer's power (Ps. 110:3), they obey willingly, and that not from legal but from evangelical motives. They study to do what the Lord requires because He commands them and in order to please and honor Him. They hate all manner of sin because it is hateful in itself and because He hates it. With holy abhorrence they forsake iniquity because He forbids it and in order that they may not displease or dishonor Him. And though their obedience will not be absolutely free till it is absolutely perfect, yet the freeness of it will always be in exact proportion to the strength and frequency of their actings of faith and love. When a man is habitually attentive to the manner as well as to the matter of every act of obedience, it is a good evidence that he is dead to the law as a covenant and is brought under the obligation of it as a rule; that the law as a covenant has begun to be erased from his heart and the law as a rule to be written on it.

CHAPTER 12

The Nature, Necessity, and Desert of Good Works

Good works are such actions or deeds as are commanded in the law of God as a rule of life. An action is a good work in the view of men when it is materially good—that is, when the matter of it appears agreeable to the letter of the law and when it is profitable either to the individual himself who performs it or to any other. But nothing is a good work in the sight of God except it is formally as well as materially good. While the matter of it must accord to the letter, the form must, in some degree, correspond to the spirit of the holy law. No man, while he is under the law as a covenant of works, can do a single action that is formally good. He must be a true believer, justified by faith, dead to the law as a covenant, under the law as a rule, and "created in Christ Jesus unto good works" before he can perform the smallest action that will be good and acceptable in the sight of God (Eph. 2:10; see also Rom. 5:6).

Good works cannot be done but in obedience to the law in the hand of the Mediator as an authoritative rule of conduct, and they cannot be performed but by persons who are vitally united to Him as the last Adam and who have communion with Him in His righteousness and fullness (John 15:5). A man, in order to perform the smallest good work, must be justified on the ground of the perfect righteousness of Christ imputed to him; and therefore his good works arrive too late to form any part of his justifying righteousness. As it is impossible for a man to be justified in the sight of God by the works of the law before conversion, so it is equally impossible for him to be justified by his good works after it. Good works will, indeed, justify the believer's profession of faith before men but not his person before God. Such works, not being performed under the law as a covenant and at the same time not being perfect, cannot enter into the ground of his justification, but they manifest him to have true faith and to be already justified by faith. And so they evidence his profession of faith before men to be sincere (Gal. 2:16; Phil. 3:9; James 2:24). As good works are strictly enjoined in the law of God, and as it is of the highest importance to the honor of God and also to the advancement of holiness and comfort in believers themselves that they understand well the nature, the necessity, and the desert of such works, I shall here briefly consider each of these in order.

<h3 style="text-align:center">♦ SECTION 1 ♦</h3>

The Nature of Good Works

Holiness of life, or the constant practice of good works, proceeds from that holiness of heart which is imparted to elect sinners in regeneration and sanctification, and it consists in their conformity of life to the law as a rule of duty. The habitual and constant performance of good works is the same as holiness of life, and it is the distinguishing character of every adult person who so believes in the Lord Jesus as to have the beginnings of eternal life. Here it will be necessary, briefly, to point out what it is that constitutes an action, a good work in the sight of God, the omniscient and sovereign Judge of all.

Much more is requisite for this purpose than merely a good intention. A man may, in his actions, propose to himself a good end or may have an apparently good intention to serve, while yet he is ignorant of the holiness and spirituality of the divine law (1 Tim. 1:7). Many, with what has appeared to them to be the best intention, have done and still do things that are expressly forbidden in the holy law of God (John 16:2). The sovereign authority of God in His law obliges men to regulate not only their ends of acting but their principles, inclinations, and the matter and manner of their actions by that divine standard (Deut. 12:32; Mark 12:30–31). The following things especially are requisite to constitute our works of obedience as good works:

1. They must be such as are required in the law of God and are performed in obedience to His holy will, expressed in the precepts of His law. "He that keepeth the commandment keepeth his own soul" (Prov. 19:16). "He that doeth the will of God abideth for ever" (1 John 2:17). The law of God is the revelation of His sovereign will, and therefore it is the authoritative rule of our obedience. No action, then, is a good work except it is performed agreeably to His will and as an act of obedience to His commands.

2. They cannot be accounted good works unless they are raised on a good foundation. Our works cannot be good unless they are works of new and evangelical obedience, and this they cannot possibly be except they are built on a new and evangelical foundation. Good works cannot stand but on a good or an evangelical ground—namely, the doctrines, offers, invitations, and promises of the gospel, and especially the glorious doctrine of justification only for the righteousness of Christ imputed and received by faith, as also the holy law, in consequence of the second Adam's fulfilling of it, divested of its federal form to believers and in and by Him given to them as the only and immutable rule of their new obedience. "If ye know these things," said our Lord to His disciples, "happy are ye if ye do them" (John 13:17). And the apostle Paul wrote, "These things"—namely, the things mentioned in the immediately preceding context—"I will that thou affirm constantly, that they which have believed in God might be careful to maintain good works" (Titus 3:8).

3. It is also requisite that they flow from evangelical principles. They cannot be spiritually good or acceptable to God except they proceed from good principles of action. But no principles are good unless they are evangelical. It is not sufficient for this purpose that our

performances be barely moral, as many of the actions of heathens were; they must be evangelical and holy likewise. They must flow from such evangelical principles as these: a soul regenerated by the quickening Spirit of Christ, a mind enlightened with the saving knowledge of Christ and of the truth as it is in Him, union with Christ and with God in Him by a living faith, communion with Christ in His righteousness and fullness and with God in Him, a conscience sprinkled with His justifying and peace-speaking blood, and a heart sanctified and comforted by His Holy Spirit (Ezek. 36:25–27; Matt. 12:35). They must proceed more immediately from principles and habits of faith, hope, and love in a sanctified soul. "Without faith it is impossible to please [God]" (Heb. 11:6). "Every man that hath this hope in him purifieth himself, even as he is pure" (1 John 3:3). "This is the love of God, that we keep his commandments" (1 John 5:3).

4. We must be excited to the performance of them by evangelical motives only. To render our works spiritually good, it is not enough that they proceed from good principles; they must, moreover, be influenced by good motives, deeply affecting and determining our hearts such as these: the astonishing love and grace of God manifested in His gospel (1 John 4:19); the sovereign authority and will of God as our covenant God and Father, declared in His law as the rule of our duty (1 Thess. 4:3; Ex. 20:2–3; 2 Cor. 5:14, respectively); our deliverance from condemnation and the ample security from eternal death that the blood of Christ affords us (1 Cor. 6:20; 1 Peter 1:17–19); the promise and the hope of eternal life as the gift of God through Jesus Christ our Lord (Titus 1:2; Rom. 6:23, respectively); and the perfect pattern of good works that Christ has proposed for our imitation (1 Peter 2:21; Heb. 12:1–3, respectively).

5. Another requisite is that they be performed in a special manner. It is necessary that the manner as well as the matter of our works be spiritually good and acceptable to God. The manner of performing them must be evangelical, suited to the state, the privileges, and

the prospects of believers. They cannot be good works except they are performed inwardly as well as outwardly; for "the law is spiritual" (Rom. 7:14), and it requires the obedience of the whole heart as well as of the whole life. They must, in order to their being good works, be performed in the exercise of trusting with firm confidence that Christ will, every moment, afford us grace to enable us to perform them acceptably (1 Tim. 1:5; Phil. 4:13; Heb. 11:6, respectively); in the exercise of a lively hope (1 Peter 1:3–4); in the exercise of supreme love to Christ and to God in Him (1 Tim. 1:5; Rom. 13:10, respectively); in the exercise of adoring gratitude to the Lord for all His benefits bestowed and promised (Ps. 116:12–14); and in the exercise also of evangelical contrition and humiliation, counting ourselves utterly "not worthy of the least of all mercies" (Gen. 32:10) and indebted wholly to His sovereign grace for all our salvation (Eph. 2:8, 10). They are good works only in proportion as they are performed in the exercise of spiritual graces and in the strength of promised grace.

6. Once more, it is no less requisite that we propose to ourselves good ends in performing them. The ends which we propose to ourselves in the practice of them must be evangelical, as well as our principles, motives, and manner. They cannot be accounted good works, except our chief or ultimate end in doing them be the glory of God in Christ, as our God (1 Cor. 10:31). Nor is it sufficient for this purpose that in them we virtually and habitually intend the glory of God; it will be necessary that, in performing each of them, we actually aim at the glory of His holy name as our highest end. It is also requisite that in our practice of them we have it ever in view, in subordination to the manifested glory of God, to advance in conformity of heart and of life to our great Redeemer (Phil. 3:10–14; 1 Peter 1:15–16); to embrace every opportunity of doing good to all around us (Matt. 5:16); and to prepare for the full and everlasting enjoyment of God—Father, Son, and Holy Spirit—as our infinite portion (Ps. 73:25–26).

Now the performances of real Christians have, in a higher or lower degree, all these requisites; and therefore they are, strictly speaking, good works. The depravity that remains in the hearts of believers hinders, indeed, their works from being perfectly good, but it cannot prevent them from being truly or spiritually good and "acceptable to God by Jesus Christ" (1 Peter 2:5). The good Spirit of God dwells in all saints and works in them "both to will and to do of his good pleasure" (Phil. 2:13). He has begun, and He promotes, a good work of grace in their hearts; and from this proceed all good works of obedience in their lives (Phil. 1:6). But, seeing their best actions are not yet perfectly good, they ought so to increase and "abound to every good work," so as constantly to press on toward perfection in holiness (2 Cor. 9:8). They are commanded to increase more and more in the strength and liveliness of their spiritual graces and in the zealous and diligent performance of their necessary duties (2 Peter 3:18; 1 Thess. 4:1, respectively).

✦ SECTION 2 ✦
The Necessity of Good Works

In this section I shall, first, endeavor to show for what purposes good works are not necessary and, next, in what respects, or for what ends, they are necessary.

In the first place, I am to show for what purposes they are not necessary.

1. Good works are not necessary to move God to be merciful and gracious to us. They are not needful to recommend us so to the favor of God so as to excite His compassion and goodwill to us or to produce the smallest change in His intentions concerning us. The change to be promoted by the continual practice of good works will be only in ourselves; it cannot be in God. "He is in one mind, and who can turn him?" (Job 23:13). He is Jehovah, and He changes not. Our holy performances do not render God more willing than He is already to show mercy or give grace to us, but they are means of rendering ourselves more and more willing to receive His mercy and grace. We

must, then, never depend on our own good works but always on the spotless righteousness of Christ and on the gracious promises of God for all the effects of His mercy and favor.

2. Our good works are not necessary to afford us a right to trust in Christ for salvation. They cannot obtain for us a right to believe in the Lord Jesus, nor is it requisite that they should. The commandment of the law to believe in the name of Jesus Christ (1 John 3:23), together with the offers, invitations, and promises of the gospel, affords us all the right or warrant that is requisite to come as sinners to the Savior and to place the confidence of our hearts in Him for His whole salvation. These afford to us, in common with all the other hearers of the gospel, a full right as sinners of mankind to approach and, with the firmest confidence, to trust in Him. And, therefore, we have no need to procure by our performances the smallest degree of right to come to Him (Isa. 55:1; Rev. 22:17). Our good works are necessary for other purposes, but not for this. "Christ Jesus came into the world to save sinners" (1 Tim 1:15) and "not…to call the righteous, but sinners to repentance" (Matt. 9:13). We must, therefore, approach and trust in Him as sinners utterly unworthy of Him, and that without looking for any good qualities or works of our own either to recommend us to His regard or to entitle us to trust that He will save us. How can our good works be necessary to afford us a right to trust in the Savior when we must begin to trust in Him before we can perform the smallest good work?

3. Neither are good works necessary to acquire for us a personal interest in Christ. So far are they from being requisite to merit, or so much as to obtain for us a saving interest in Jesus Christ, that our being previously interested in Him is indispensably necessary to our being capable of performing so much as the very smallest of them (Eph. 1:6; John 15:5, respectively). Good works, then, can have no place in procuring for us a personal interest in the Savior. It is necessary to qualify us for them, but they are not necessary to confer on us a right

to it. They are indeed an evidence of it but not a procuring cause; they follow it but do not go before it. They can have no existence before it, and therefore they can neither entitle us to it nor qualify us for the reception of it. A personal interest in Christ must either be received as a gift of sovereign grace, by faith only, or not received at all. Many convinced sinners err greatly in this matter. They hope that their reformations, their frames, and their performances will so recommend them to God as to procure for them a saving interest in the person and work of Christ. Thus, they themselves try to begin the work of their salvation and then to trust that the Savior will help it forward. But this is to seek righteousness "not by faith, but as it were by the works of the law. For they stumbled at that stumblingstone" (Rom. 9:32). No man can attain a saving interest in Christ until he is made willing to receive it as a gift of infinitely free grace.

4. Good works are not requisite to acquire for us a right to increasing degrees of sanctification. We ought, indeed, to employ them diligently as means of growing in habits of grace, but we must not hence conclude that they are needful to procure for us a title to those influences of sanctifying grace which are every moment requisite for increasing our habits of grace and exciting them to exercise. They are necessary as means and also as evidences but not as procuring causes of progressive holiness. It is not the good fruit that makes the tree good, but, on the contrary, it is the good tree that produces the good fruit. It is not the good works of believers but the infinitely perfect righteousness of the second Adam that entitles them to increasing holiness both of heart and life. And, therefore, while they ought to be diligent and zealous in performing all good works, they must not presume to place the least dependence on their performance of them for a title to continued supplies either of sanctifying or comforting grace. Instead of trusting to their own endeavors for a continued increase of inherent holiness, their duty is to rely on the righteousness of Jesus Christ for their whole title to it. They ought to rely on His surety-righteousness as much for a title to sanctification as for a right to

justification. It is by faith in the Lord Jesus as their "righteousness and strength" that they are sanctified as well as justified (Isa. 45:24; see also Acts 15:9; 1 Cor. 6:11; Col. 2:12). While then they trust constantly in Christ Himself for continual supplies of sanctifying grace, they must, instead of depending on their own works, rely daily on His righteousness alone for all their title to those supplies. Though good works are indispensably necessary in them who are sanctified, yet they are so far from being requisite to procure for the saints a title to progressive sanctification that these could not perform so much as one of them till after they began to be sanctified.

5. Once more, good works have no place in obtaining for the saints a right to eternal life in heaven. "The gift of God is eternal life through Jesus Christ our Lord" (Rom. 6:23). It is a "purchased possession" (Eph. 1:14), purchased for all His spiritual seed by the obedience unto death of the second Adam. It is an inheritance that He, the "heir of all things" (Heb. 1:2), bequeaths to them and of which they attain possession not on the ground of their own good works but by union and communion with Him. It is not their own good deeds but His righteousness that is meritorious of eternal life for them. "Not by works of righteousness which we have done," says the apostle Paul, "but according to his mercy he saved us" (Titus 3:5). It is Christ only who has "obtained eternal redemption" for believers (Heb. 9:12). They are accepted as righteous in the sight of God and entitled to eternal life not for their own good works but "only for the righteousness of Christ imputed to us, and received by faith alone."[1] It is "by the righteousness of one" that grace, or "the free gift[,] came upon all men" who believe "unto justification of life," for "by the obedience of one shall many be made righteous" (Rom. 5:18–19). Were the good works of believers to entitle them in the smallest degree to salvation, their salvation would, in the same degree, be of debt to them and not

---

1. Westminster Shorter Catechism 33.

of grace. But it is not by any merit of theirs but by the sovereign grace of God that they are saved (Eph. 2:8–9).

Besides, if their good works afforded them a right claim to eternal life, it would inevitably follow that they could not have a right to it till after they had performed them all. But the infinitely perfect righteousness of Jesus Christ gives them in their justification a complete right to life eternal, and that before they begin to do one good work (Rom. 4:4–6). Indeed, believers, although they could perform even perfect obedience, could yet yield no degree of obedience but what they owed to the Lord; and therefore, even their perfect obedience could not merit the least favor from Him.

And as their good works can give them no meritorious right to eternal life, so neither can they afford them a pactional title to it; for by the consummate righteousness of Jesus Christ imputed to them they have already both the one right and the other, and that in the highest possible degree. Though good works, then, are not necessary in order to procure or obtain a right to eternal salvation, yet they are the necessary duties of all who are justified and entitled to that salvation. They are the consequences of salvation already procured, and they are the antecedents that prepare believers for the salvation to be still attained. At the same time, however, they are not causes of obtaining the possession either of the beginning, the progress, or the consummation of salvation. They are indispensably necessary in all adult persons who shall be saved, but not necessary to obtain or acquire salvation. Believers are saved not *by* their good works but *to* them, as effects and evidences of their salvation already begun. These words of the apostle Paul, "They do it to obtain a corruptible crown; but we an incorruptible" (1 Cor. 9:25), will not prove that good works are necessary to obtain eternal salvation; for the verb in the original properly signifies "to receive or apprehend," and it is so rendered by our translators in the verse immediately preceding. Believers are not saved either by their works or for them or according to them. Not by them: "Not by works of righteousness which we have done, but according to his mercy he saved us" (Titus 3:5). Not for them: "Not for your sake do I this, saith the Lord GOD, be it known unto you" (Ezek. 36:32). Not according to them: He "hath saved us, and called us with an holy calling, not according to our works, but according to his own purpose and grace" (2 Tim. 1:9). Men are, indeed, to be judged according to their works but are not to be saved according to them. The rule of judgment will be the law, but the rule of salvation will be the gospel.

I proceed now, as was proposed, to show in what respects or for what important purposes good works are indispensably requisite.

1. They are necessary as just acknowledgments of God's sovereign authority over believers and as acts of obedience to His righteous commands. "For this is the will of God," says an apostle, "even your sanctification" (1 Thess. 4:3). The infinite Majesty of heaven has not laid aside His right of dominion over believers by affording them deliverance from condemnation and a right to eternal life but, on the contrary, has, in that wonderful way, laid them under additional obligations to be "holy in all manner of conversation" (1 Peter 1:15). The glorious liberty to which He has called them is given them for this purpose: that they "might serve him without fear, in holiness and righteousness before him, all the days of [their] life" (Luke 1:74–75). He has delivered them from the law as a covenant for this very end: that according to the law as a rule they might serve Him "in newness of spirit" and "be careful to maintain good works" (Rom. 7:6; Titus 3:8). The sovereign will of God as the supreme rule of duty is expressed in His commands, and therefore universal and perpetual obedience to them is necessary.

2. Good works are indispensably requisite as being one special end of the election, redemption, regeneration, and effectual vocation of the objects of God's everlasting love. They are one design of the election of sinners. "The God and Father of our Lord Jesus Christ...hath

chosen us in him," said the apostle Paul, "that we should be holy and without blame before him in love" (Eph. 1:3–4). They are also one end of the redemption of elect sinners. For the same apostle said, "Christ…gave himself for us, that he might redeem us from all iniquity, and purify unto himself a peculiar people, zealous of good works" (Titus 2:13–14). They are one of the designs, too, of the regeneration of God's elect. "We are his workmanship," said our apostle, "created in Christ Jesus unto good works, which God hath before ordained that we should walk in them" (Eph. 2:10). Good works are the native and necessary operations of a regenerate and sanctified soul. Grace in the heart is a living, operative principle of holiness in the life. Good works are likewise one of the ends to be attained by their effectual vocation. "As he which hath called you is holy," said the apostle Peter, "so be ye holy in all manner of conversation" (1 Peter 1:15).

3. Good works are also necessary inasmuch as they are one great design of the gospel and of the ordinances and providential dispensations of the Lord. As for the gospel, it is "the mystery of godliness" (1 Tim. 3:16), "the doctrine which is according to godliness" (6:3). The doctrine of the gospel is not speculative merely; it is also transforming and practical. It is not only the instrument of enlightening the mind but also of renovating the will and of rectifying the affections of the soul. In the hand of the Holy Spirit, it is a fire that penetrates, warms, softens, quickens, purifies, and comforts the heart. It is a light that assimilates (2 Cor. 3:18) and truth that sanctifies (John 17:17). It is also "the law of the Spirit of life in Christ Jesus," which, by making believers "free from the law of sin and death" brings them "under the law to Christ" (Rom. 8:2; 1 Cor. 9:21). The design, too, of the ordinances of the gospel is that sinners may be converted to the love and practice of holiness and that saints may be enabled to abound more and more "in every good word and work" (2 Thess. 2:17; see also Phil. 1:9). This is the design likewise of all providential dispensations to the children of God. If they are favored with prosperity, it is that the goodness of God may constrain them to "bring forth therefore fruits

meet for repentance" (Matt. 3:8); or, if they are visited with adversity, it is that it may yield "the peaceable fruit of righteousness unto them" (Heb. 12:11).

4. It is indispensably requisite that believers perform good works as expressions of gratitude to their God and Savior for all His inestimable benefits vouchsafed to them. They are bound to always be grateful and thankful to the Lord for His great goodness to them in creation, in providence, and especially in redemption. It is He who has made them and not they themselves (Ps. 100:3). He has preserved them amid innumerable dangers and has liberally supplied their various wants. He has distinguished them from all others of the sons of men by the greatness of their privileges and the inestimable value of their enjoyments and by the innumerable instances of His kindness and the rich abundance of His favors. He has also, in the immensity of His love, sent His only begotten Son to redeem them to Himself by His blood and to merit for them the full and endless fruition of Himself in the mansions of bliss. Moreover, He has sent His Holy Spirit to dwell in them, to apply redemption to them, and by His sanctifying and comforting influences, to prepare them for every good work and advance them to the full enjoyment of eternal life. How boundless, then—how inexpressible—is the debt of adoring gratitude that they owe to the Father, to the Son, and to the Holy Spirit!

Now, what does the Lord require of them in return for all His benefits? Nothing but that they should "be ready to every good work" (Titus 3:1) and be "zealous of good works" (2:14). Having been bought with a price of infinite value, they are no more their own but are indispensably bound to glorify God in their body and in their spirit, which are His, by a spiritual, universal, and cheerful obedience to Him (1 Cor. 6:19–20). It is the will of their sovereign benefactor that they express their gratitude to Him for the inestimable blessings of His grace by taking pleasure in keeping all His commandments and by showing themselves patterns of good works (Titus 2:7).

5. Good works are no less necessary, as they are our walking in the way that leads to heaven. Jesus Christ is "the way" (John 14:6). Faith and holiness are our walking in Him as the way. This way, accordingly, is called "the way of holiness," or the holy way (Isa. 35:8), inasmuch as none can walk in Christ other than by faith and by that holiness of heart and life which is "the obedience of faith" (Rom. 16:26). As no man can arrive at heaven but by Christ, so without "holiness," or walking in Him, "no man shall see the Lord" (Heb. 12:14). None is in the way to heaven but he who, by a life of faith and the practice of those good works that are the fruits of faith, is advancing toward perfection of holiness. It is the order immutably fixed in the everlasting covenant that a man be made holy in heart and in life before he is admitted to see and enjoy God in His holy place on high. The love and practice of good works, then, in one who has an opportunity of performing them are necessary as appointed means of disposing or preparing him for the holy enjoyments and employments of the heavenly sanctuary. The redeemed, therefore, who are in the way to the celestial city, are zealous for good works and "fruitful in every good work" (Col. 1:10).

6. They are also indispensably requisite in order to evidence and confirm the faith of the saints. Wherever a living and a saving faith is, good works are, in every adult believer, the native fruits and proper evidences of it. "Shew me," said the apostle James, "thy faith without thy works, and I will shew thee my faith by my works" (James 2:18). Sincere obedience is the necessary consequence, and therefore a necessary evidence, of justifying and saving faith. Good works are "your work of faith" (1 Thess. 1:3)—works performed in faith and proceeding from it as the living principle of them. Whatever seeming evidences of true faith, then, a man may have, they are all to be regarded as counterfeit and delusive if he does not, at the same time, love and practice good works. Such works not only evidence a living faith, but they also encourage the believer resolutely to persevere in renewing his exercise of faith; and so they prove to be means of confirming his faith.

7. Good works are necessary to believers for making their calling and election sure to them. Although such works afford a man no right to eternal salvation, yet they are an infallible proof to him that he has a personal interest in it and a sure title to it. They, under the witnessing of the Holy Spirit, supply the believer with arguments that not only serve to confirm his assurance of faith but to increase his assurance of personal interest in Christ and His great salvation. "Hereby we do know that we know him," said the beloved disciple, "if we keep his commandments.… Whoso keepeth his word, in him verily is the love of God perfected: hereby know we that we are in him" (1 John 2:3, 5). To the same purpose, the apostle Peter says, "Giving all diligence, add to your faith virtue; and to virtue knowledge; and to knowledge temperance; and to temperance patience; and to patience godliness; and to godliness brotherly kindness; and to brotherly kindness charity.… Give diligence to make your calling and election sure: for if ye do these things, ye shall never fall" (2 Peter 1:5–7, 10). Without the diligent performance of good works, no believer can attain assurance of his personal interest in eternal salvation, far less establishment in that assurance.

8. Good works are indispensably requisite for the maintenance or continuance of peace and joy in the Holy Ghost. Though such works are not procuring causes of spiritual peace and joy, yet, as fruits of righteousness imputed and fruits of faith, they always accompany that peace and joy which issues from the lively exercise of faith (Ps. 119:165; 2 Cor. 1:12). The consolation that flows from the vigorous exercise of an appropriating faith and from cheering discoveries of personal interest in the covenant of grace cannot be retained without unwearied diligence in the exercise of spiritual graces and in the performance of good works. If believers would know by experience that wisdom's "ways are ways of pleasantness, and all her paths are peace" (Prov. 3:17) and if they would enjoy a continued sense of redeeming love and a sweet foretaste of heavenly felicity, they must be habitually careful not only to maintain but to be rich in good works.

9. Good works are no less needful in order to adorn the doctrine of God our Savior and our profession of that holy and heavenly doctrine. The apostle Paul gave this charge to Titus: "Exhort servants to be obedient unto their own masters, and to please them well in all things; not answering again; not purloining, but shewing all good fidelity; that they may adorn the doctrine of God our Saviour in all things" (Titus 2:9–10). Believers cannot otherwise be a credit to the gospel and to their holy profession of it than by a cheerful and diligent performance of every good work. It is only by the love and practice of universal holiness that they can strike a conviction of the holiness, excellence, and efficacy of the gospel of God our Savior on the consciences of hardened sinners around them. No other practice than that of good works in all their variety becomes the gospel of Christ. It is only "the beauty of holiness" that is suitable and ornamental to His glorious gospel (Ps. 96:9). If believers, then, would not afford occasion to the enemies of the Lord Jesus to blaspheme His glorious name, to speak evil of the way of truth, and to conclude that all who profess faith and holiness are hypocrites and impostors, they must "have diligently followed every good work" (1 Tim. 5:10). "If, while we seek to be justified by Christ, we ourselves also are found sinners," this reflects much dishonor on our great Redeemer and makes Him "the minister of sin" (Gal. 2:17).

10. Good works are also requisite to stop the mouths of wicked men and to prevent offense. "For so is the will of God," said the apostle, "that with well doing ye may put to silence the ignorance of foolish men" (1 Peter 2:15). They are necessary likewise to gain over unbelievers and other enemies of the truth and to recommend faith and holiness to their esteem. It is, by the faithful and cheerful performance of every good work, that believers commend the Lord Jesus and the way of truth and holiness to the consciences of all around them.

11. They are necessary, moreover, for the edification and comfort of fellow Christians. Our blessed Lord, therefore, gives His disciples

this high command: "Let your light so shine before men, that they may see your good works, and glorify your Father which is in heaven" (Matt. 5:16). And the apostle Paul informed the believers at Corinth that their zeal, in contributing readily and seasonably for the poor saints at Jerusalem, "hath provoked very many" (2 Cor. 9:2). The same apostle informs us that the doctrines of grace and the good works to which they tend "are good and profitable unto men" (Titus 3:8). Such works are highly necessary not only for the edification and comfort of individual believers but also for the peace, security, and glory of the church.

12. Finally, good works are indispensably requisite for promoting before the world the manifested glory of Christ, and of God in Him. The apostle Paul prayed for the believers at Philippi that they might be "sincere and without offence till the day of Christ. Being filled with the fruits of righteousness, which are by Jesus Christ, unto the glory and praise of God" (Phil. 1:10–11). The Lord Jesus said to His disciples, "Herein is my Father glorified, that ye bear much fruit" (John 15:8). Believers, then, must endeavor, whatever they do, to "do all to the glory of God" (1 Cor. 10:31). To this purpose it is requisite that they care for the things of the Lord, "that [they] may be holy both in body and in spirit" (1 Cor. 7:34), diligently following every good work, and that they "follow not that which is evil, but that which is good" (3 John 11).

These appear to be the leading purposes for which good works are necessary; and so indispensably requisite are they to subserve those designs that, according to the order unalterably fixed in the covenant of grace, it will be impossible for the latter to be attained without the former. Though good works, as has been observed, are not necessary out of their proper place, yet, in the place assigned to them and for the purposes intended to be served by them, they are absolutely indispensable. No man can warrantably conclude that he is instated in the covenant of grace except he finds that he is disposed and enabled daily to perform them.

♦ SECTION 3 ♦

The Desert of Good Works

Although the good dispositions and actions of one fellow creature deserve to be commended and, in some cases, to be rewarded by another, yet no good qualities or works of mere men can merit the smallest blessing or good thing from the infinite Majesty of heaven.

With respect to the works of unregenerate persons, they are destitute of everything that can render an action good and acceptable in the sight of God. They are not done from true faith as a principle (1 Tim. 1:5; Titus 1:15; Heb. 11:6), nor are they performed from a principle of love (Rom. 8:7; 13:10). Neither are they done by persons who are "accepted in the beloved" (Eph. 1:6). They are not performed in obedience to the will of God expressed in His holy law (Zech. 7:5; Rom. 8:7–8), nor are they done to His glory as the chief end of them. All unconverted persons are said in Scripture to be sinners or workers of iniquity (Ps. 53:1–4; Rom. 3:9–19); and their works, however advantageous many of them may be to themselves or others, are all, notwithstanding, represented as sins in the account of an infinitely holy God (Prov. 21:4; Isa. 1:13–14). For although many of them may be materially good, yet all of them are formally evil, and therefore they are an abomination to Him (Prov. 15:8; 21:27). Consequently, the very best works of unregenerate persons, instead of deserving the favor of God, "deserveth God's wrath and curse, both in this life, and that which is to come."[2] Such works deserve eternal death and cannot surely, at the same time, merit eternal life (Rom. 6:23); and yet so deplorably ignorant and self-righteous are unregenerate sinners that they all rely, either wholly or partially, on their own works for a title to the favor of God, and even to endless felicity. Nay, so gross is

---

2. Westminster Shorter Catechism 84.

their ignorance of themselves and of the righteous law of God and so inveterate is their pride that they depend on such works not only for a title to eternal life but even for security from that eternal death which is already due to them for their innumerable sins and to which they are already condemned.

As for the good works of regenerate men, these also cannot merit from the high and holy One the smallest blessing, much less eternal life. So far as they are spiritually good, they do not, indeed, like the works of the unregenerate, deserve the wrath of God; but still they do not merit the smallest favor at His hand. Merit of condignity, or merit strictly so called, necessarily requires that the works which can merit from God such a reward as would, in strict remunerative justice, be a reward of debt be performed in our own strength; that they are more than we owe to God or more than He requires from us; that they be at least absolutely perfect, and that both in parts, degrees, and continuance; that their value be equal to that of the promised reward; and that the reward be, according to the strictest rules of justice, due for them. Hence, it is manifest that the very best works of the holiest of men can merit no favor, no benefit for them at the hand of God. The perfect works of Adam in innocence could not merit any good thing at the hand of the Lord; much less can the imperfect works of holy men now.

These works cannot, by their own intrinsic value, merit the smallest blessing from God. For first, all the performances that are spiritually good proceed from the almighty agency of the Spirit of grace in believers (1 Cor. 4:7; Phil. 2:13). Second, according to the precepts of His holy and righteous law, believers owe perfect and perpetual obedience to the Lord (Matt. 5:48; Rom. 8:12). Third, the very best of their works in this world are far from being answerable to the high requirements of the holy law of God (Isa. 64:6; Gal. 5:17). And fourth, their best actions, suppose they were perfect, could bear no proportion to any divine blessing, especially to the inestimable blessing of eternal life. The former are the works of finite creatures; the latter, being endless felicity, or the eternal enjoyment of God and of the Lamb, is an infinite reward (Rom. 8:18; 11:6). It is evident, then, that to believers it is wholly a reward of grace and in no degree a reward of debt. "The gift of God is eternal life through Jesus Christ our Lord" (Rom. 6:23).

As the good works of believers cannot, by their own intrinsic value, merit eternal life or even the smallest blessing from God, so they cannot, by paction, procure the smallest right either to the one or to the other. For first, the law as a rule of life, under which believers are, is a perfect law of liberty; and therefore, it cannot contribute to or admit of pactional merit. The man who "looketh into the perfect law of liberty" and who is "a doer of the work...shall be blessed in his deed" (James 1:25; see also 1 Cor. 9:21); but he shall not be blessed for it. Second, the good works of believers, during their state of imperfection, are never correspondent in a perfect degree to the law as a rule of life (Matt. 22:37–39; 5:48; Eccl. 7:20, respectively). Third, the principles of faith and union with Christ, from which all the good works of believers do flow, imply that the infinitely perfect righteousness of Jesus Christ is imputed to them, which alone merits for them a complete title to the progress and consummation of eternal life (2 Cor. 5:21; Gal. 2:16, 20; Rom. 5:21, respectively). The infinitely spotless and meritorious righteousness of Christ, therefore, which is placed to their account, as well as the infinite grace of God which abounds toward them, leaves no room for the pactional merit of their own works (Eph. 2:7–9; Rom. 5:16–19, respectively). And fourth, we read nowhere in Scripture that God ever makes a covenant or paction with believers in which He promises to them eternal life, or even the smallest favor, in consideration of their own sincere obedience. The only covenant that He makes with them is the covenant of grace, according to which every spiritual and temporal blessing is wholly a gift of free and sovereign grace (Eph. 2:8–9).

The good works of believers, then, do not, either by their own intrinsic value or by paction, procure for them a right to the smallest favor at the hand of God, much less to eternal life. It is only the surety-righteousness of Jesus Christ, imputed to them and received by faith alone, that merits and so procures for them a complete title to the beginning, progress, and perfection of eternal life (Rom. 5:21).

◆REFLECTIONS◆

It is evident from what has been said that Christ, who lives in believers, is the only source of all their good works. Having in regeneration entered by His Spirit, He dwells in their hearts by faith as the only fountain of holiness and the sole cause of good works (Eph. 3:17). If adult persons, then, are vitally united to Christ, they will certainly be renewed in the spirit of their minds after His holy image and will perform good works as the necessary fruits of holiness implanted in their hearts (Eph. 4:24–25; Col. 3:10). Where vital union with Christ is, good actions, by persons capable of them, will be the certain consequence; and where it is not, such actions cannot be performed, and it will be in vain to pretend to the practice of them. All the performances of believers that are spiritually good flow from Christ dwelling in their hearts by His Spirit as a spirit of faith, and whatever works proceed not from this principle have nothing more than the mere appearance of good works. "Without me," said our blessed Lord, "ye can do nothing" (John 15:5). No works are good and acceptable to God but those that have the Spirit of Christ for their main principle and the glory of God for their chief end. And no man is "careful to maintain good works" (Titus 3:8) but the man who has the Spirit of Christ in him, causing him to walk in His statutes, to keep His judgments, and do them (Ezek. 36:27).

It is from the gracious work of the Spirit of Christ in the saints that all their good works proceed. If He did not work in the heart "both to will and to do" (Phil. 2:13), they could not work in the life; and if He did not rest on them as "the spirit of glory and of God" (1 Peter 4:14), they could not perform a single action to the glory of God. The only way, then, in which either ministers in the gospel or private Christians can effectually promote the interest of good works among others around them is not only to exhibit a bright example of them in their own conduct but to endeavor diligently to be instrumental in conducting sinners to Jesus Christ and in teaching them how to walk in Him (Col. 2:6).

Can a man perform no good works till after he is justified in the sight of God? Hence, it is manifest that those who rely on their own obedience for a title to justification are strangers to good works. Their continued and avowed dependence on their own works for a right to justification is a sure evidence that they have never performed a single good work; it demonstrates them to be totally destitute of that "holiness, without which no man shall see the Lord" (Heb. 12:14). To pretend to sanctification and then to rely on it for justification is to derive the fountain from the stream, the cause from the effect, and so to invert the order of the blessings of salvation. It is necessary that our sins are forgiven and our persons accepted as righteous in the sight of God in order to our being capable of yielding the least degree of acceptable obedience to Him. As long as a man is not justified, he is under the curse of the law. But how can a man who is under the condemning sentence of the law, and consequently under the dominion of sin, perform good works? The apostle Paul informs us that "as many as are of the works of the law are under the curse" (Gal. 3:10). It is evident, then, that as long as they rely on their own works of obedience to the law for justification, they are utterly unable either to love or perform the smallest good work. It is the distinguishing property of all good works that they are performed from, and not for, justification. Oh, that secure sinners and self-righteous formalists would believe this and flee speedily to the compassionate Savior for righteousness and strength!

The notion of a sinner's justification before God by his own works is an absurdity; it is contrary not only to Scripture but to reason. Every condemned sinner, being under the dominion of sin, is, as was already observed, unable to perform the smallest good work;

yet he flatters himself either that his ability is so great or that the conditions of his justification and salvation are so easy that he can, especially with divine assistance, fulfill them. "If righteousness come by the law, then Christ is dead in vain" (Gal. 2:21); and yet, while the self-righteous formalist seeks righteousness by the works of the law, he professes to believe that the death of Christ has satisfied divine justice for his offenses. If righteousness is by the works of the law, then remission of sins is unnecessary (Rom. 4:6–7); and yet, while he is establishing his own righteousness for his justification, he professes to pray for the pardon of all his sins. He expects justification for the merit of his own works, and at the same time, he professes his belief that they who are justified are justified by grace. In a word, he professes to believe that good works follow justification and that "without faith it is impossible to please [God]" (Heb. 11:6), and after all, he depends on his own works for his justification, as a blessing that he expects will follow them. Ah, how inconsistent, how irrational is the conduct of a self-righteous professor of Christianity! How plainly does it appear that his understanding is darkened and that he himself is under the dominion of the Prince of Darkness!

Are we never to perform good works in order to recommend ourselves to Christ or to afford us a right to trust in Him? Then how dreadful is the condition of multitudes in the visible church! There are many—very many, alas—who, if they grow remiss in performing duties or fall into open sins begin to suspect that Christ will not accept them! But when they labor to mortify their lusts and reform their conduct, they then presume to hope that He will receive them and that God, for His sake, will accept them. Now what is this but to hope that they shall procure the favor of Christ and an interest in His salvation by their own performances and that His merits will render their own works so valuable as to recommend them even to the acceptance of God. They suppose that if they themselves but begin the work of their salvation, they may warrantably trust that the Savior will carry on and finish that work. Thus, they proudly and sacrilegiously presume to divide the work and the honor of their salvation between Christ and themselves. This legal temper is a sure evidence that they are under the dominion of the law of works and that they are totally destitute of evangelical holiness. It is an infallible proof that they have no part in that salvation of the Lord Jesus, the glory of which is to be ascribed wholly to Himself and to God in Him.

We also learn from what has been advanced that good works are to be considered as the fruits of a believer being already saved and, at the same time, in subordination to the glory of God as the end for which he is saved. They are the fruits of his being already in a state of salvation. "Not by works of righteousness which we have done," said the apostle Paul, "but according to his mercy he saved us, by the washing of regeneration, and renewing of the Holy Ghost" (Titus 3:5). Here our apostle argues against salvation by our own works of righteousness on the ground that our good works are the fruits, or effects, of salvation already begun in our souls. He shows that inherent holiness from which all our good works spring is an essential part of our salvation, for he says that we are saved "by the washing of regeneration, and renewing of the Holy Ghost."

Holiness of heart, then, is a necessary part of salvation by Jesus Christ; and holiness of life, or our being careful to maintain good works, is the necessary fruit springing from that salvation (Luke 1:74–75). Good works are also the end for which believers are saved. They are "created in Christ Jesus unto good works" (Eph. 2:10). The great end, in subordination to the glory of redeeming grace, for which they have been saved or created in Christ Jesus is that they might perform and persevere in the practice of all good works. Such works, then, are so far from being grounds of title to salvation that they are the fruits, or consequences, of being already in a state of salvation. True saints are actually, though not completely, saved, and their fruits of righteousness are the evidence of it. They are not saved by their good works, but they are saved to them; nor are they sanctified in order to be justified but are justified in order to be sanctified.

The reader may hence learn how to understand aright this proposition: good works are necessary to salvation. If the term *salvation* is, by some, and that without any warrant from the Scriptures, restricted to the perfect blessedness of saints in heaven, then good works, in the case of persons capable of them, are necessary to or toward salvation. They necessarily exist before it not indeed as procuring causes or federal conditions but merely as antecedents of it. They must of necessity go before it inasmuch as that which, according to the covenant of grace, is first imparted to the spiritual seed of Christ must with its genuine effects precede that which is last of all conferred on them. Personal and progressive holiness is necessary to perfect holiness, and happiness begun is requisite to happiness consummated. At the same time, I dare not say that holiness either of heart or of life is necessary to procure or obtain the felicity of heaven. But if the word *salvation* is taken in its large and scriptural sense, as comprehensive both of a state of grace in time and of a state of glory in eternity, then good works are, properly speaking, not necessary *to* it but necessary *in* it. As imperfect, they are indispensably requisite in a state of grace; and as perfect, they are necessary in a state of glory. They are needful in progressive as well as in perfect salvation. They are indispensably requisite in every adult person who is justified and saved. That the term *salvation* ought to be taken in this comprehensive meaning is evident from this, among other passages of Scripture: "I endure all things for the elect's sakes, that they may also obtain the salvation which is in Christ Jesus, with eternal glory" (2 Tim. 2:10). Here the salvation which is in Christ Jesus is distinguished from eternal glory.

What has been advanced may serve to show us the difference, or rather the opposition, between a reward of debt and a reward of grace. In the law of works, eternal life is promised to the man who yields perfect obedience. If man had yielded this obedience, that would have been a reward of debt (Rom. 4:4), a recompense due by stipulation for the work done. In the gospel, the reward of eternal life is promised to the obedient believer not for his good works but considered as united to Christ in whom he has righteousness for his justification and in whom all the promises of God are yea and amen. This is, indeed, a reward of debt to Christ, to whom the believer is united and in whom he is justified; but it is a reward of infinitely free grace to the believer himself. It cannot be a reward of debt to the believer and at the same time to Christ. A reward of debt is promised to the act or work, but a reward of grace is promised only to the agent or worker. The former is adjudged as a recompense for the work performed; the latter is awarded in and after the work.

If the reward is given to a man for his works of obedience, then it is not of grace; otherwise, work is no more work. But if it is given him of grace, then it is not for his works; otherwise, grace is no more grace (Rom. 11:6). If the reward corresponded to the exact value of the work done and if it followed on work to which man was not bound or which was more than he owed to God and which he performed in his own strength, independent of God, then it would be a recompense strictly merited by him and so would, in the highest sense of the phrase, be a reward of debt to him. Or even though the value of the work done bore no proportion to that of the reward, and though it were work that man previously owed to God and that he performed in strength received from Him, yet, if God had made a covenant with man in which He promised to him the reward of eternal life for the perfect performance of that work, then eternal life would be a reward of pactional debt to man on his complete performance of the work.

On the other hand, when the reward is given not according to the intrinsic worth but according to the spiritual nature or quality of the work and of the work as already due to the Lord, and when it is conferred not in consideration of the work done but because of the free favor of God to the believer who has done the work, it is in that case a reward of grace. Although eternal life is given to the true Christian not as a recompense for his good works but only as a gift of infinitely free grace, yet in the Scriptures it is called a reward to him because it is conferred on him in and after his works.

While the gospel teaches us that good works are unnecessary to the justification of a sinner before God, it affirms that they are necessary in the life of a saint. It, indeed, excludes them from being federal conditions or procuring causes of salvation, but it includes them in salvation both as parts and as consequences of it. We are not saved on the ground of them, but we are "careful to maintain" them because we are saved (Titus 3:8), and saved by grace through faith (Eph. 2:8). "The grace of God" exhibited in the glorious gospel enables as well as teaches us to deny "ungodliness and worldly lusts" and to "live soberly, righteously, and godly, in this present world"; nor have we truly discerned or received that grace which "bringeth salvation" if it has not effectually taught and enabled us to do so (Titus 2:11–12).

Reader, let it be your diligent endeavor to trust at all times in the Lord Jesus for that great salvation which He has brought near to you in the offers and promises of the glorious gospel and to trust in Him for it in order that you may thereby be enabled to perform good works. You can do nothing that is spiritually good except you trust and pray daily for grace to enable you. Let "the life," then, which you "live in the flesh," be "by the faith of the Son of God"; and in this way you shall so die to the law in its federal form as to "live unto God" (Gal. 2:20, 19, respectively). Rely on His consummate righteousness, and on that only, for all your title to salvation; trust His overflowing fullness for all supplies of grace necessary to make you advance daily in the love and practice of every good work. Faith in the adorable Redeemer is the first act of acceptable obedience and the root of all other spiritual graces. Implanted by the Holy Spirit in the heart, it is the principle and primary means of that evangelical "holiness, without which no man shall see the Lord" (Heb. 12:14). Trust, then, and trust with all your heart in the compassionate Savior for justification by His spotless righteousness and for sanctification by His Holy Spirit. Come to the Lord Jesus and, on the warrant afforded you by the unlimited offers and calls of His glorious gospel, place the confidence of your heart in Him for that holiness which is the beginning and the very essence of salvation by Him, which instead of being the proper condition of salvation is salvation itself.

Thus, by grace derived from His fullness, you shall become "zealous of good works" (Titus 2:14)—zealous for performing them and equally zealous for placing no dependence on them for a title to divine favor. And so you shall be "filled with the fruits of righteousness, which are by Jesus Christ, unto the glory and praise of God" (Phil. 1:11). United by faith to the second Adam as your head of righteousness and life, you shall live a life of progressive obedience in time and of perfect obedience through eternity.

Oh, be persuaded that union and communion with Christ as your righteousness and strength are indispensably requisite to your being capable of performing such works as will be good and acceptable to an infinitely holy God. You yourself must, in union with Christ, be accepted as righteous and have a right to eternal life before any of your works can be accepted as sincere. The great Redeemer is in the gospel freely offered to you that you may have a warrant so to believe in Him as to be united to Him, and it is to your peril if you reject the gracious offer. Do not say, "I cannot believe in Him, and why should I be doomed to more dreadful destruction for not doing what I cannot do?" You cannot believe in the Savior because you *will* not, just as Joseph's brethren could not speak peaceably to him because they hated him. Were you really willing to believe in Christ and yet were not able, you could not be an object of blame. But it is quite the reverse with sinners: they are not able because they are not willing (John 5:40), and they are not willing to come to Christ because their carnal mind is enmity against Him (Rom. 8:7). Their inability is moral and, therefore, sinful impotence. Nothing renders them unwilling but the sin that reigns in them. If you are willing to come to the Savior, you will, in the same proportion, be able. No sinner was ever willing to come to Him and yet was not able. In order, then, that you may be made willing to come, you ought, without delay, to trust and plead this absolute promise that, in and with Christ Himself, is graciously offered to you: "I will take away the stony heart out of your flesh, and I will give you an heart of flesh" (Ezek. 36:26); and also this one: "In his name shall the Gentiles trust" (Matt. 12:21).

If Christ is the way to God and to glory, and if He is the way of holiness, or the holy way, then you who have believed through grace ought to take heed that you walk constantly in that way. "As ye have therefore received Christ Jesus the Lord, so walk ye in him" (Col. 2:6). In union with Him, go forward daily in the exercise of faith and love and in the practice of holiness. Depending on His grace and strength, advance with holy diligence and with increasing ardor in the daily practice of those good works that are "your work of faith, and labour of love" (1 Thess. 1:3). Make constant progress in your exercise of faith, and by sanctifying and comforting influences from the fullness of Christ, walk on with cheerfulness and resolution in Him as your way to the perfection of holiness and of happiness.

To walk in Christ is, in consequence of union with Him and by communications of grace from Him, to walk in the unwearied exercise of trusting and hoping in Him, to walk in His commandments (2 Chron. 17:4), and to walk in the love and practice of all good works (Eph. 2:10). Having, then, become dead to the law as a covenant by the body of Christ, apply and trust the promises of His gospel; and in the faith of the promises, walk in all the commandments of His law as a rule. In the humble confidence that He performs the promises of His glorious gospel to you, and so "worketh in you both to will and to do" (Phil. 2:13), keep the commandments of His holy law. Keep them diligently, and "whatsoever ye do in word or deed," do all in His name and to the glory of God in Him (Col. 3:17). Thus, shall you "walk worthy of the vocation wherewith you are called" (Eph. 4:1) and "worthy of the Lord unto all pleasing, being fruitful in every good work" (Col. 1:10). Thus, you shall both adorn the gospel of God your Savior in all things and honor His righteous law (Titus 2:10–12).

Oh, believer, much depends on your behavior! The men of the world around you will always be ready to spy out every blemish in your conduct in order to justify their contempt of you and their disapprobation of your sentiments. Others may commit many sins and escape censure, but if you do anything wrong or discover inconsistency even in a single instance, every mouth will be open—not against you merely but against your principles and all who profess them. Take heed, then, that you "give none occasion" to the enemies of the Lord "to speak reproachfully" (1 Tim. 5:14); but rather, on every occasion, study "with well doing" to "put to silence the ignorance of foolish men" (1 Peter 2:15). You are one of the children of light: "Let your light so shine before men, that they may see your good works, and glorify your Father which is in heaven" (Matt. 5:16).

In conclusion, from what has been said we may see how good works are related both to the law and to the gospel. Four things are to be remarked concerning such works—namely, obligation to them, assistance in them, acceptance of them, and reward according to them. The first proceeds from the law as a rule of duty in the hand of the Mediator, and the other three proceed from the gospel in its strict acceptation. The obligation to perform them arises from the sovereign authority of God our Savior revealed in the law; assistance in performing them is afforded by His strength promised in the gospel; the acceptance of them flows from His righteousness revealed and offered in the gospel; and the reward according to them proceeds from His boundless grace displayed and tendered also in the gospel.

Much more, therefore, is requisite to the performance of good works than merely to know that they are enjoined in the law. That, indeed, is requisite to the right performance of them, but it is far from being all that is needful.

Many think it sufficient for them only to know their duty, and no sooner do they seem to themselves to know it than they immediately and inconsiderately attempt the performance of it. But all they who have "the spirit of wisdom and revelation in the knowledge of him" (Eph. 1:17) and so are made "wise unto salvation through faith which is in Christ Jesus" (2 Tim. 3:15) know that much more is requisite to the right performance even of the smallest duty than to know that it is commanded in the law. They not only look, therefore, to the law as a rule for authority to oblige them to the practice of good works, as well as for direction in performing them, but they look also to the gospel and to the Savior offered in it for strength to perform them, for merit to render them acceptable to God, and for a reward of grace to crown them. If the true Christian, then, would "be ready to every good work" (Titus 3:1), he must be excited and resolved not only to receive the law of Christ as his rule of direction but to believe with application to himself the gospel of Christ and, in believing it, to trust with firm confidence in Him for assistance, acceptance, and a gracious reward. Thus, he will be enabled, while he sojourns in this valley of tears, to serve God acceptably; and at length he will be graciously rewarded with the inexpressible honor of serving as well as enjoying God and the Lamb forever and ever in the holy place on high. For there, "his servants shall serve him: and they shall see his face" (Rev. 22:3–4).

Study Questions

BOOK INTRODUCTION

1. Who was John Colquhoun?

2. According to the summary of chapter 1, how did the law function differently for Adam as a covenant of works than it does for those in Christ?

3. After reading the summary of chapter 7, how would you explain the main differences between the law and the gospel?

4. How would you summarize in a few sentences the main idea of the book, based on this introduction?

5. Of the four closing applications, which is most helpful to you right now? Why?

6. What is something that you hope to gain from reading this book? After writing it down, take it to the Lord in prayer and ask Him to do a good work in you.

CHAPTER 1A
(Chapter Introduction and Sections 1–2)

1. How do the Holy Scriptures show that God created man with the law written in his heart?

2. What are the definitions of (a) the law of creation, (b) the law of nature, and (c) the moral law?

3. Why is all mankind under obligation to obey the law of nature?

4. Someone says, "I wish you Christians would stop trying to force your morality on everyone!" Based on what you have read in this chapter, how do you respond?

5. What is the covenant of works, and what are its three main components?

6. How can we prove from the Scriptures that the covenant of works included a promise of life?

7. What is the "penal sanction" of the covenant of works? Why is it just and reasonable?

8. Consider that we were born fallen in Adam under the covenant of works and are obligated to fully obey God's law, corrupted by sin, and condemned to be punished. How should the knowledge of this affect unsaved people? How should it affect those saved in Christ?

CHAPTER 1B
(Section 3 and Reflections)

1. How much authority does the moral law have for believers in Christ? Why?

2. What is the "law of Christ"?

3. How is the law as a rule of life to believers different from the law as a covenant of works?

4. What is the difference between heathen morality, pharisaic righteousness, and true holiness?

5. How do two sorts of sinners, legalists and antinomians, especially offend against the law?

6. How can a Christian set his heart to keep all God's commandments without falling into legalism or an unbiblical guilt and shame over the sins he still commits?

CHAPTER 2

1. What declares the covenant of grace in the preface to the Ten Commandments?

2. How does placing the stone tablets in the ark reveal the covenant of grace?

3. Why was it impossible that the Lord made a covenant of works with Israel?

4. How does God's grace to Israel under the law of Moses encourage you to trust Christ?

5. What was God's purpose in displaying aspects of the covenant of works at Mount Sinai?

6. What visible signs of God's wrath did God manifest at Mount Sinai? Why?

7. How do these Scripture passages show that God displayed the covenant of works in the law given to Israel: (a) Matthew 19:17–19; (b) Romans 10:5; (c) 2 Corinthians 3:7; and (d) Galatians 3:10?

8. Someone says, "God put the Israelites under both the covenant of grace and the covenant of works when He gave them the law at Mount Sinai." How do you respond?

9. How did the Lord make a national covenant with Israel in terms of (a) conditions, (b) promises, and (c) penal sanctions?

10. How has reading this chapter given you a clearer understanding of God's ways with Israel?

CHAPTER 3

1. What does it mean that God's moral law is universal?

2. Given that the law is "perfect," or complete in its moral instruction, what does that imply when people try to add to or subtract from it?

3. How does the moral law's being "spiritual" relate to (a) the human spirit and (b) God's Spirit?

4. Where does the Bible teach that the moral law is holy, just, and good? What does that imply if we resent any of God's commandments?

5. How does your heart respond to the thought that since the moral law is "of perpetual obligation," you must obey God forever? What does your response show about your heart?

CHAPTER 4

1. What is an example that illustrates each of the following principles of interpreting the law?

   (a) Where a duty is required, the contrary sin is forbidden; and where a sin is forbidden, the contrary duty is required.

   (b) Where a duty is required, every duty of the same kind is also required; and where a sin is forbidden, every sin of the same sort is prohibited.

   (c) Whatever we are commanded to do or not to do, we should do what we can according to our position in relation to others to influence them to do or not to do the same.

   (d) Where a duty is required or a sin is forbidden, the use of all lawful means to do the duty and avoid the sin is also required.

   (e) All our obedience should aim at the ultimate goal of all the law, which is the glory of God in the holiness of His people.

2. What are some ways that these principles of interpreting the law show that mankind, apart from the saving grace of God, is completely destitute of true holiness?

CHAPTER 5

1. What are the general meaning and the specific meaning of *gospel*?

2. What doctrines of grace and promises of grace are part of the gospel?

3. What offers and invitations are included in the gospel?

4. According to Colquhoun, do the commands to repent and believe in Christ belong to the law, the gospel, or both?
Do you agree? Why or why not?

5. Why is it wrong to say that the gospel gives us a new law that is easier to keep?

6. How can you test whether you have an experiential knowledge of the gospel?

CHAPTER 6

1. What is the first and greatest use of the gospel?

2. How does the gospel reveal to sinners their warrant to trust in Christ for salvation?

3. In what way does the Holy Spirit use the gospel to continue to apply Christ to believers?

4. How does God use the gospel to display His glory? How have you experienced that, and how has it affected your life?

5. How does God use the law to restrain men from sin, and how does that benefit mankind?

6. What is the law's special use for unregenerate sinners?

7. How can the law as a covenant of works make believers appreciate Christ more?

8. What uses does the law have for believers as a rule to direct their lives? Select one of these uses and describe how you have experienced this by the Spirit's power.

CHAPTER 7

1. Why is it a serious error to confuse the law (as a covenant of works) with the gospel?

2. How is the law related to God's nature and the gospel to God's will?

3. How is the law made known to mankind, in contrast to the gospel?

4. How is the gospel different from the law when the latter says, "Do this and you shall live"?

5. How is the gospel different from the law's works to convince and condemn sinners?

6. How does boasting relate to the law and the gospel?

7. What did Colquhoun mean when he said, "We should always take heed that we do not apply to ourselves the gospel where the law should be applied, nor the law where the gospel ought to be applied"?

CHAPTER 8

1. How does the law in its command for perfect obedience agree with the gospel?

2. How does the law in its condemnation of sinners agree with the gospel?

3. How does the law as a rule to direct a believer's life agree with the gospel?

4. Why is every enemy of the gospel also an enemy of the law?

5. In your own experience, how has your knowledge of the law increased your love for the gospel? How has your knowledge of the gospel increased your love for the law?

CHAPTER 9

1. What Scripture declares that the doctrine of justification by faith establishes the law?

2. What are three ways that the doctrine of faith establishes the law as a covenant of works?

3. How does the doctrine of faith establish the law as a rule of life to believers?

4. How does the grace of faith establish the law as a covenant of works?

5. How does the grace of faith establish the law as a rule of life to believers?

6. How does the establishment of the law by the gospel show God's intention to honor His law?

7. How do these truths show the depth of human depravity and horrible evil of sin?

CHAPTER 10A

(Chapter Introduction and Sections 1–3)

1. When Paul says believers are "dead to the law" (Rom. 7:4), why should we understand him to refer to the moral law as distinct from the ceremonial law?

2. Why should we understand "dead to the law" to refer to the covenant of works as distinct from the law as a rule to direct the believer's life?

3. What does Colquhoun mean when he says believers are dead to the law both "relatively" and "really"?

4. How are believers dead to the law as a covenant of works in its (a) commanding power, (b) promising power, (c) condemning power, and (d) irritating power?

5. How does becoming dead to the law affect the believer's hopes, anxieties, and spiritual rest?

6. How does the law itself become the occasion of a believer dying to the law experientially by its revelation of the holiness, justice, and majesty of God?

7. How does the law become the occasion of dying to the law by its revelation of the law's own authority, holiness, spirituality, vast extent, and perfection?

8. How does the law become the occasion of dying to the law by its revelation of the evil of sin, the wrath of God, and the justice of God in eternally damning sinners?

9. How does the law become the occasion of dying to the law by driving a sinner to Christ?

CHAPTER 10B
(Sections 4–5 and Reflections)

1. What is the result of dying to the law and being united to Christ (Rom. 7:4)?

2. What does it mean to serve God in newness of spirit (Rom. 7:6)?

3. To live unto God consists of what four things?

4. Why is it impossible to live unto God without first dying to the law?

5. How does being dead to the law bring about a spiritual influence to live unto God?

6. How does being dead to the law bring about a moral motivation to live unto God?

7. How does the law in the hand of Christ reveal the love and grace of God?

8. If dying to the law is the only way to be united to Christ and His benefits, what does that imply about the state of unregenerate sinners?

9. Since believers are wholly delivered from condemnation from the law, in what sense are they guilty when they sin and need to ask God for forgiveness?

10. Why should we never say to the law, "Have patience with me, and I will pay you all I owe?"

CHAPTER 11

1. Why does God's being the Lord, or Jehovah, obligate believers to obey His law?

2. How does the doctrine of creation bind believers to obey God's law?

3. How does the doctrine of providence, or preservation, oblige believers to obey the law?

4. Why does God giving Himself to believers in covenant obligate them to keep the law?

5. Someone says, "I think we don't have to keep the law anymore because God has loved us so much that He sent His Son to redeem us." Why is the opposite true?

6. What did Colquhoun mean when he said, "The law in the hand of Christ is…not only the rule but the reason of their duty"?

7. What did Colquhoun mean by saying, "Holiness is not only connected with happiness but is itself happiness"? How does this truth obligate believers to obey the law?

8. What is a "legal spirit"? How does it hinder believers from growing in holiness? How have you seen it in yourself?

CHAPTER 12A

(Chapter Introduction and Sections 1–2)

1. What is the first requirement for an action to qualify as a good work pleasing to God?

2. What does it mean that good works must be done with *evangelical* principles and motives?

3. What is the ultimate purpose to which all good works aim?

4. For what purposes are good works *not* necessary?

5. How are good works necessary to honor our God and Savior?

6. How are good works necessary to benefit believers who do them?

7. Why must believers do good works for the sake of other believers and unbelievers?

CHAPTER 12B

(Section 3 and Reflections)

1. Why is it impossible for unregenerate persons to merit the smallest blessing from God?

2. Why is it impossible for regenerate persons to merit any blessing as well?

3. Why can't the good works of believers merit God's blessings, if not by their intrinsic value, at least by God's covenant promise ("by paction")?

4. Someone says, "Good works are necessary to salvation." How should you respond?

5. Why should believers diligently endeavor to trust in Christ at all times for both justifying grace and sanctifying grace?

6. How has reading this book helped you both to trust in Christ more and obey the law more?

Scripture Index